CAB 10

The West Coast Cabbie

Randy Collenberg

CHECKOUT CAB10 ON THE WEB
WWW.WESTCOASTCABBIE.COM

TO CONTACT CAB10 BY EMAIL
CAB10@WESTCOASTCABBIE.COM

ISBN: 0-9676505-0-X

First printing   November 1999

COVER DESIGN BY MIKE CRAGHEAD

COVER PHOTOS BY RUSSELL WEAVER

INSIDE PHOTOS BY DANNETTE COLLENBERG & RUSSELL WEAVER

PROOFREADING BY JANET M. CUNNINGHAM

TYPESETTING BY ELIZABETH A. WHITLEY OF SENIOR NEWS GRAPHICS

Printed in the United States by:
Morris Publishing
3212 E. Hwy 30
Kearney, NE 68847
1-800-650-7888

Dedication

I dedicate this book
to my mother and father,
Tony and LaVina Collenberg -
the best parents a child could have.

Thank you, mom, for always being there
when I needed someone to talk to, for your
love, and for always believing in my dreams,
no matter how outrageous some of them
were. Thank you, dad, for all the things you
taught me, from ranching to playing sports.
Thank you also for your love and for always
providing inspiration for me to meet my
challenges and to forge ahead and achieve
my goals.

Acknowledgements

Thanks as well to my family, my lovely wife, Dannette, and my sons David, Zachary and Benjamin. Your love, patience and sacrifices have helped make this book a reality. I love you all very much.

Thanks also to Kevin Hoover, editor and publisher of the *Arcata Eye*. You took a chance, ran my column every week and introduced me to the world of deadlines and public recognition. You always found time in your busy schedule to help me and offer advice.

Thanks to all those too numerous to mention who aided in the editing and production of this book.

Thanks to all the readers for their interest, support and encouragement.

Lastly, thanks to the passengers who provided me with the raw material for my columns and this book.

Randy Collenberg
September 23, 1999

Table of Contents

Foreward

Randy Collenberg wants to talk to you, the Plaza hot dog vendor said. He drives a cab and wants to write a column. That was back in November, 1997. I'd been doing the newspaper long enough at that point to know better than to drop everything and chase after a new columnist. Lots of people say they want to write, and for most, that's as far as it goes. Writing isn't easy, and producing a newspaper column is even harder. Deadlines tend to scare away all but the most fearless. And then there are length limits and the inevitable disagreements about editing, style, headlines and horrible typos, along with innumerable other details which make newspaper writing such a dreadful undertaking. Plus, the pay for columnists is hardly enticing– basically pennies per drop of sweat.

But those with something to say, and the attention span to say it, will find the editor, bring a useable product, put up with all the nonsense and perhaps return to punish themselves in this fashion again and again.

And so it was that Randy Collenberg walked in the door of the *Arcata Eye* office bursting with stories. And he's turned one in without fail every week since then. Any editor can understand the appeal of a writing cabbie. Readers like – no, love – true grit told in plainspoken fashion. A cab driver encounters so many different types of people with such fascinating stories and problems and needs and agendas; people one might not necessarily want to meet up with, much less smell, except in print. Which is not to say all of Randy's fare are malodorous hoodlums. Apparently some of them do bathe. But even the normal people who hop in Cab10 often turn out to have something wonderfully strange going on, or special problems which give readers great delight, or some human quality we can identify with.

Of all the columnists featured in the *Arcata Eye*, Cab10 has consistently stirred the most comment, both favorable and otherwise. And unlike other writers who may appeal to a certain niche, Randy has fans across a broad demographic. His verité accounts have drawn comment from college students, seemingly prim seniors, brawny blue-collar workers and others who defy categorization. The thing is, everyone who can read likes a good read, and for them, Cab10 is at the ready.

As it turns out, Randy is the perfect anthropologist/journalist to document the weird wiles and ways of the special people who troop in and out of his cab, and then turn it into a column which captures their essence. That's because he instills trust in people. Randy is unabashed about pumping passengers for their stories, and it's uncanny how readily they cooperate. Why people spill their innermost, often embarrassing personal problems to a total stranger remains something of a mystery. Maybe it's Randy's winning personality, the rhythm of the road, the confession-inducing confines of the luxurious yellow cruiser/mobile anthropology lab or the universal appeal of hearing one's own voice. Or maybe it's Randy's boisterous, winning laugh and good grooming. The results of Randy's field research is recorded in these pages. So take a ride with Randy as he roves the byways of California's North Coast. And help yourself to some salami and cheese.

Kevin L. Hoover, Editor & Publisher, *Arcata Eye*

CAB10's Map of Humboldt County

CHAPTER 1

Getting Crazy

THE KIND OF STUFF YOU SEE IN THE MOVIES

On TV and in the movies you often see someone running out of a building chasing someone. The person that they're chasing jumps into a car and takes off. They then flag down a taxicab and tell the driver to "follow that car!" This call is a lot like that, except it happened after I picked someone up. So sit back and enjoy the ride.

I had just taken someone to the Bayshore Mall when I was called to Carl's Jr. on Broadway. I arrived a few minutes later and picked up two ladies who had just finished eating and wanted to go home. One of the ladies was talking about her ex-husband and was very angry. She was telling her friend that her ex-husband was a drunk, a low life and a few other choice names.

She then started telling me about their lunch. The ex-husband had gone with them to lunch at Carl's Jr. to talk things over. He decided to go outside and have a cigarette while waiting for their food (so they thought). When he didn't return, they realized that he had taken off with the car.

As I was pulling up to the stop sign to cross Broadway and take these ladies home, we noticed a car in the far lane going north at a high rate of speed. The lady in the back seat started yelling, "There goes that S.O.B.; hurry up and follow that car!" And the chase was on.

By the time I got out on Broadway I was about six cars behind the ex-husband's car. All of a sudden he runs a red light, swerved to miss a car and hit a telephone pole head on, going about 55 m.p.h.. I pulled over to the shoulder and into the gas station on the corner to watch all this action.

There were cars and people everywhere. The lady in the back seat is going ballistic, she's yelling and screaming and jumps out of the cab. She runs over to the crash scene to probably kill her ex-husband (if he isn't already dead).

The police are now on the scene. A couple of guys pry the car door open and the husband crawled out and was standing by the

1

car. This guy was lucky he didn't get killed, but may not be so lucky when she gets to him.

The other lady in the cab tells me that her friend was very upset because the car her ex-husband stole from them and just wrecked, belongs to her friend. She had borrowed it for the day and her friend had just bought the car last week.

The police are trying to keep this happy couple from killing each other. The man appears to be drunk. After about 30 minutes the Eureka Police Department (E.P.D.) handcuffed this guy and walked him towards the police car. He's yelling at his ex- wife that he wanted her to come down to the police station and get him out. She tells him to go to hell and that he would have to be crazy to think she would do that after what he just did to her.

The lady gets back into my luxurious yellow cruiser and was very upset and crying. She said, "I can't believe what he did." (I couldn't either.) "I think I better go home and have a drink; I need to call my girlfriend and tell her that her car was totaled." "I'm sorry you had to wait for me," she said. I told her it was no problem. I didn't want to tell her I enjoyed all the excitement.

POLICE SAVE BULLY'S BUTT FROM GALLANT CABBIE

I have seen a lot and learned a lot about people while driving around in my luxurious yellow cruiser. When I hear that famous line, "You ain't seen nothin' yet," I believe it because just when I think I've seen almost everything, the next call could be a new experience in my life.

Almost every day something crazy happens. That's the case of my next call.

I had to go to a local motel and pick up the motel owner's wife and little girl and take them to the girl's dancing lessons. I have been doing this twice a week for three weeks because their car's in the shop.

On this beautiful day I pulled up to the lobby of the motel and honked my horn. Usually they come right out. Well, I waited for a couple of minutes then decided I had better go see what's the problem. Just as I opened my door, I noticed them coming out from their apartment into the lobby. I opened the doors for them and turned around, thinking they're ready to go.

The husband started yelling at his wife that he needed to talk to her. So I had the little girl get in and I turned on the meter; now they can talk all day, and it won't cost me. As I was asking the little girl about her dancing lessons, I was looking into the lobby and watched her parents yelling at each other.

The next thing you know, the husband grabbed his wife around the neck, from behind and started yanking her up and down off the floor. I couldn't believe it. I pulled ahead a little so the daughter couldn't see her parents fighting, and I radioed for the Arcata Police Department (A.P.D.).

I was pretty mad and disgusted by now. I decided it was time to get involved in this mess. I jumped out of my cruiser and ran into the lobby. I'm about 100 pounds bigger than this coward. When he saw me coming, he stopped jerking his poor wife and yelled, "WHAT THE HELL DO YOU WANT?" He then says, "Here's a Ten for the cab, now beat it."

I told him to put the $10 where the sun doesn't shine; and if he doesn't let his wife go with me, I'm going to yank on his neck for awhile. His wife told me not to hurt him (classic), just leave. At this time Mel Brown's (Arcata Police) Army showed up. They questioned all of us about what happened. Guess what. The wife denied her husband did anything to her. Well (I was mad at her now), how come you have big red marks around your neck and your makeup is running down your face? That's all it took. They arrested the coward.

I then got the lady in the cab. She was still mad at me for calling the police. I took her and her daughter to where they were going. Case closed.

HONKING REVENGE

One of the most important and most used assets of my luxurious yellow cruiser is its horn. I use it often, especially when arriving at a location to pick up a fare. Most people come right out when they hear my horn. Some look out at me and give me some kind of signal that they will be right out, others open their door and go back in and finish getting ready.

Then there are the people that hate my horn. I have run into at least two people that hate my horn, and I want you to know about them.

The time of day was approximately 11am. I had to go to a

3

trailer court in McKinleyville to pick up one of my regular ladies that I take to Mad River Adult Day Care. She's a really nice lady who can't hear very well so I need to honk a few extra times.

On one particular day I was feeling a little crazy (which is pretty normal), so I honked about eight or nine times instead of four or five. I jump out of my luxurious cruiser and start walking towards the trailer so I can help the lady get into my cruiser because she uses a walker.

As I'm walking to her trailer, I notice a guy from a trailer across the street approaching me. He had coveralls on. I don't know why, because he looked like he never worked a day in his life. He's sort of a long hair, lazy bum, scared-of-work looking type of guy.

I asked the guy, "How are you today?"

"I was doing good until you violated my airspace," he said.

"What do you mean by that?" I asked.

"That damn horn honking you did," he said.

By now I was getting a little upset with this brainless wonder. "I'm picking up your neighbor who can't hear well, and she likes me to honk a few extra times," I said. He said that it was more than just a few times. (Well, I was starting to feel like Mike Tyson, and his ears were starting to look good.) I'm just trying to do my job and have a little fun, and I have to put up with this kind of harassment.

I told him the extra honks were for all the lazy people in the trailer court that should be working instead of going around complaining at this time of day about someone who is working and paying his taxes to support them.

He didn't like that, and walked off bitching about what just happened. (He probably had to go back and watch some more TV.)

My other horn hater is a lady that lives in the Greenview area who really hates my friendly taps on the horn. She is one of the numerous Dial-A-Ride (share a ride program) persons, and I pick her up a lot; she goes to the senior lunch at the Community Center. She always has a chip on her shoulder, has a very dry personality, is rude and tells me boring stories.

When I first started to pick her up, she told me not to honk the horn next time because she hates it, and it's not necessary as she will be watching for me. I said OK. So, she gets in and we are off to pick up the next Dial-A-Ride a ride customer.

As usual, I honk for the next person (of course, I give the horn a few extra beeps). I load this customer next to Mrs. Personality who asked her, "Doesn't that horn bother you?" The other lady said no. "It bothers me," said the first lady. The other lady, who is her friend, told her, "You complain to much." I was thinking to myself, "All right!"

About a week later I picked up someone that needed to go to Fortuna. On my way to Fortuna, I heard the dispatcher tell one of the other drivers to go to Greenview to pick up Mrs. Personality and take her to lunch. I couldn't resist, (I have to do it-you knew I would) I called the dispatcher and told him to tell Greg (the other cab driver) when he picks her up make sure he honks loud and several times, because she can't hear too good. (boy, that felt good). I told my passenger the story and about what I did, he laughed.

A few days later I saw Greg. He asked me "Were you being a smart ass last week about honking my horn loud for that lady in Arcata?" Not me! Greg said she was hot. Then we laughed for about five minutes. I love this job!

CAB 10 IS NUMBER ONE IN NEW YORK TOO!

I want to share with you a couple of stories that didn't have anything to do with Cab10, but I thought you might enjoy. Once in a while someone will ask me for my personal favorite experience riding in a cab as a passenger, instead of as the driver. I have several. My favorite was when I went to New York several years ago.

A friend and I went to New York for two weeks for the unveiling of the Statue of Liberty after they refurbished it for its 100th birthday as a gift from France. We saw the Yankees play, saw the Empire State Building, rode on the subways, saw the Rockettes, went to Times Square, ate a $10 hamburger, went to Madison Square Garden; we did everything.

Two weeks went by so fast and it was time to check out of our Hotel. We were going to Washington, D.C. so we needed to go to Grand Central Station to catch the train. It was only about four blocks away; but we had a lot of luggage so we had the bellman get us a cab.

The cab arrived and the driver and the bellman loaded our luggage into the trunk. We get in and told the driver we want to go to Grand Central Station to catch the train to Washington. The cab driver never said a word; he just jumped out of the cab opened up the trunk and threw our luggage out. He then opened our doors and told us to get the hell out. We look at each other like, "What the hell is going on?" Then we start laughing, and look over at the bellman and he's buckled over laughing too. The cab driver gets in his cab and drives off. We are all still laughing because it was funny. You had to be there, I guess.

The cab driver didn't want to waste his time with such a small fare. The bellman finally stopped laughing and came over and said, "You guys must not be going far." I told him, "What was your first clue?" He smiled and said that he'd get another cab for us, but this time we should tell him we are going to the airport (which is a good fare).

He told us, after we go about a block, to tell the driver that we changed our mind and tell him where we wanted to go and he'll take us there. He won't be happy, but that's New York for you. So we did that and I couldn't believe how quickly our drivers smile and humor disappeared. You could almost see smoke coming out of his ears.

We get to the station and he hit his brakes hard, got out, and threw our luggage out as fast as he could. I would never do that to one of my customers. So I take a long time getting out my wallet out to pay him. I wanted to make sure he'll never forget me. And I just had to ask him, "Hey, what's your cab number? I'll call you when we need a ride back to the hotel."

He turned around and, I couldn't believe it; he gave us the finger. My friend and I started laughing again. At least we knew we're number one on his list.

A SPATULA-WIELDING PRANKSTER

Have you ever had a religious group stop by your house and share the word of the Lord with you? One day I was driving through McKinleyville and I noticed several car loads of one of our very popular (yeah, right) religious groups knocking on doors.

They were everywhere. They must be predicting the end of the world again, or maybe they're just spreading the Lord's word. I have nothing against them or their religion. I think it's good that they go out and talk to people about what they believe in.

Once in a while I'm parked somewhere and one of them will give me one of their pamphlets to read. I always tell them thank you, and I do read it. But I've got to tell you, if you don't already know, they can be a pain in the butt. Then I start thinking about a few times that always make me laugh, and I want to share them with you.

When I was a bachelor, I had several different roommates over the years, but one seven year stretch I had the same one. We had a lot of good times together, and once in awhile we would play tricks on each other. This particular religious group came to our house one Saturday morning.

I happened to be cooking some breakfast for my roommate and me after a night of partying. I was in the kitchen cooking some eggs and homemade hash browns.

All I had on was my shorts and I probably looked like hell after drinking Jack Daniel's and dancing all night. I was cooking up a storm.

I didn't hear anyone knock on the door, but I sure was going to find out that someone did. My roommate was in the other room watching the football game, when he yelled, "Hey Randy!" I had a spatula in my hand facing the stove when he yelled at me.

I turned around to see what he wanted. There are two women all dressed up carrying briefcases, standing in the kitchen staring at me. I must have looked like the devil in my shorts, hair all messed up, and my spatula in my hand.

My roommate was behind them laughing his ass off. I was embarrassed, and they were speechless. Then one of them told me that they would come back at a more convenient time. I told them that I was sorry, and they left.

My roommate was hiding in the bathroom. He came out and we laughed and laughed. But revenge came about a year later.

One morning, about 10 am., the phone rang and it was for my roommate. I yelled at him that the phone was for him but didn't get an answer. So I walked into his room to find him and his girl-friend passed out naked on the bed.

I went back to the phone and told his friend to call back; then I went back to watch TV. A few minutes later, someone knocked on the door. I didn't look out the window like I usually do. Big mistake. I opened the door and their were three young ladies from our favorite religious group standing there. I was trying to get rid of them, when I got this great idea. (You didn't guess what it was did you?) I tried not to laugh.

I told these lovely ladies to come on in. I told them that I'm a

Catholic (which is true) and I'm not interested, but my roommate would enjoy their visit. They said, "OK, is he home?" I told them to wait just a minute, and I would check with him to see if he wanted them to go back to his room to talk to him. I pretended to go to his room and came back and told them that he said it was OK for them to go on back.

They then walked right into his room, and I'm just rolling on the floor. Those girls started screaming. They woke up my roommate and his girlfriend. The three girls ran out of the house and I'm in my bedroom with tears running down my face. My roommate ran into my room and saw me laughing. Then he knew that I had returned the favor. We still laugh about those tricks today.

UNPLUGGED ROMANCE

I won't forget this next story for a long time. I had to go to the airport to pick up someone. He was about 35 years old, well dressed, and seemed like a pretty good dude. He told me he needed to go to Eureka to take care of some important business.

"Where are you from?" I asked him. He told me that he used to live here about a year ago, but he's getting a divorce and is now living in the Midwest. He owns a business—one of the largest producers of cotton candy in the world.

I thought that was sort of interesting, but what he was going to tell me next was even more interesting.

He asked me if I could help him out with a few problems he needed to deal with while he's here, and he handed me a $20 bill. I told him, "No problem! What kind of help do you need?"

He told me that when he was living here he thought he had a happy marriage until one day he discovered his wife was having an affair with another man.

So he packed his bags and moved to the Midwest. I wanted to know more about his wife's affair, so I asked him, "How did you find out about your wife's affair?"

He told me it all started a couple of years ago when he bought his wife a computer. She was on it all the time. After a few months he was getting a lot of strange phone calls, and his wife was getting a lot of gifts from her "boss!"

He did some research and found out his wife was having an on-line affair with a guy in Texas. He told her he knew what was going on, and she had better end this nonsense right away! She told him she would!

A couple of months go by. One day he found a letter from the guy in Texas which was sent to his wife; it was about them running away together plus a few other juicy suggestions. When his wife got home that night, he confronted her with the letter, and she told him that she was in love with this guy from Texas. So he packed his bags and moved to the Midwest. He came back to town today to take care of some unfinished business.

First he wanted to go and pick up his two kids at a local daycare center because he hadn't seen them for a long time. His wife had told him he could have the kids for a week.

On our way to get his kids he told me that he's taking them for good, and she doesn't know it. After we picked up the kids and their suitcases, he wanted to go to his wife's work.

After a few minutes he showed up with the car. Now he wanted me to follow him with his two kids to his house where his wife is living so he can get the rest of what belongs to him. She doesn't know he's doing this either, he told me.

When we got to the house, he wanted me to help him carry his stuff out to the car. When we walked into the house, he told me he was going to terminate his wife's boyfriend before we did anything else.

Well, I didn't say anything for a couple of minutes. I was getting nervous now.

Then he told me, "You're still going to help me, aren't you?" I was thinking. This guy just kidnapped his kids, stole a car, broke into his wife's home, and now he wants to terminate his wife's boyfriend.

"I don't want to go to jail; I'm leaving," I told him. He started laughing! "It's not as bad as it sounds," he said. "This guy has cotton candy for brains," I thought.

"I think I better leave," I told him. "You're going to have to do the rest of your dirty work by yourself."

He started laughing again! "What's so funny," I asked. He told me, "I'm not going to hurt anyone." I asked him, "What's all this talk about terminating your wife's boyfriend then?" "Come in the house; I will show you what I meant by that!"

When we got into the house, he grabbed his wife's computer and tore the wires out of the wall. Then he said, "I wish I could see my wife's face tonight when she comes home to use the computer to talk to her boyfriend. I just terminated their on-line relationship."

I just shook my head, and told him I had better wait outside with the kids. After he got everything he wanted out of the house and into the car, he told me thanks. Then he and his kids drove off. Just when I thought I had seen and heard it all!

WRONG WAY RANDY

Once in a while someone will ask me if I have ever been in an accident. The answer is no, but one time I came close.

I was in Eureka, and I had to go to Winco and pick up someone. We were really busy. I picked up a nice older gentleman. While I was loading up his groceries, he was talking up a storm. He wanted me to take him to Cutten, as soon as possible, because he needed to go to the bathroom. After I load up his stuff I start driving through the parking lot to Harris Street, which is a one-way going to my left.

Just as I approach the one-way, my dispatcher told me to go to the Bayshore Mall, which is to my right, and pick up someone else who is also going to Cutten. I told the dispatcher OK.

At this time I'm ready to enter Harris Street, but I was thinking, I needed to go right to get to the mall. My passenger was still talking, and for some reason I went brain dead and turned right on Harris going the wrong way.

About a second later I'm sort of in both lanes of traffic facing the wrong way. I hit the brakes, and so did about 15 other cars that were barreling towards me. Two cars almost hit me—it was close.

All I could hear were people slamming their brakes and lots of horns going off. And there were a lot of dirty looks and some fancy hand language too. I looked at my passenger and he's OK, but staring at me. I could see he's relieved in more ways than one that he was still alive.

I'm thinking, "He probably didn't need to go to the bathroom anymore." I asked him, "Are you OK?" He said in a calm voice, "Were you trying to take a shortcut?" We both laughed. I told him, "Looked that way didn't it?" As I was backing up into Winco's parking lot, everyone driving by was giving us dirty looks, like I'm an idiot or something. I finally got my luxurious yellow cruiser going the right way and took my passenger home.

ARE YOU AN UNDERCOVER COP?

As a cab driver we meet all kinds of people with all kinds of fantasies. These next two guys had big plans. I picked them up at the Sidelines in Arcata. They wanted to go to Eureka. On our way there they're whispering to each other in the back seat. They're talking about picking up one of the local hookers.

Pretty soon one of them asked me, "You aren't an undercover cop are you?" I laughed! Then I told them, "What do you guys want to do? Pick up a hooker, some booze, and go party?" "You guessed it," one of them said.

About twenty minutes later we saw a couple of the "girls" walking on the sidewalk. We pulled over so these two lover boys can line up some action. In about five minutes they came back with one of the young "ladies." I asked them, "Is the other "girl" coming with us, too?" They told me no; they were going to share the one. I just shook my head.

We now go to a store so they can buy some beer. "We're all set, cabbie; take us to a motel," one of them said. When we got to the motel, they wanted me to wait while they got a room.

Then I drove them around back to their love nest. One of the guys told me to wait a minute while the three of them go into room. About a minute later one of the guys came out and told me they made a deal with the "lady" to have sex with me in trade for the $28 cab fare. I had to refuse the generous offer.

CAB10 BECOMES A VAN OF WORMS AND CRAWLY CRITTERS

This next story is one for the record books. Cab10 has set a new world record.

A few months ago there was a movie on TV called *Noah's Ark* which most of you probably watched. I'm sure almost all of you know the story of Noah's Ark.

If you don't know anything about Noah's Ark, that tells me two things: you don't read two of the most important reading materials ever written—the Bible and the checkout-line rag tabloids where someone every week claims to have found the famous ark on some hilltop.

Those stories about finding the ark are all lies. Only I know where it is at, and it's right here in Humboldt County. You're probably wondering what Noah's Ark has to do with Cab 10. Well, I'm going to tell you so we can get this mystery solved before the millennium bug gets here.

I have delivered and moved a lot of things for my customers, but I bet I'm the only cab driver in the world who has delivered a whole zoo.

I received a call to pick up a young lady in McKinleyville who needed a van because she was moving to a motel. On my way there I had thoughts running through my head about what I might be moving. Usually when I move people's things, it's because they just got evicted or booted out by some loved one. I was imagining broken dishes, dirty dishes, dirty clothes in garbage bags, old pots and pans, open food containers and other valuable possessions that I can't wait to load into my luxurious yellow cruiser.

When I pulled up in front of the house, I knew I was at the right place. There were a couple of garbage bags of clothes and a few priceless household things on the ground. In addition there were a few animal cages with animals in them. I honked my horn and a young lady came out carrying two more cages.

"Could you help me load this stuff?" she asked. "I need to go to a motel in Arcata where my husband and kids are."

"I don't think the motel is going to allow those animals in their rooms," I said.

"We're not going to tell them, are we, so how will they know?"

"You're the boss. Let's load up your things."

I was putting her clothes and others things in the cab, when I noticed her coming back out of the house with more cages. I couldn't believe it. I had to ask her, "What do you have, your own private circus or zoo?"

She laughed and then said, "Looks like it, doesn't it? I just love animals."

I have had dogs, cats, mice, and even snakes (we're talking animals here) in my cab before, but never a whole zoo of animals. I kept loading and she kept on bringing more cages.

There were also three containers of fish. One was a big jar which was really cool. It had all kinds of stuff in it so the fish would feel like they were living in the ocean. All the cages and animals were very clean and very well taken care of.

It took us about 20 minutes to load my luxurious ark, but we did it. On our voyage to a local motel, which I don't want to mention for obvious reasons, I asked her to tell me how many animals we had on board because this had to be a world's record.

Here's the list of animals that we loaded. One big cage had two parrots, parakeets and a few other exotic birds for a total of nine. Three rabbits, six mice, four kittens, two snakes (I hate snakes), an iguana, four chicks, three ducklings, 21 gold fish, nineteen other fish varieties, a jar with thirteen worms, and two big dogs. You're probably wondering what happened to the elephants and the giraffes; I was afraid to ask. I had a total of 87 animals.

As we got close to docking at our destination, I was trying to talk to this lady of the jungle. You can imagine the different noises we were competing with. But she did tell me that she and her menagerie had been evicted and were staying in a motel for a couple days until they got another house. Maybe a compound would be more appropriate.

As we approached the new animal kingdom of Arcata (a motel), she told me to drive around back so the person in the office wouldn't see us. When we got to the motel, we drove around to the back of the motel to her room. I couldn't believe it; there were five maids taking a break, standing in the road and smoking cigarettes.

When I saw them I told her, "I think we better take our chances and go the other way." She agreed.

As I was backing up, she said, "You must have done this before."

I started laughing, "Yeah, but not with a whole zoo in my cab."

She laughed and said, "You must think I'm weird or something."

"No, you're OK. People like you make my job more interesting."

As I'm driving by the office I wanted to duck, because I just knew someone was going to see us or hear us.

We pulled up to her room where her husband and kids were waiting and started unloading. I had backed up to the door as close as I could get.

A few minutes later we were finished, I thought. Her husband was looking over the animals like he was making sure they were all there. I turned to walk out to my cab to see what they owed me when her husband asked, "Where is the ocean?"

I turned around and said, "It's about three miles from here."

He laughed and said, "No, not that ocean—our ocean."

I was lost; I didn't know what he was talking about. His wife came out of their room laughing and told me, "You know that big jar of fish we put in your cab, that you thought was cool."

"Yeah, what about it?"

"We call that our ocean." I have heard everything now. That must be another world's record. The smallest ocean in the world has ridden in Cab10. I opened up the door and in the corner by the back seat was their ocean. She grabbed it and took it into the motel room.

While she was doing that, I was looking around just in case anything else was squirming or crawling around in my cab. I didn't see anything.

I then told them what they owed me. They paid me and gave me a good tip. Before I left I had to ask them if they could check to make sure both snakes were accounted for. They told me not to worry; they were both in the bathtub, getting some exercise.

I couldn't help but laugh as I was leaving. I would hate to be the people to rent their room next.

As I was driving off they told me, "Thank you."

I hollered back, "I wish you guys luck, and I recommend that you don't have maid service." They both laughed as they turned around and went into their animal kingdom.

As I was leaving, I was thinking if that motel had room service, it would be interesting to see what that couple would order for lunch.

Speaking of lunch, I better go eat. That sounds good after a long voyage in the ark.

So if you're ever sleeping in a motel and are suddenly awakened in the middle of the night by wild animals in the room next to you, you better just turn over and go back to sleep. Don't call the office to complain because nobody is going to believe your story. Bon voyage!

CHAPTER 2
Hard Luck

TRAVEL TROUBLE

I'm sure you have all heard the saying, "If it wasn't for bad luck, you wouldn't have any at all!"

I picked up this guy at the airport, and he wanted to go to a car repair shop in Eureka to pick up his truck. He told me that he has had a bad week, and he was probably the unluckiest person in the world this week.

"What happened?" I ask.

He told me that some of his family from Florida came to see him. They flew into San Francisco and he had to drive down there to pick them up. They came to spend a week with him. Then after their visit he had to take them back down there so they could fly home.

Here's what happened. On his way down there to pick them up, he stopped at a store to pick up a few snacks for his trip. When he came out of the store he was in for a rude awakening. Someone had smashed into his truck, bent the fender down onto one of the tires, and driven off. His truck couldn't be driven, so he had it towed to the repair shop. He then rented a car and drove it to San Francisco. After he picked up his family he started back to Eureka.

When he was passing through Santa Rosa the traffic was pretty heavy. Before he knew it, the cars in front of him were putting on their brakes. He then hit his brakes just in time, but the car behind him didn't and smashed into him and pushed him into the car ahead of him.

He told me it was a big mess, but his car was still driveable. After he talked to the police he continued on his way back to Eureka in his wrecked rental car, which he returned the next morning. He said it was embarrassing when the rental representative came out and saw the car smashed in front and back. When he told me that, I was wondering if that's how Rent a Wreck car rentals got started.

After the week was over, he went to the airport to rent another car to take his family back to San Francisco. After he dropped them off, he drove to San Rafael to stay with some friends for the night.

15

The next morning he went out to get in his rental car and go home. He was in for another big surprise. Someone broke the driver door's window and stole his CD's that he had left on the seat.

I told him, "Next time your family comes to see you, tell the tightwads to spend the extra money and buy an airplane ticket all the way to Eureka." He laughed.

When we got to the repair shop so he could get his truck, I asked him, "Are you sure you don't want me to take you home? It might be safer." He told me he's going to drive very carefully straight home, and hide for a few days. I laughed.

BAD LUCK COMES IN BUNCHES

Driving a taxi you run into a lot of people that are down in their luck. Every once in a while it seems like everyone I pick up has bad luck for some reason or another. Have you ever combed your hair, drunk some coffee or talked on your cell phone while you're driving and almost got into a wreck. Maybe after you read this next story you will quit taking so many chances of getting into an accident and wait until you get to your destination first.

One day I had to pick someone up on Dows Prairie Road in McKinleyville. When my fare came out of his house, I wanted to laugh, but I held my composure. This guy looked like he had just finished fighting World War III all by himself.

He looked like hell. He was about 25. He was on crutches, had a black eye and was trying to hold one of his hands and use his crutches at the same time. It looked like he was in a lot of pain.

I thought I better get out and help this guy before he hurts himself some more.

After I got him stuffed into my luxurious yellow cruiser, he told me that he needed to go see his doctor. I asked him what the heck happened to him?

He told me it had been a bad week. "I can tell," I said.

He told me the other day he was driving to work, and his coffee was spilling on the floor. So he reached down to grab it, lost control of his van and hit a telephone pole, smashed his van, and broke his foot.

A couple of days later, he was just getting used to his crutches and was walking through his house when he slipped and fell down, hitting his head on his coffee table. Then today, he was in his garage gas welding, and grabbed a hot piece of metal by accident and burned his hand really bad. He needs to see his doctor so he can look at it. I told him," After you get back home you'd better take it easy for a while." He laughs; "It can't get any worse, can it?"

WEDDING PARTY BLUES

Have you ever been part of a wedding party and everything that could go wrong did?

I picked a lady up one day at the Quality Inn in Arcata. She was dressed to kill and was even wearing a fancy fur coat. She wanted to go to Budget Rent-A-Car at Mickey's Quality Cars in McKinleyville.

On our way there I asked her, "Are you here on business or visiting someone?"

"I really don't know at this point, because you won't believe what I have been through the last few days!" she said in a very excited voice.

"Try me, I think I have heard everything," I told her.

She then told me what had happened to her. She's from Washington, D. C. and came out to San Francisco on Friday to be in her best girlfriend's wedding on Saturday. She was going to be the maid of honor.

After her plane landed she went to get her luggage. One of her suitcases was missing. It was the one her maid of honor dress was in. She wasn't too worried about it, because it was only Friday. But on Saturday it didn't show up either. So she ended up going to a bridal shop and buying another dress which cost her $400.

The dress she bought was close to the wedding's colors, but looked a little out of place. But it did the job. The bride was upset, but at that point she didn't care. Then on Sunday she rented a car to go to Tahoe to go snow skiing for a couple of days.

When she got to Donner Pass on Highway 80 it was snowing so bad that chains were required. She didn't have any chains, so she turned around and decided to go to Crescent City to see a good friend that she hadn't seen in about ten years.

When she left Donner Pass she went back to Sacramento. There she called her girlfriend and told her she was going to come see her the next day. She then took Interstate 5 up to Redding.

From Redding she took Highway 299. When she got up into

the mountains by Weaverville she came around a turn and didn't see a rock that was in the middle of the road. She told me it was raining really hard and it was very dark. After she hit the rock it pushed her off the road into another rock and dented up her rental car. She somehow got her car back on the road and then realized she had a flat tire. She got out and found out she had three flat tires. It was really dark, windy and cold. She was a little scared being alone, too. A couple of cars came by a few minutes later and stopped. One of them called a tow truck for her. After about half an hour the tow truck came. After the tow truck driver got her car ready to transport they headed for McKinleyville.

It was about 2 a.m. She didn't know it, but just down the road there were two other cars that had hit the same rock and had flat tires. The driver called for another tow truck to help these other people out. When they got to Arcata she decided to get off at the Quality Inn. She had the tow truck driver take her car to Mickey's in McKinleyville. The next morning she called her girlfriend to get directions, but for some reason couldn't get hold of her until late afternoon.

When she finally reached her, her girlfriend told her that her father-in-law died early that morning and she and her husband had to leave town to go to Utah. So she then decided that was enough and spent the night in Arcata.

After she told me her story, I asked her, "I bet it's going to be a long time before you come to California again."

After all that she still managed to laugh and then said, "I hope I can get a rental car so I can get back to San Francisco and can fly home. They're supposed to have one for me when we get to Budget."

I didn't want to get her hopes up about her rental car, but I did tell her, "I could give you a ride to San Francisco if it came to that."

"Well, if I can't get a car, you're hired," she said. When we got to Mickey's they had a car waiting for her. The car she wrecked the night before was there too.

When she got out I wished her a safe trip home. She smiled and said, "Thanks for the ride and I hope I didn't bore you with my depressing story." I just smiled back and took off thinking about writing this story.

A SELF-INDUCED TRAGEDY

One of the strangest and saddest stories I wrote was this next one. I received a call to go to Mad River Hospital Nursery to pick up someone and take him home. A nurse came out and told me to take home this guy named Bill. (He's about 40 and well dressed.) She told me to try to cheer him up, because he's in a bad mood. He looked like he was depressed.

Bill got in and I told him my name and of course I start asking him a million questions. He said he's very depressed because his wife just had a baby and that they just drove off with her father and left him there. He was crying a little and didn't act like he wanted to talk too much. I waited awhile; then I asked him why his wife and baby left. He told me he doesn't know why. He said he works hard, has a nice house, and never did anything to hurt his wife. I'm getting a little suspicious now that he's not telling me everything, and we need to know what's going on.

Just before we got to his house he said he doesn't know what he's going to tell his friends. I told him to tell them the truth and if they are his friends they will understand and help him. (If you didn't know it, a cab driver is sometimes a counselor, too. People are always asking me for some valuable advice and it's free.)

We got to his house and he wanted to show me something. We went inside house and it was a nice place. He took me into a room he just built for his new baby. It was all ready with baby stuff everywhere. After he showed me everything, I wished him good luck.

On my way back to Arcata, I kept thinking I needed to know more about Bill. I had to go back to the hospital later in the day and thought maybe I could find out some more details then.

Later, I drove back around to the hospital nursery to do a little investigating. I needed to find the nurse. I was getting out of my cruiser when a guy I know comes running out of the shop. He's all excited and asked, "Did that guy tell you everything that happened to him?" I said, "No, do you know?" He told me to come into his office for all the details.

What happened was, Bill and his wife have been married for about five years. His wife's parents came out from Florida about a week before the baby was born. They stayed at Bill's house to give them support and help them get ready for the baby. They went out to dinner one night and had a good time all week.

Then it was time to go to the hospital. So Bill and his wife and his in-laws got in the car and drove to the hospital. One big happy family. The first night at the hospital they all had dinner in the cafeteria and were all talking about the baby that would be born any time.

The next morning the baby was born. Everyone is at the birth. Bill is very proud and excited about his new little boy.

After a couple of days it's time for everyone to take the baby home. So they all load up everything into Bill's in-laws' car and everyone gets in. Just when Bill was going to close his door, a couple of policemen walked up and told Bill they needed to talk to him.

So he got out and was wondering what was going on when he heard the door close. He turned around and watched as they drove off leaving him there. They were going back to Florida without him. The police explained to him what was going on.

What happened was Bill was abusing his wife and her dad wanted her out of the relationship. He had told her how he had this big plan about how to get her out of there (this was all planned weeks ahead). He had the police there just in case Bill lost it and tried to harm someone.

It's not right for a man to hit a woman. Even though he probably knows he was wrong, he probably still loves his wife and to take his new baby away, that has to be tough. I wish people would think before they get themselves into a bad situation like this.

GAS LOCK RAGE

I encounter a lot of different types of people, and see a lot in my daily travels. And almost everyday I witness something new. You have all heard or read somewhere about "road rage" on our freeways. Nowadays, especially in big cities, you could get shot just by getting too close to someone in your car, or by giving someone a dirty look. Rage in the workplace and in schools are in the news almost every week.

Now we even have rage in the skies. Lots of airlines are having problems with unruly passengers on planes. What's next?

Well, I have a new problem to add to the growing list of rages in America. The other day, I went to fuel up my luxurious yellow cruiser at the Renner card lock on West End Road. For those of you that don't know, a card lock fueling station is just like a regular gas station, but nobody works there, and you use a fuel card to purchase your gas. I use a Renner card lock card. It works like an ATM card, but you get gas and not money in return.

As I was pulling into the gas pump area, I noticed a big Ford truck parked on the other side of the pumps. Then I saw a guy kicking, beating and cussing at the card lock machine. He was dressed like a logger and was as big as a tree. He probably stopped to fuel up before he headed to the woods to work.

When I pulled up next to him, he's still going nuts, and it seems like he's getting madder by the minute. I assumed he was upset because his card wouldn't work. After a lot of use, the magnetic stripe on your gas card can get worn down and won't work every time, or not at all. Then it's time to order a new card.

Every time I fuel up, I have to fill out some paperwork for the cab office. While I took care of that I kept an eye on this guy, especially after I noticed he had two rifles in his gun rack in his truck. This was the first case of fuel card lock rage I had ever seen.

After I finished filling out my gas log, I decided it was time to fill up my cruiser, and see if I could help Paul Bunyan get his card to work. When I got out he told me "Good luck, my card won't work, and I don't have enough fuel to get to another damn gas station."

I wanted to tell him I could give him a ride in my cab, but I decided I didn't want to be the first person in America to be shot while fueling up by an outraged card lock customer.

After I got my card to work, the guy was mad again. I tell him, "Let me see your card; maybe I can make it work."

"Here, go ahead," he told me.

After about five tries, it worked! He was relieved now. When I was leaving, he told me thanks, and asked me what my name was. I told him just remember Cab10! He said OK.

OVER THE HILL

Every once in awhile, do you feel like you're over the hill? Do you wish you could think of something that would make you feel younger?

Here's a Cab10 idea for you, if you can't think of anything. Here's how David Oehler solved his over-the-hill problem.

I had to pick up his lovely wife, Deborah, at David's doctor's office and take her to work at Mad River Community Hospital

Adult Day Center. She's one of the many special women and men that help run the Adult Day Center, which has an excellent program. I take a couple of van loads of people there every day to participate in all the fun activities they have available. I have known Deborah for a couple of years now.

Deborah told me that she was at the doctor's office talking to her husband, David, who injured his ankle trying to be a kid again.

I asked Deborah, "What happened to him?" She told me that her husband just turned "50" last week, and was feeling like he was over the hill. He kept telling her he needed to do something fun or exciting to get his mind off his age.

Then he remembered that his mother-in-law had given him some money for his birthday, so he bought a skateboard.

Earlier that morning he was feeling like a kid again. He took his new skateboard outside in the rain (in the rain!) to prove to the world and himself he's still a kid at heart. He tried and tried, and finally felt comfortable enough to give his skateboard a test of the youthful energy he was feeling. He was going along pretty good, when all of a sudden he fell down, severely twisting his 50-year-old ankle.

I told Deborah, "Maybe if you bought David some training wheels for the skateboard, he would feel like a kid again."

So if any of you see a guy at the Arcata Skate Park with training wheels on his skateboard, make sure you tell David hi!

MR. WONDERFUL

I had to pick up a lady about 40 years old at the Pantry Restaurant in Valley West. As she was getting in my cruiser I could tell that she had been crying because she had makeup running down her face.

She wanted to go to Korbel. After we took off she asked me, "Will $20 be enough for the cab fare? That's all I have."

"That will be more than enough."

After I told her that, she started crying again. When she stopped, she told me a man at the Pantry felt sorry for her and gave her the $20 so she could get home. I had to find out what was going on here, so I asked her, "Did your car break down or something?"

"Nooo!"

Then she started crying again, holding her face in her hands.

"Are you going to be OK?" She couldn't answer me. A couple

of minutes later she put her hands down and said, "I can't believe my boyfriend took off and left me in Klamath. I thought he was the man of my dreams. He sure fooled me."

"Why did he leave you there?" I asked.

"We spent the weekend in Crescent City. Last night he started drinking and got real drunk. On our way home, I told him that I was upset with him and he got really mad at me. He then started hitting me and calling me names."

"How often does he get drunk?"

"Only a couple of times a month, which is an improvement for him because he used to drink everyday until we started living together."

She said that when they got to Klamath, she told him that she wanted to drive because he was too drunk and it was her car. He got really mad at her but pulled over. When she got out to walk around to drive, he took off and left her there.

"So what did you do, hitchhike?"

"I walked for over an hour before someone finally picked me up and took me to the Village Pantry."

"Where do you think your boyfriend went? Do you think he will be waiting for you at home?"

"I hope so, unless he went to buy some drugs." I was thinking this is the man of her dreams. I wanted to tell her my opinion, but I knew it wouldn't do any good. Before we got to her house she wanted to go to her bank and get some money. A few minutes after we got to the bank, she came out crying again and was very upset.

"What's the matter now?"

"I had $400 in my account. The teller told me my boyfriend, came in about an hour ago and took all my money."

I didn't know what to tell her. I don't think anything I would tell her would make a difference.

When we got to her house, her boyfriend and her car were missing. She started crying again. As she was getting out I asked her, "Are you going to be OK?"

"I don't know. My car's gone, I'm supposed to go to work in a couple of hours, my boyfriend's probably at the bars drinking and spending my money. Can't get any worse, can it?"

I didn't know what to tell her but good luck. It's amazing how many people have relationships like this lady. I hope she figures it out and gets rid of this scumbag or gets him some help.

If you or someone in your life that is abusing alcohol or drugs needs help, call the California Department of Alcohol and Drugs 1-800-879-2772. People are waiting to help you, so what are you waiting for? Call today.

THE DRIFTER

The other morning I picked up a drifter near Dows Prairie who had missed the bus! He had a bed roll, a walking stick that was made from a tree branch and a dirty backpack with a couple of pans hanging from the back of it. He looked beat.

He was mad because he missed the bus. He wanted to go to Arcata. I thought he might have some interesting things to write about, but I found out different. I started asking him questions, and here are the responses I received.

"How are you today?" I asked.

"If I want you to know I will tell you!"

Friendly kind of guy, don't you think?

Then I asked him. "Where do you want to go in Arcata?"

"To a place called Wildberries!"

"Are you going to have something to eat there? They have some good stuff there!"

"It's none of your damn business what I'm going there for, is it now?"

This guy had no personality at all, but I had to ask him one more question!

"Sir, where are you from?" He looked at me again and said, "Are you writing a book or something? Quit bugging me!"

I started to laugh to myself. I wanted to tell him that I was writing a book at that time, but I figured he might use his stick on me if I didn't shut up. So I didn't say another word, except of course to tell him how much he owed me for his excellent ride in my luxurious yellow cruiser.

CHAPTER 3
Drinkers Delight

"FASTER" HE SAYS

Some of my most interesting and crazy stories are about my passengers who have consumed too much alcohol. I like to pick people up at bars. I get some of my best stories from bar customers.

Usually when I go into a bar, everyone just stares at me because everyone has been drinking, and they're all wondering who I am, standing there staring at them. Then the person that called will usually figure out who I am and tell me that they're the one that called. They're usually never in a hurry, and nine out of ten times they just got a fresh drink.

I always tell them to enjoy their drink because the meter's on; I can wait. Then they usually will offer to buy me a soda. So, I usually will accept the offer and sit down and enjoy my drink, I mean my soda, because you never know, I might meet some new friends while I'm waiting.

I had to go to the Alibi Bar and pick up a drunk. He's a regular. He's usually really funny. This time he's really drunk. He can hardly talk. "Take me to Jimmy Dunn's in Eureka," he belts out. "Here's a $10, get this heap (I don't like anyone calling my luxurious yellow cruiser names) going fast."

Well, for ten bucks, I guess its OK. We're on the freeway and it's raining I'm going about 55 m.p.h. when he says, "Here's another $10, kick this cab in the ass! Lets go!" So I sped up to 65 m.p.h. About three miles later I let up on the throttle a little; I'm now going about 60 m.p.h. and he asks, "How fast are we going?" I told him 70 m.p.h. (I didn't really want to lie). He says, "Here's another $10; go 80 m.p.h." So I pump on the throttle again, and he's happy.

We arrived at the bar and the guy handed me a couple of twenties. He can hardly talk at this point. "This is for you if you go in the bar and hire me one of the girls to take care of me," he said.

I had to refuse that generous offer. With my luck I would ask an undercover cop. Then again, that would be a good story to write. Well, he gets out and rolls into the bar, and its time for me to roll on.

GOING SOUTH

This next story is a sad one for me. I had to go Toby & Jack's cocktail lounge and pick someone up. When I got there, I went inside; the bartender told me my customer was at the other end of the bar. When I walked to the other end of the bar, I was in for a big surprise. There sat an old bowling buddy of mine; I will call him Jerry.

I hadn't seen him in about four or five years. He was so drunk he could hardly walk. If you knew Jerry you wouldn't have believed what bad shape he was in. He had a nice family and a good job. The bartender told me that he had been drinking heavy for a couple of years.

Jerry and I used to bowl together on the same league at Arcata Bowl back in the '70s and '80s. Fred and Don Vanni owned the bowling alley back then. I used to have a great time bowling and partying afterward with all of the guys. I met a lot of friends there, and Jerry was one of them.

I remember the night I first met Jerry. Fred Vanni's son, David, was bartending that night. David is a good friend of mine, and we were always doing crazy things. One night he started smoking a cigar and wanted to know if I wanted one. I was having a good time, so I said OK.

A few minutes later Jerry walked in and sat down by me. We never really talked much before, but after an hour or so, we were having a good time. He asked me if I liked cigars, and I told him I was just smoking one for fun. He wanted to smoke one, too; so David gave him one. He doesn't drink, and I think that was the last cigar he ever smoked because he kept coughing and gagging. It was funny.

We bowled on the same league for at least 10 years. A few years ago I quit bowling, and this is the first time I had seen Jerry in quite a while. When Jerry saw me, he asked, "What the heck are you doing here, Randy?" I told him I'm the cab you called for, so lets go so I can get you home. He said, "OK!" As we're walking, (I'm walking, he's stumbling) out of the bar, he grabbed the arm of a girl sitting at the bar. He asked her, "Are you going to Mexico with me, Debbie, or not?"

She handed Jerry a note, and told him, "I have written down my conditions, so let me know what you want to do, Jerry."

"Conditions for what?" he asked.

I told Jerry it's time to go, because he could hardly talk, or stand. I finally got Jerry in my cruiser, and he started telling me why he's in the condition he is in. I think he was embarrassed, even though he was about ready to pass out.

A couple of years ago, his doctor told him that he only had a little time left to live. So he got depressed and started drinking. He then lost his job, and soon after his wife left him.

He told me he wants to move to Mexico and live his last days there so no one will see him in the condition he is in, or feel sorry for him.

We're now almost to his house, and he was reading the letter the girl at the bar gave to him. While he was reading the letter he was cussing and getting angry. As I pulled up to his house, I asked him, "What's the matter Jerry?" He handed me the letter, and told me to read it and tell him what I thought about it.

The letter was a handwritten contract made out by the girl at the bar. In the letter she told Jerry she will go to Mexico with him, as long as she has her own apartment, and he pays her $2,000 per month. The first $2,000 must be paid to her in cash before they leave.

I told Jerry she's trying to pull a fast one on him. I told him as soon as he gives her the money, she will probably skip town.

"You are probably right," he said.

He told me that he asked his wife to go with him, but she's fed up with him. He wanted to have some companionship so he asked this girl at the bar. He had met her about a month ago. "Go to Mexico by yourself," I told him, "I'm sure you will make news friends down there." He told me that is what he's going to do. After I helped him into his house, I wished him good luck and told him to take care of himself. It's sad to see someone you know turn out like Jerry.

A BORN FIGHTER

Here's what happens when you don't pay attention on the job. I had been going to a local trailer court almost every day at 3 p.m. to pick up this guy named Jim who is having tests done at the hospital.

I got a call to go to the same trailer court, and I didn't pay attention to the dispatcher when he was giving me the address. I just assumed I was picking up Jim again for his appointment. When

I got into the trailer court, I passed by a trailer where there were two guys who looked like a couple homeless drunks. They were giving me a dirty look and waving their arms at me when I drove by them.

I pulled up to Jim's house, which is about three houses down from where those two guys were having a fit, and honked my horn a couple times. Then I jumped out of my luxurious yellow cruiser and went to open the door for Jim when ever he came out. About this time the two drunks are walking up to me yelling and screaming.

"You guys have a problem with me?" I asked.

"Yeah, I do," one of them said. "You're a jerk. And I'm going to kick your ass!"

Now of course I'm wondering why I'm so lucky to get all this attention from this drunken weirdo.

"Are you having a bad day, or what?" I asked him.

"You know what you did," he said. "You drove right by us just so we would have to walk down here instead of picking us up back there where we were standing."

I tried to explain to them that I thought I was picking up a regular at the trailer where I was parked. Well, the one guy didn't believe me, but the other guy did and tried to calm down his lowlife friend.

They finally got in. They wanted to go to Fickle Hill. That's a good place for them, I thought. On our way there, the one guy was still being rude; plus he was drunk as a skunk. He's telling his buddy, "I want to kick the cabbie's ass; he drove by us back there on purpose. I'm going to call his boss and have him fired, too."

I had had about enough of this guy, so I told his friend, "You better calm him down or I'm going to call the police."

After a couple of minutes everything was quiet. I finally got these two guys where they wanted to go and was happy to get them out of my cab.

COUCH LAUNCHING

One day I picked up one of my regular customers at the Quality Inn. He wanted to go to the Plaza and have a few drinks. It's only 8:00 a.m. so I asked him, "What are you doing here?" He said he and his wife got into an argument the night before and the police brought him to the motel to cool off. He likes to drink a lot and is always raising hell everywhere he goes.

The guy said that yesterday he went home drunk again, and

his wife told him she was fed up with him. They got into a big yelling and screaming match. He said he started throwing things all over the house. She was trying to make him stop. He then threw the couch through the big front room window. That was enough for his wife; she called the police.

When the police got there they told him to calm down so they could talk. He told the police, "This is my house and my furniture and I can do whatever I want with it." He then told the police to go to hell and get out of his house.

The police handcuffed him and started questioning his wife. They found out that she hadn't been harmed by him in any way, except for being yelled at and breaking her furniture. The police told him that they were going to take him to a motel so he could sleep it off; otherwise he was going to jail. Another marriage out the window.

DRUNKEN SAILOR STORY

I got a call to go to Budget Rent-A-Car at Mickey's Quality Cars in McKinleyville.

When I got there, I saw a guy inside the showroom talking to someone at the Budget window. I assumed he was my fare. When I went inside, the guy turned and saw me.

"Hey you got here quick," he said. "That's good, because I'm in a hurry."

"Where do you want to go?" I asked.

"I need to go to Samoa to catch a ship that I work on; hopefully it's still there." After he got, in he told me he is from Seattle and has been down here for about 40 days. He is a seaman on a salvage ship that is doing a job for Louisiana Pacific.

There are 25 seamen and fifteen divers on his ship. He works for Crowley Salvage out of San Francisco; they do work all over the world. In this case they are working on L.P.'s drainage pipe that drains into the ocean. It's about 250 feet long and has a lot of debris built up in it.

The divers go down and repair the outside and clean the inside. He told me the opening of the pipe is only 32 inches. A diver will work his way through the whole pipe cleaning it out. He told me it's tough, but they have divers that do a good job.

While he was talking to me I could smell his breath. He must have been drinking all night because he smelled like Marino's Club at 2 a.m. I was going to tell him that he smelled like he had been partying all night, but he beat me to it.

"I hope I get to my ship in time," he said. It was about 9:45 a.m.

"What time is it leaving?"

"It's supposed to leave around 10 a.m., but the captain will wait for me, I hope."

"Is he a good guy?" I asked.

"He's really an ornery old goat. He's real pushy and is always ordering us around, but the pay makes the job worth it."

"Why didn't you get an earlier start back to the ship?"

He laughed. "I just got out of the 'cop shop.'"

"What's a cop shop, the police station?"

"Well, I'm from Boston and that's what we call a police station back there."

"So what happened to you last night?"

He started laughing again. Then he told me that he got arrested the night before for being drunk and disorderly in

Arcata. He had been drinking with some girl he is nuts over.

When I picked him up at Mickey's he was returning a car he had rented when he got off the ship a few days ago. After he got out of jail and went back to Arcata he couldn't find his rental car because he couldn't remember where he left it.

"What did you do?" I asked.

"After a couple of hours of walking around, I called Mickey's hoping that someone had brought the car back because I couldn't find it."

They told him they had no idea where it was, and to call the police and see if they knew where was at. So he called A.P.D. and asked them where he had been arrested to see if they knew where his car was. They told him his car was at 4th Street Market.

Then he walked to the market, got the rental car and took it back to Mickey's. Then he called me.

"If I could have found that damn car two hours ago, I wouldn't be in such a hurry now," he said.

When we got to Samoa, his ship was gone. He was not a happy camper. I asked him, "What are you going to do now?"

"I don't know. I guess I'll get out and walk around and think about it for a while."

"Where were you guys going next?"

"To the Panama Canal."

I wanted to laugh, but I held it back. As he was getting out, I wished him good luck.

GETTING LOOPED AT THE HOSPITAL

Just when I think I have seen it all while driving a taxi, something I never experienced happens. I bet this will be a new experience for you, too.

I picked up this guy at the Mad River Community Hospital who smelled like a bottle of whiskey, cheap whiskey at that. He wanted to go to the nearest liquor store to get some booze and then go back to the hospital.

I was wondering if he's going to have a party in the hospital, or what. As soon as we took off, I had a lot of questions going through my mind because this character was half looped already.

Before I start asking him what he's up to, I told him, "The closest liquor store is the Liquor Still in Valley West. Will that be OK?"

"That will be fine," he said.

"Are you having a party at the hospital?"

He laughed, "No, well sort of; we have a family tradition among the guys. Any time one of us in the family is having an operation, we all take turns going to the hospital and supporting him.

When I asked him where the booze comes in, he laughed again and told me that they always get some booze to drink while they're waiting during the operation in the waiting room.

"You drink in the waiting room?"

"Why not? It's just as good as anywhere else."

I started laughing. "I don't think the hospital will like that."

Just before he got out at the Liquor Still, he told me, "They will never know because we each get a glass full of ice from the cafeteria

31

and mix our drinks in the bathroom. Nobody knows the difference."

While he was in the store I was thinking, "I bet this guy is more worried about drinking than about the guy who's having surgery."

After a few minutes he came back with a big bottle of whiskey and two airline-sized bottles of whiskey.

After he got in he said, "I'm all set, let's go back."

"OK, but what's the reason for buying those two small bottles of whiskey when you have that big one?"

"Oh, that's a family tradition too. We always sneak two shots of booze in to the guy who is having the surgery so he can relax and feel like he's part of the party."

I couldn't believe this guy. The hospital would have a fit if they learned of this.

When we got back to the hospital, he wanted to go to the waiting room by the Emergency Room. When we pulled up, four guys come out with glasses in their hands.

"Are those your relatives?" I asked.

"Yeah that's them. Can we make our drinks in your cab?"

"The meter's on; go ahead." I was thinking I hope the surgery doesn't take too long because these guys will probably be pretty loaded in an hour or so.

As they were making their drinks, they flipped a coin to see who was going to sneak the two bottles of whiskey into their relative.

After they made their drinks, they paid me and told me "Thank you."

I told them as they were leaving that I hope their relative has a successful surgery.

One guys said, "I'm sure everything will be OK." Then one other guy said, "As long as we don't run out of whiskey, everybody will be happy."

SUBSTANCE ABUSE AND CAB10 CODEPENDENCY

One day I picked up Al, one of our loveable old drunks who rides with me once a month or so. The last time I picked him up was a few weeks ago at Marino's Club. It was one of the craziest adventures I ever had with someone who has had too much to drink.

Every time I pick up Al, no matter where he is, he wants to go to the nearest bar and today was no exception. This time he wants to go to the Sidelines to drink.

32

The time I picked him up at Marino's Club he was super drunk. When I walked into the bar that day it was hard to see. It was sunny outside and the bar seemed darker than usual because my eyes weren't adjusted yet. I asked the barkeep where my fare was and she pointed to corner booth where Al was sitting. I walked over to him.

"Al, are you ready to go?" I asked.

"I'll be out in a minute," he stuttered.

"OK, Al. I will be outside waiting for you."

As I was walking through the bar, people started laughing. I turned around and Al is stumbling behind me. They must have thought that was funny. I smiled and turned around and continued out to my cab.

When I was going through the bar door, I could still hear people laughing and talking about Al. When he got outside of the bar, I found out what was so funny. He must have gone to the bathroom earlier and not zipped up his pants, because his manhood was hanging out. It was pretty funny.

I then pointed at his crotch and said, "Al, you're not riding in my cab like that." He looked down and laughed. While he's trying to zip up his pants, a couple of ladies walk by. They were all embarrassed. He finally gets his barn door shut and slowly gets into my cab.

He was totally blitzed. It was the first of the month. He must have gotten his check, and he's out blowing it on booze.

After he closed his door he said, "Let's go to a liquor store so I can buy a bottle of vodka."

"OK, Al."

When we got to the liquor store he opened his door, rolled out and staggered into the store. I figured he was probably buying a bottle of booze to take home with him.

A few minutes later here comes Al. Before he got out of the liquor store door he had the lid off his bottle and was chugging on it. I just shook my head. I decided I'd better get out and help him get back into my cruiser.

After I got him in, I asked, "Ready to go home now Al?"

He gave me a funny look, like I was crazy or something. "Take me to the next town," he stuttered.

I couldn't believe he was going to keep on drinking.

"Al, do you want to go to McKinleyville or Eureka?"

"I don't care." Then he paused for a moment. "Let's go to

Central Station in McKinleyville."

As I'm driving to McKinleyville's most luxurious cocktail lounge, old Al's sucking down his vodka. He was trying to talk to me between gulps, but he was so drunk I could hardly understand him.

When we got to the bar, Al told me, "You wait for me while I have one drink."

"OK, I'll be here waiting for you." About two minutes later the bar door opened and out came the bartender with Al. The bartender, who I know, came over to me and said, "Randy, get this guy the hell out of here, I can't serve him a drink; he's too drunk."

Al was mad and was giving the bartender a bad time. I had to laugh; it was funny. After Al got in he said, "Let's go to Eureka to Jimmy Dunn's; they'll give me a damn drink."

On our way to Eureka he finished off his bottle of vodka. When we got into town, Al wanted to stop at Spadoni's Market so he could buy another bottle of Vodka. After we stop at the liquor store, Al goes in and a few minutes later he's back in my luxurious yellow cruiser drinking from his new bottle as we're driving to Jimmy Dunn's. I told him he shouldn't drink in my cab. I might get a ticket. He gave me a dirty look as he put the lid back on his bottle.

When we got to Jim Dunn's Bar and Grill, Al got out and told me to wait for him again. I just sat there watching him stumble towards the bar. We were about a block away. Just before he went in the bar he took another drink from his bottle and then set it down along the wall by the main entrance.

As the door of the bar closed behind Al, I was wondering how long it would be before they throw him out of there, too.

While I'm waiting for Al, a couple of other drunks walked towards the bar. As I watched them they pointed at the paper bag on the ground that had Al's bottle in it. They walked over, picked it up and looked in the bag. They were all excited. They looked around and didn't see anyone, so I guess they figured the bottle of vodka was now theirs.

They took the lid off and were smelling the contents; then I could see their eyes light up. As they're walking off, they were all smiles, taking turns drinking from Al's bottle. While I'm laughing at these two drunks, I notice the bar door opening and here comes old Al. It took him awhile to get to where I was parked, but he made it.

As he was getting in my cab, he's grumpy as ever. "They serve you a drink in there, Al?"

"No, let's go to Loleta."

"Aren't you ready to go home now?"

"Hell no. My friend bartends at the Gilded Rose in Loleta. We're going there. He'll serve me a drink."

I then told him the devastating news—someone took his bottle. He didn't care.

Before I go any farther I thought I better tell Al what his cab fare was. I wanted to make sure he had enough money for it. "Al, your cab fare is $80."

He didn't say anything. He just looked at me and tried to put his hand in his pocket to get some money.

"Al, don't you think I should take you home now so you can get some sleep?"

A few seconds later he pulls out a big handful of crumbled-up bills and hands it to me.

"Here," he said. "Take what you need. Shut up and drive." I took $150 and told him I would give the difference back to him when we got to our final destination. I know he doesn't know where that's going to be and neither do I.

We were on Broadway, almost out of Eureka, and Al told me to pull into Ray's Food Place at the Bayshore Mall. He wanted to buy another bottle of Vodka. When I pulled up to the store, I told Al I would go inside to get his bottle. I think he thought that was a good idea. A few minutes later we're on our way again to Loleta. When we got to the Gilded Rose, I gave Al back his change for the cab fare and was happy that I would be on my way back to Arcata.

As I was turning around, I saw Al putting his bottle of vodka on a bench in front of the bar as he was going in the front door. I was glad to get out of there.

About 10 minutes later I was on the freeway by the College of the Redwoods when the dispatcher came on and told me to go back to Loleta and pick up Al.

I wanted to ignore the call, but I turned around and went back to pick up Al. When I got back to the Gilded Rose, old Al was sitting on the bench drinking from his bottle. I never saw anyone in my life drink as much as this guy and not pass out or get sick.

After I threw him back in, he told me, "Take me to Fortuna." I couldn't believe old Al was still functioning.

Then I told him, "If they kick you out of the bar in Fortuna, don't call, because we're not going to come and pick you up." He gave me a dirty look and told me to get going.

When we got to Fortuna I took him to the first bar on Main Street. He got out and staggered over to the bar.

He put down his bottle by the front door and walked in. I fired up my super-sonic cruiser, turned off my radio and headed for home.

When I got back to Arcata, I asked the dispatcher if Al called back, and he said no. They never heard from him any more that day.

DRUNK AND OBNOXIOUS

I picked up another one of our famous drunks at Everett's Club and he wanted to go to Eureka. He was really upset because all the bars kept kicking him out. I wondered if it had anything to do with to the fact that he was really drunk and was obnoxious.

As we're leaving the Plaza, he told me he wanted go to stop at 4th Street Market to get some more liquor (as if he needs more) so he can drink on our way to Eureka.

When we got to the store he told me he would be right out. A couple of minutes later a police car pulled up next to me. The officer told me he received a call from one of the bars and that they wanted someone removed from the bar who had too much to drink and was causing a lot of problems.

The barkeep told the officer that the drunk just left in Cab10 and they were going to 4th Street Market. The officer asked me if I was waiting for the guy he was looking for. I told him the guy's in the store. So he waited until my customer came out and they then had a few choice words. It was fun to watch.

Then the officer handcuffed the guy and put him in his patrol car. I asked the officer, "What about my cab fare?" He told me he would get it for me. When he came back with my money he told me he was taking the guy to jail and thanked me for my help.

I told the police officer he should have followed me to Eureka and then arrested him there so I could have gotten a bigger fare.

He laughed. "Maybe next time," he said.

CHAPTER 4

College Calls

DON'T DRINK AND DRIVE

There's one advantage in driving a taxi in a University town. It's not hard to find something to write about because of all the college kids and the crazy things they do.

One thing college kids like to do is party and so do I. But sometimes these kids do some real crazy things. I don't think these three guys you're going to read about planned what happened to them, but it was fun to write about it.

I have to go to Bayside to pick up someone who wants to go shopping. I find the house and go up the driveway, which must have been engineered by a idiot because it was so steep, and it wasn't very smooth either.

I honked my horn, and someone opened the door and waved at me that they will be right out. I turned my luxurious yellow cruiser off and waited. While I'm sitting there I noticed that there are five vehicles; which are all pretty new, parked in front of the house, and I was wondering why someone needed a cab.

After about five minutes, three college guys come out and get into my cruiser. They want to go to Safeway and get some groceries. I had to ask them why there were so many cars, and yet they called a taxi. They started laughing.

The five cars belong to them. They're all from Los Angeles and are best friends that came up here to go to college. One of the guys owns one car. The other two each have a car and a truck.

I told them they have some pretty nice cars for college kids. They said they all come from wealthy parents who hope they can get an education and earn their own way.

Then they told me that they had to call for a cab, because in the last four months they have all been arrested for a DUI and won't get their drivers license back for a while. They started laughing about it, and I did too.

One of the guys told me that about four months ago they were coming back from a party in Eureka. They had been drinking a lot

37

and were pulled over for speeding. The driver was arrested for a DUI. Then, about a month later, they were coming home from the Central Station Bar in Mckinleyville when some lady ran a stop sign and smashed into their car.

While the police were investigating the accident and interviewing everyone, the police realized that these guys were drunk. It was the lady's fault for causing the accident, but one of them was arrested anyway because he was driving under the influence. The guy who was arrested told me it was about the worse luck you could have. "My truck had $4,000 damage, and I got a DUI," he said.

I couldn't help but laugh at these guys. I couldn't wait to hear the third guy's story. He told me that the other night they were driving around the Plaza about midnight, getting ready to go home, when they noticed two good-looking girls that they had drinks with earlier walking down the sidewalk. So they pulled over to see if the young ladies wanted a ride home.

They were talking to them when someone pulled up behind and started honking the horn at them so they would get going because they were stopped in a red zone. It was one of Mel Brown's troopers(A.P.D.). He came up to them and told them to move along. They tell the officer to give them a couple of minutes, and about this time a friend of theirs who was in the back seat tells the officer some smart ass remark.

The officer tells the driver to get out, and after a few minutes, he's arrested for a DUI. I had to laugh again—it was so funny.

SKIRTING THE ISSUE

I love asking people about their jobs, because almost everyone has a story to share about their work. Some of the funniest stories I have heard in my taxi have come from people who work in restaurants.

I picked up a lady that goes to San Diego State; she wanted to go to the airport. I asked her, "Do you live here or are you just visiting?" She told me, "I wish I did live here!" She told me that she has to go back home and go to work. She told me that she had the most embarrassing moment of her life last week at work.

She works for an exclusive dinner house in San Diego. She's a waitress, and all the girls have to wear short wrap around skirts.

The other night she was working, and the restaurant was busy as usual. She had just cleaned off a couple of tables and had a big tray of dirty dishes that she needed to take to the kitchen to have cleaned. She grabbed the large tray, put it over her head and started walking through tables working her way to the kitchen. She came to a couple of tables where the people are sitting real close together. She turned sideways, sucked her stomach in and made it through. She's walking along and people are laughing and pointing at her. She then realized what all the commotion was about. When she squeezed through the two tables, her skirt fell off. She walked right out of it and didn't know it.

"It was so embarrassing," she said, "I dropped all the dishes and ran for the bathroom!" That made it even worse, because most of the dishes broke, and it was really loud. After a couple of minutes one of her co-workers brought her skirt to her and told her that the boss said she could go home if she wanted to. She was out of there in a minute. The next day she bought an airplane ticket to come here to visit a good friend.

I couldn't help it, but I had to laugh at her.

She looked at me and laughed too. I told her, "I bet your boss will be happy to have you back. I'm sure everyone in San Diego has heard about what happened. Everyone will want to come to his restaurant and see the excellent entertainment." She told me, "Thanks a lot," and laughed as she was getting out.

DISTRACTION FRACTION

A university student takes girl watching to a different level. I picked up a Humboldt State University student at Mad River Hospital. He came walking out, and has a cast on his arm. He told me he broke it and wanted to go home. I asked him, "How did you break your arm?" He told me he was riding his bike at a high rate of speed on 7th Street towards Healthsport, when he noticed a very attractive young lady walking on the opposite side of the road.

He was checking her out when he lost control of his bike, went over the embankment and fell on his arm and broke it. He told me it was pretty embarrassing.

HOW NOT TO GET OUT OF BED

When your telephone rings do you run to your phone or do you take your time to answer it? I picked up a young lady in Arcata who was using crutches. She wanted to go to the doctor to have her ankle checked. She told me it was really sore. I asked her, "How did you hurt your ankle?" She told me, "This is embarrassing."

"I don't care; what happened? Everyone tells me everything, so you might as well tell me your story too."

"OK, I fell out of bed!" She laughs.

"Sounds like you were having fun."

"No, I wish!" She said. "The other night I was sleeping, and the phone rang. The phone is on the other side of the house. I tried to jump out of bed, but I got all tangled up in the sheets and fell on the floor and fractured my ankle."

I laughed! She then told me she needed to get a job for the summer before she goes back to school at Humboldt State University. I told her, "You're not going to get a job if you can't stand up. By the time your leg heals, it will be time for school to start. If anyone hires you, they probably won't give you any time off! They would probably be afraid you would go to sleep and fall out of bed again."

She said, "Thanks a lot," and went on her way.

THE TRUE MEANING OF COOL

The next Cab10 adventure is one of the coolest. Being a cab driver, you have to know everything! If you ask my two younger sons, Zachary or Benjamin, they will tell you their dad does know everything.

(Of course I trained them.) But if you ask Mrs. Cab10, you will get a different answer.

In this next cab story Mrs. Cab10 is right again. I pick up a cool young lady, Jenny Shaver, in McKinleyville. She needed to go to work at the Rocket Station in Valley West. She moved up here to go to College of the Redwoods. She told me that she loves it here in our beautiful area. She also told me it's a cool place. I told her I think it's a pretty cool place too!

As most of you know I always ask my customers lots of questions, because it's the cool thing to do. Sometimes I get a cool story, and sometimes my inquiries lead to a dead end.

As I was saying earlier, I know everything. I asked this young lady where she's from. She told me she's from Cool. I sort of laugh, then I ask her again, "Where did you say you're from?" She told me, "I'm from Cool." I was thinking, "that's cool." But what or where is Cool? I never (OK, so I don't know everything) heard of Cool, California before. "It's east of Sacramento, she says."

"I thought I knew every town in California, but I guess I was wrong." I reply.

She laughed, "It's a cool town."

"I wonder why," I told her. "I bet you have heard a lot of cool sayings about your cool town."

She told me she has heard them all. But I just had to ask her a few cool questions, and here are some of the ones that I asked her.

"Was it cool to live there? Is it always cool there in the winter? Are the people that live there cool? What's not cool about your home town? What's the coolest thing to do in Cool?"

Then I thought I better cool it, or she won't call for Cab10 ever again, and that wouldn't be cool.

When she got out she told me, "I will probably call you again sometime, because I don't have a car yet, and because you're (you guessed it) a cool cab driver."

Well, I hope you liked this cool story, because I got to cool it and go back to work.

ROLLING BLUNDER

When was the last time you saw someone naked in a wheel chair along side of the road. I picked up a guy at Mad River Community Hospital at the emergency room. He's about 25 and sitting in a wheel chair in a hospital robe. He wanted to go home. While we're heading towards his house I asked, "What were you in the hospital for?"

He asked me if I read the police log about the naked guy in the wheel chair. I started laughing, "No, I missed that story. He tells me that yesterday he took too many drugs and started feeling real bad.

He decided he needed to go to the hospital. He wanted to call for an ambulance but had no phone.

41

He had no clothes on and tried to get himself dressed, but couldn't. Finally, after struggling for quite a while, he got into his wheelchair and started for Mad River Community Hospital. The last thing he remembered was leaving his house. He had gone a few blocks and blacked out.

Someone found him and called an ambulance. (That must have been a strange sight—a naked guy in a wheel chair passed out on the sidewalk.)

When we got to his house I helped him in, and he tells me thanks. He told me if I ever see a naked guy in a wheel chair, it's probably him, and to call an ambulance. What a character he was.

HEAD OF THE CLASS

I had to pick up Emily Jacobs, an Anthropology student at Humboldt State University. She needed a ride home, because it was raining real hard. (I'm lucky I have a speller check on my computer, because anthropology is a tough one to spell.)

Before I took her home we picked up her 3 year old daughter, Raven. She was as cute as her name. After they got in, we headed for Emily's home.

I asked her, "How's school going?"

"It's going really good; I just got out of my anthropology class. It's a great class and my teacher, Professor Mary Scoggin, is great also," she said.

Then she told me something that was very interesting. "The other day in my anthropology class one of my classmates used one of your columns as an example of "urban legions."

I was thinking, what are "urban legions?" I never went to college so I had no idea what she was talking about.

So I asked Emily, "What are "urban legions" and what does my column have to do with it?"

She laughs and then says, "We're studying "urban legend storytelling to folklore to poetry performance, and myths in American, Chinese, and Middle Eastern Cultures. We consider contemporary practices, histories, and ways of viewing folklore, oral storytelling practices, and the different relationships between oral and literary narrative in each of these distinct and elaborate traditions."

Now if you're confused, I'm totally lost. "So how does my column fit into all of what you just told me?" I asked.

She told me every day a different student brings in a story which they read to the class. The stories can come from a book, newspapers, articles or even be made up. Then the students will question the person to see if it's a myth, or if maybe it's an "urban legion." They can look at a certain time in history and learn from the different writings of that time what was common in that time period.

For an example, the column they used that I wrote was one of my more outrageous ones, it was almost unbelievable (a possible myth?) to some people, but it did happen. Emily told me my column was a hit with the class and raised a lot of interesting questions. Such as, "Is that a true story?"

"When was that written?" "Who wrote the column?" Emily told me her classmates were surprised that I was from Arcata. The other thing Emily told me that was interesting about my column was that automobiles and cell phones were mentioned.

So, for an example, if someone reads my column a hundred years from now, they will learn that automobiles and cell phones were in use at this time in history. I thought that was interesting.

I also asked Emily, "What else are you doing in your class?"

"We're reading a book called "The Baby Train and other lusty "urban legions."

Now I was in left field again. "What's the book about—babies?" She laughed. "It's about trains going through small towns all over America early in the morning blowing their horns, waking up the adults who make more babies. All these towns are experiencing population explosions." She tells me then the question is, "Is it a myth or not?"

Just before Emily got out she asked me, "You should come to my class some day and give a lecture on your writing and take questions from my classmates."

"That would be fun, I would be interested in doing that. Just have your professor contact me." Well, a few days after I wrote this story, and before I sent it to the newspaper, I received an invitation from Professor Mary Scoggins inviting me to her class at Humboldt State University to give a lecture on how I collect my story ideas and represent them in written text and other storytelling techniques I use.

I never dreamed when I started writing that I would be giving a lecture at a university on my work.

Hard Luck Driver

Have you ever had your car impounded? I'm going to show you how to save time and money if you are ever in this situation.

I picked up this guy at about noon the other day at the University. He needed to get his car out of an impound yard but wanted to go to the DMV office in Eureka first.

As we're getting ready to go I asked, "What happened; did you get a DUI?"

In a very depressed tone of voice he said, "No, they towed my car off a few days ago because it wasn't registered."

"Did you forget to pay your registration?"

"No, I have two cars. I drive one every day and my other car is in storage. The car I drive everyday had to go into the shop for two days. I needed a car to go to work, so I decided to get my other car out of storage. I haven't registered it for a couple of years because I'm trying to sell it. I figured I could drive it for a couple days and get away with, but I was wrong and got stopped. I explained my situation to the police officer, but he wasn't listening and had it towed off."

On our way to the DMV office he told me he had a date later and was wondering how long it would take us to go to Eureka and back. I told him I had no idea how long it would take because anytime you go to the DMV office, it depends on how many blocks long the line is.

"I need to be back at the university in a couple of hours. This is the first date I have had in almost two years."

"That's a long time."

"Yeah, I don't have too much luck with the ladies."

All the way to the DMV office he was rattling off about his whole life, which was one big mess. After listening to him for a while, I came to the conclusion that most of his problems were his fault, and the girl that was going to be his date later must be desperate to go out on a date with this guy's outlook on life.

After he stopped talking for a second to breath, I asked him, "What do you have to do? Pay for your registration and then you can get your car out?"

"Yeah, I need to pay for my registration or they won't let me have my car."

When we get to the DMV office, he gets out and goes inside. I grab my newspaper to read while I wait. About twenty minutes later, he comes out, fit to be tied. "What's the matter?"

"I can't pay for my registration unless I have insurance on my car. I need to go to an insurance company to buy some."

"Which insurance company do you want to go to?"

"I don't care. This is ridiculous. It's going to cost me a fortune for all this."

On our way to find an insurance company he's telling me more about his exciting life. I have come to the conclusion that this guy could win the lotto and still think he's got it bad. Besides that I think he's a few sandwiches shy of a picnic.

A few minutes later we find an insurance office. He gets out and tells me he will be back as soon as possible. "I'll be here," I said.

About 15 minutes later I see him coming through the insurance office door carrying some papers. Then for some reason he stopped and turned around and started talking to someone inside the door. It turned into a yelling match. About a minute later he threw his papers on the ground, told the insurance agent to stuff it, and got back into my cab. He was steaming.

"They want $500 for six months, that's ridiculous. Then the guy tried to talk me into coming back into his office to see if he could find something that might work that I could afford."

"I was wondering what you guys were arguing about."

"The heck with those guys; let's go somewhere else," he said disgustedly. After a couple of more places he finally buys some reasonably priced insurance. We then go back to the DMV office.

About an hour later he comes out with his registration. You

would think he would be smiling a little bit, but he wasn't. He had to pay $235 for his registration. After he gets in, we go to McKinleyville to A & M Body Shop to pick up his car.

When we get to A & M Body Shop his cab fare is $75. He has to go inside the office to break a hundred dollar bill so he can pay me, because I don't carry much change. When he comes back out he's steaming again. "What's the matter now?"

"They won't let me have my car until I take my proof of registration to the Arcata Police Station and have my ticket signed off. I can't believe this."

"Do you want me to take you to Arcata?"

"I have no choice. Let's go."

On our way to Arcata this guy is really going off. "This is the biggest joke I have ever seen," he says.

When we get to the police department he has to pay them about $100 for the towing which he wasn't aware of. So you can imagine what he told me when he got back into my cab this time, ouch, my poor virgin ears.

On our way back to McKinleyville, Mr. Personality tells me that when he was getting change at the impound yard earlier, the secretary told him it was going to be $150 for the storage of his car.

When we get back to A & M his cab fare is now $120. As he's paying me he's adding up what he has spent to get his car back.

"My insurance was $250. My registration was $235. The towing was $100, storage was $150 and now my cab fare is $120. I spent $855. I hope you know that I can't afford to give you a tip today."

I didn't care at this point if he gave me a tip or not. I thought I would cheer him up, so I told him, "Hey don't worry about the tip, you have a date tonight." He gives me a funny look as he's leaving and says, "The heck with her; I'm broke."

CHAPTER 5

Rough trade

DEADBEAT DILEMMA

What happens when you don't have any money for your cab fare? I get asked that question a lot. You have three choices: get the money, be arrested or deal with me, the 280 lb nightmare. (I'm almost as big as one of our famous Redwood trees).

I picked up a lady at Mad River Hospital Emergency Room; she wanted to go to Blue Lake to her home. She told me that she didn't have any money, but that her husband would pay me when we get there. I agreed.

When we got to her home, we pulled into the driveway. Her husband saw us but just kept on walking the other way. I caught up with him and told him that his wife said that he would pay the cab fare.

He told me she has called the ambulance three times this week to take her to the hospital for no major reason. He told me he is fed up with her and her problems. His wife told me now to take her to Arcata, to a friend's house, and she will pay me. I said, "OK," but I was getting a little nervous.

We arrived at her friend's house and the fare was now $18.50. She went up to the door and her friend came out and told me she is not paying either, that she is tired of this lady's problems, too. I decided it's time to call the police.

The lady got back in the cab and asked me, "What are we going to do now?" I told her the police were on their way to talk to her. She said, "OK," like no big deal.

I told the lady's friend if she doesn't pay, the woman will be arrested and fined $470. She finally agreed to pay. When the police arrived, they talked to the lady in my cab anyway and found out she has warrants for her arrest for something else. I got my money and she got a free room at the County Jail.

CRAP HAULING CAPER

Cab10, the luxurious yellow cruiser moving van at your service. Yes, we do move people's belongings. Have you ever had to move something, such as a TV, stereo, bed, etc., but you had no truck, and your friends who had trucks weren't available. Next time call for Cab10 and get the job done quickly, safely, and professionally.

This call was one of those moving jobs that all cab drivers hate to get. This time, I have to go to a motel in Eureka to help someone move out. Sometimes it's not too bad, but most of the time, it's just a waste of energy. When I pulled up to the motel, it was raining pretty hard. I saw three people waving me towards them.

They looked like the normal group of people that moves from one motel to another all the time. They told me to back up towards this little corridor that leads to their room. There is no roof over the corridor, and their room is about 50 feet from my cab. There is a big pile of junk, I mean their belongings are stacked outside their room, all wet from the rain. They wanted to move their stuff from here to another motel that is three (wow)blocks from here. So I opened up all my doors and we started loading up all their stuff. I was getting soaked. I wasn't a happy camper. After about five minutes two of the guys quit helping and the other guy was slowing down.

I finally told them that I needed to organize the loading of my cab, and they can bring the rest of their stuff. They didn't like the idea, but they agreed.

You should have seen this stuff. Dirty moldy clothes, broken flower pots, dishes and pans with old food stuck in them that smelled terrible. There were broken toys, torn books, loose clothes and blankets, and a lot more valuables too numerous to mention. It would take three full cab loads to move it all.

When we came back for the second load, the owner of the motel was at the motel room yelling and screaming at the two lazy guys that waited there for us. The owner was in the room throwing the rest of their stuff out into the rain. It was sort of funny. You should have seen the room. They had destroyed it. Everything was stained, and there were holes in the walls.

The owner told them to hurry up and get out of his sight before he called the police and filed a complaint for the damages. We finally got the last two loads over to the other motel where there are three ladies (ladies might be the wrong word) and a few kids to help us unload.

They were smoking pot and drinking beer.

We were almost done unloading the last load when this car drives up and this guy gets out screaming and yelling. I thought he was going to lose it. Then I realized it was the motel owner, who happened to own this motel too. There was a lot of yelling going on. The motel owner didn't know that they were moving to his other motel.

It was time for me to get out of there. I told one of the guys to pay me so I can get back to work. He yelled into the motel room for someone to pay me. I'm waiting and watching these guys scream at each other. What a mess.

Then this girl asked me, "How much do I owe you?" I turned around and this girl was standing there with a fishnet top on and no bra. She paid me. I went to close the doors to my luxurious yellow cruiser and there's dirt and other crap on the floor of my cab. I just shook my head and headed for the car wash to clean up the mess.

I told the dispatcher, "Thanks for a great call!"

A LOWLIFE GETS A 280 LB REALITY CHECK

The scariest thing about driving a taxi is getting robbed or getting stiffed. In this next story a runaway scumbag gets a 280 lb. reality check. I had to pick someone up at General Hospital. It was about 7:15 a.m. When I pulled up to the hospital, a guy about 25 came out of the lobby and got into my luxurious yellow cruiser.

He's a clean cut, quiet type of person. He's wearing a white baseball hat with a marijuana leaf on the front of it. He told me he was in the hospital for two days for minor surgery and was just released. He wanted to go to his home on 14th Street.

When we got to 14th Street, there was a big house. He told me that he needed to go into his apartment that's in back of the house and get some money to pay me. I said, "OK!" I could see from where I was parked, the apartment he was talking about. I had no reason to doubt this guy's word. But when you're a cab driver, I have learned, anything can happen.

I was watching this guy walk towards the back of the house, when all of a sudden he started running. I could tell that the reason he was running wasn't because he wanted to hurry and pay me. He was going to try to get away without paying.

I was steaming now. I fired up my cruiser, hauled ass down to the next street and headed for the alley that he probably was using for his getaway. I couldn't find him. I was really mad now; this was the first time someone got away from me. It was a good thing for him, because if I had caught him, he would have found out what 280 lbs. of hell would be like. The cab fare was only seven dollars, but it was my seven dollars.

Three other times I had people not pay, but I had them all arrested. I learned a lesson again. I wish someday that we could all trust each other again in America, but I doubt that will happen. Little did I know that the next day, I was in for a big surprise.

The next day I had to go to Eureka to deliver some truck parts to someone. After I dropped off the truck parts, Gary our dispatcher, told me to go to the Cinema 8 movie theater and pick someone up.

When I got there, I pulled up in front so whoever called could see me. They're probably about 50 people in the lobby buying their tickets or some snacks for the show. I waited about five minutes and no one came out. I walked around inside the lobby, but still no one showed up. I was about to leave when I remembered I needed to make a phone call.

I went back into the lobby to use the phone. As I was talking I was watching all the people. There were about 20 people in line for snacks. I happened to notice a guy wearing a white hat. I couldn't really remember what the guy who ran on me the day before looked like, but this guy was acting funny. It looked like he was watching me out of the corner of his eye. Then he turned enough that I could see a marijuana leaf on his hat. I was thinking it has to be the same guy. He must have called for a cab, and when he saw me get out (280 lbs. of his worse nightmare) got in line and hoped that I would not find anyone and leave.

I hung up the phone. I was on a mission. I don't get mad very often, but I was fired up now. I walked through the people that are in line, and I yelled at the manger to call the police, that I wanted to make a citizen's arrest. He gave me a funny look but told me, OK.

Everyone was getting out of my way and was watching what I was up to. I walked up to this punk and grabbed him by the shirt.

"Do you remember me?"

"No, I don't know you!"

"Let me remind you; I'm the cab driver you ripped off yesterday, and I want my money!"

He told me that I have the wrong guy! I then told him that he has two choices, either pay me, or I'm going to drag him outside and beat the hell out of him. He was shaking a little now. Finally he said, "How much do I owe you?" I told him $7. He handed me a ten, and said, "Are you happy now!"

I wanted to stick his hat where the sun doesn't shine, but I controlled myself, like the professional that I am. I started walking away with my $10, when he yelled at me, "Where's my three dollars change!" At this time, Eureka Police were coming into the lobby. I pointed at the police officer and I told this scumbag, "Ask the police; they'll be happy to help you." I called my boss and told him what happened. He laughed! He told me he wished he could have seen that guy squirming in his shoes.

SUICIDAL MANIA

One day I had to pick up someone on Humboldt Hill. When I got there, a lady about 35 years old came walking out with a very large backpack on. She's growling and complaining about something. When she saw me she said, "Get me the hell out of here, I'm tired of my ex-husband and my kids' crap!"

When I heard that I knew I was going to be in for an earful. After we got rolling, she told me to take her to Cloney's drug store so she can pick up her prescription. Then she wanted me to take her to Arcata so she can start hitchhiking to Michigan.

After we go to Cloney's and she got her prescription, she got back in my cruiser and we headed for Arcata. Then she started telling me why her life was all screwed up just what I wanted to hear.

Her husband left her a few years ago because she was on drugs and tried to commit suicide. When he realized she wasn't getting any better, he went and got custody of their three kids. In the last year she has gotten her life back to normal, but her husband doesn't want her back and neither do the kids.

Today was her last try begging her kids to come with her, but they refused. She told me at one time even her husband was on drugs and tried to kill himself, but he got help and she never did, so he gave up on their relationship.

So she told them she was leaving the state and never coming back.

About this time we were passing by a house on our way out of Eureka, and she ducked down real low in her seat. "What's the matter?" I asked. "My mother lives in that house right there, and I

51

told her I might be leaving the state and never coming back. She told me if I leave she would kill herself because she couldn't stand it without me, because I'm all she has left."

The rest of the way she told me more details about her exciting life, and said, "Now do you understand why I want to move to another state?"

I asked her, "Don't you ever get scared hitchhiking?"

"I try to ride with truck drivers because they seem to be safe to be with, and once in a while they even let me clean their trucks so I can make some extra money," she said.

Then she reached into her backpack and pulled out a can of mace and a pistol. "I'm prepared," she told me.

"I see that you are," I said, and told her to put her weapons away because they make me nervous.

When we got to Arcata she jumped out and has her thumb out before I drive off. As I drive away I was thinking, "Doesn't Dr. Kevorkian, the suicide doctor, live in Michigan?"

THE RUDE JERK ACTUALLY LEFT A TIP

I had to go to the airport to pick up a package to deliver to a business in Eureka. There was a long line, so it took me about 45 minutes before I finally made it to the counter.

While I was in line, someone from the airport had called for a cab. I didn't know it yet, but I was going to find out soon enough.

When I finally reached the counter, I was giving the clerk the information on my package so she could go find it when some guy starts yelling, "Is there a taxi driver anywhere?"

So of course I turned around, wondering if he wanted me, because my cab is out front and he probably wanted a ride. There were a lot of people in the terminal and the line behind me was pretty long also, so this guy probably couldn't see my cab shirt.

I raised my hand up and yelled, "I'm right here; I'll be with you in a minute."

He yelled back, "I called over half an hour ago; what the hell are you doing over there?"

I didn't know he had called, but I guess he thought I was there looking for him. He was very rude and was making a big scene in front of everyone.

I then told him, "Hey, I'm picking up a package and after I get it, I will be able to take you wherever you want to go."

"You can get your package later, I have an important meeting I need to be at."

This guy was pissing me off, so I told this jerk in a very firm voice, "I came to the airport for a package and haven't been back to my cab so the dispatcher could tell me that you called for a cab. If you want a ride, you can go get in my cab and I will be out as soon as possible."

He didn't like that, but he went and got into my cab. I finally got my package and headed out to my cab. I got halfway there and decided that it would be a good time to go to the men's room. (Ha Ha!) It took longer than I thought, but that's nature for you.

When I got out to the cab I knew I was going to get grilled again, but it's part of my job. The customer is always right.

I opened the back door to put my package in and this guy lit up again. "I thought you said you would be right out. I've got to get going!"

"What time and where is your meeting anyway?"

"It's in Eureka and it started an hour and a half ago."

"Well, how come you flew in here at the last minute and expect to be in Eureka on time?"

He didn't like that, and said. "I didn't know that Eureka was in Timbuktu and that I would have to wait for a cab, too. Didn't your dispatcher tell you I called?"

"No, I came here to pick up a package. You must have called while I was in line so I haven't got the message yet that you called, because I have been in line for 45 minutes."

I was closing the back door when this guy said, "Can't you move any faster?"

I was getting pretty tired of this guy's crap, so it was time to give him some of his own medicine without lowering myself down to his low level.

I decided I needed a soda, so I walked back into the terminal. My fare was right behind me.

"What the hell are you doing now?" he yelled.

"I'm thirsty, and I see you're not ready yet anyway because you're following me around. I will meet you out in my cab in a couple of minutes."

He was coming unglued.

It was fun watching this guy foam at the mouth. I decided it was time to take this creep to his meeting. It was a long ride to Eureka, but he did calm down and even gave me a tip.

RANDY'S SECRET IDENTIFY REVEALED

This next story is a combination of one of mine and one of our Eureka drivers. The other day I was talking to Dave Frazier, who drives Cab1.

He was telling me about one of his crazy adventures with one of our regulars who lives in Cutten. He asked me if I have ever been lucky enough to pick him up. I told him I have, but it's been along time. After he told me what happened to him, I told him about one of my experiences with the guy. We had a good laugh.

It's been about six months since I've seen this guy. I knew when I picked him up the first time that there was something unusual about him by the way he looked and acted. He always wears all black clothes and talks about weird things. And his house looks like it should be condemned. It has no paint left on it. The grass has never been mowed. The curtains are all stained, it's just a weird place. Maybe he's related to the Addams Family.

Anyway, every time I have picked him up he wants to go to the bank, Longs Drugs, McDonald's and then home. It always takes him about an hour to take care of his business.

The last time I picked him up he was acting really strange. I asked him if he wanted to do his normal routine. He said, "Yes," in a real low voice.

On our way to the bank I asked him, "How have you been?" He didn't say anything. I looked in my rearview mirror at him and asked him again, "How have you been doing?"

In a loud voice he said, "I know who you are, you're not fooling me!" As I was driving I turned around to see what this guy's problem was and he said, "Turn around. You don't think I know who you are? Well I know."

I wanted to laugh, but I held my composure and asked him, "Who do you think I am?'

"You're the devil. You're not fooling me. Quit talking to me and quit looking at me in the mirror with those evil eyes of yours."

I wanted to give this guy a bad time, but I was polite and didn't say anything else to him. After an hour of fun we arrived back at his house.

After he paid me I watched him go into his house, because I have noticed in the past that he has to push really hard on the door so he can squeeze himself into the place. It looks like the door has a bunch of stuff behind it making it hard for him to open.

As I was driving off I was wondering how anyone could live like that. After I told Dave about my last experience with this guy, he told me the other day he also took him to his usual places and the guy was also acting stranger than usual.

When Dave took him home he refused to pay. He told Dave he didn't have any money and for him to pay the fare because he has a job and can afford to pay it. Then he got out of the cab and went up to his front door and pushed and pushed on the door and finally squeezed himself inside and closed the door. Dave couldn't believe it.

Dave then knocked on the door, but the guy wouldn't answer. So Dave called the police. When the police arrived, they knocked on the door, but got no answer. They then went around to the back of the house and after about 10 minutes had our friend handcuffed and hauled him off to jail.

Dave told me a few days later he was after a call and was driving by this guys house. There their was a big sign on the front of the house saying, Keep out. This house has been condemned.

Then the very next day he drove by again and there was a fire truck and a special kind of truck which had hazardous signs all over it. What was really weird, Dave said, was that there were two guys in space suits going inside the house to check on something.

There was also a big garbage bin in the front yard. He said it was really weird. I told him it's not weird, not in our business it's not. I told him what would be weird is if those guys in space suits are there because of some kind of hazardous materials and our cabs start melting or something.

IDIOT DRIVER NO. 3,972

Driving a taxi 200-300 miles every day I run into a lot of crazy situations with other drivers. Of course they're the crazy drivers, not me. If they can't see my big luxurious yellow cruiser coming towards them, they must be blind or they're an idiot with a drivers license. If that's the case, they shouldn't be allowed to have a drivers license.

I'm sure you have all encountered one of these crazy drivers at one time or another in your travels.

I encountered one of these idiots the other day. I was at the stop sign at the intersection next to Cahill's Gas and Mini Mart on 11th street in Arcata. I was going to the hospital so I had to turn right on K Street, which is a two way street. Just after I made my turn I see a pickup coming right at me in the wrong lane. He must have thought both lanes were one-way. I slowed down hoping that this moron would move over into the proper lane, but he kept coming towards me.

So I drove over into the bicycle lane next to the sidewalk hoping that he would get the hint and get the hell out of the way. When he saw me do that he must have gotten mad and started driving right at me like I'm the guy with the dead brain cells. So like a very intelligent, professional, and courteous driver I stopped.

He swerved in front of me like it was my fault we almost got into a wreck. He was cussing, waving his arms and yelling at me, because I wasn't as stupid as him I guess. Then he gave me the finger too. I didn't know if that meant I was the number one cab driver or if it meant I was the number one worse driver he has ever seen.

As he was pulling along side of me to add a few more compliments on my driving, a couple of cars stopped behind me, I guess he never noticed them or just figured everyone was going the wrong way.

Because I'm such a nice guy and a very courteous person I rolled down my window to tell him thank you for all the nice compliments and he continues with even more praise.

By this time they're cars everywhere honking their horns. The guy must have finally heard the cars honking their horns and turned his head to see what all the honking was about. He must have finally realized that he was in the wrong lane.

Just before he drove off he looked at me one more time, because I'm sure he thought he was in the right. I gave him a big smile and a wave. He gave me one more four lettered compliment and reminded me that I was indeed the number one cab driver in America.

CHAPTER 6

Kids Corner

DO ALL CAB DRIVERS TALK TOO MUCH LIKE YOU?

I get a lot of calls to pick up kids. They are my favorite fares. Most of the time it's to take them to, or from school. Either the parents' car is broken down, or they're running late for work. Then the luxurious yellow cruiser is transformed into a school bus.

Some of the kids even think my cruiser is a small school bus. Some of the places I have to take kids to are their grandma's, or soccer practice, and other times to the dentist or the doctor.

One day I had to go to Mad River Children's Center to pick up a little girl and take her to her grandma's house because her mom was getting off work late. My Dispatcher, Randy Hendricks, told me the little girl's mom said to pick her daughter Jenny up and stop somewhere along the way and buy her an ice cream cone. Then take her to her grandma's. Her grandma will pay for the cone and the cab fare.

RANDY'S BOYS - BENJAMIN & ZACHARY

When I got to MRCC, I told one of the employees, "I'm supposed to pick up Jenny. Her mom wants me to take her to her grandma's house." She told me, "Your son Ben is showing her and a few other kids the art of baking."

"Baking?" I asked.

"Go out to the sandbox, and you will see what I'm talking about," she said.

I didn't have to go that far, and I knew what he was making. He loves to make mud pies. When I got to the sandbox, there were about 6 kids making mud pies and they were covered with mud. They were having lots of fun.

My son loves it here at Mad River Children's Center. It's a great place for kids, and they have a great staff. Cab10 recommends that you stop sometime, and say hi to the staff—Pam, Darcy, Steven, Sunshine, Kimberly and Christina.

I had to wait for a few minutes because they had to clean up Jenny so she wouldn't look like a human mud pie, or dirty up the pristine luxurious yellow cruiser.

I finally got her on board and told her that her mom told me to buy her an ice cream cone, and then take her to her grandma's house. Her eyes lit up when I mentioned an ice cream cone.

She was all excited. While she's eating her cone, I asked her how old she was. She told me, "I'm four-thirty!" I thought that was pretty funny. I didn't know if she's four or four-and-a-half.

She was a sweet little girl. When we got to her grandma's house she started getting out, and she asked me, "Do all cab drivers talk as much as you?" I laughed! Kids, they're the best!

KIDS STILL SAY THE DARNEST THINGS

One time I had to go to a local children's center. They called and ordered another cab and me to take two van loads of kids to Gymnastics Express. They go there to do gymnastics and play. They were all excited about riding in a cab. The kids were acting pretty silly and giving me a bad time on the way there.

I asked one boy, "Where does your dad work?" He told me that his daddy is a minister for a big church in Eureka. I asked him, "Do you help your dad collect the money on Sundays at church?" He said, "No!" Then he told me that his mom asked his dad one day if the people at church gave very much money that day. He told her that the people are so tight they squeak. I laughed about that one.

Another boy told me his dad is an attorney. I asked him, "Is that a very important job?" He said, "I think so, but I don't really know. I know every time my mommy takes me to see him he's always whispering to someone in suits." I asked him, Does he whisper to you and your mommy too?" He said, "No, silly!" Then he said, "Last night my mom and dad got into a big fight." "What happened?" I asked. "My dad told my mom she needed to lose weight, because she has a big butt," he said. All the kids, the teacher, and I got a good laugh about that one. I wish I had more fares like that one. Those kids were pretty smart.

KID ON BIKE CAREENS INTO THE LUXURIOUS YELLOW CRUISER

One day I was driving in Eureka on a back road that doesn't have any sidewalks. It was dark outside, and I saw a young boy about seven or eight riding a bike in front of me on the shoulder of the road. He was weaving back and forth, goofing off.

When I caught up to the boy, I moved over to the center divider to make more room for him, just in case. As I was moving away from him, he turned towards me and rode his bike right into the side of my cab. I don't think he heard me coming.

I looked in my mirror, and I saw the boy lying on the ground. I stopped and backed up to see if he was OK. He was watching me back up when all of a sudden he jumped up and took off on his bike like there's no tomorrow. I jumped out and yelled at him to see if he was OK, but he kept going. He was probably scared because he knew he was in the wrong.

I jumped back into my luxurious yellow cruiser and continued on to my next call. We're always suppose to call in when something happens, no matter how small an incident it is. So I decided I'd better tell the dispatcher about the kid that ran into me with his bike. I told the dispatcher what happened. The dispatcher said, "OK, but make sure you fill out a report before you go home." I told him, "OK!"

About five minutes later, the dispatcher told me to come to the office right away. The police are on the phone and want to talk to me. I was thinking, "what now!" When I got to the office, I had to explain to the E.P.D. what happened.

They told me that the boy's mom called and filed a complaint. She told E.P.D. that her son told her that I ran a red light and knocked him down and left the scene. I was getting a little upset now.

About that time I was getting off the phone with E.P.D. when I got another call. The dispatcher told me that some lady was on the phone and wanted to talk to me. It's the boy's mom!

She told me that she talked to her son again after she had called E.P.D., and realized her son was lying to her about what happened. She told me she was sorry for what happened.

I asked her, "Why was your son riding his bike at his age after dark?" I told her it's very dangerous, and she was lucky that something worse hadn't happened. She agreed with me and then said her son wanted to apologize to me.

He got on the phone crying, and told me, "I'm sorry," and then said, "Because of you I'm grounded for a whole month." I told him, "That's good, and I hope you learned a lesson!"

A LITTLE BOY HATCHES A PLAN TO SAVE HIS MOM

Last Christmas I picked up a young boy with high hopes that Santa's elves will come to his house, but he is living in a home that has a lot of violence.

I wish Christmas could be a great time for everyone, especially the kids. When you read this little boy's story, and you're in the same situation, please ask yourself why you are doing this to your children and yourself.

I had to pick up a little boy that missed his school bus. When I got to his house, his mom came out with him to my cruiser. She was talking to him and telling him how disappointed she was that he had missed the school bus. After he got in, his mom told me her son had the money from his piggy bank for the cab fare. She then gave him a kiss good-bye and we took off to his school.

The little boy was crying. I felt bad for the little guy so I thought I'd better try cheering him up.

"What's your name?" I asked.

He looked at me with his big sad eyes and said, "Kenny."

"Kenny, how old are you?"

"I'm five years old."

After he told me his age, I asked him how old he thought I

was, because you never know what kids will say. He looked at me and said, "You look about as old as my grandfather."

I sort of laughed. "Well how old is your grandfather?"

"I don't know, but my sister told me once that our grandfather was older than the hills." I was thinking, "thanks a lot." It was time to change the subject.

"Kenny, what grade are you in?"

"Kindergarten."

"Do you like your teacher?"

"She's pretty nice most of the time."

I didn't know that my next few questions were going to take us out of the spirit of Christmas to a living hell that this little boy has to live in.

"So, Kenny are you excited that Santa Claus will be here soon?"

He looked at me and said, "Santa doesn't go to people's houses; his little elves do. "Well, are Santa's little elves going to bring you a lot of presents this year?"

"I don't know."

Another question I like asking kids is what they want for Christmas. You get all kinds of answers, but once in a while you hear they want something that is more unusual than what the rest of the kids want.

Before I go on, I want to tell you about the time I took my son David, who was three at the time, to see Santa Claus.

We lived on our ranch and my son loved farm machinery. So when he sat on Santa's lap I assumed he was going at ask for a tractor or maybe a truck. When he was done he walked back to where I was standing waiting for him. Just before he got back to me, Santa waved for me to come over to him. So I walked over wondering what he wanted.

"Your son just asked me for something I never heard of, and I was wondering if you can explain to me what it is that he wants," Santa said.

I sort of laughed and then I asked, "What did my son tell you that he wanted for Christmas?"

"A manure spreader."

I laughed. I then explained to Santa that a manure spreader is used to haul the cow manure from the barn and the corrals to the fields. It spreads the manure out of the back of the machine into the air and onto the field. My son gets a kick out of watching that. You just have to have one if you're a farm boy. I have told that story a lot since then.

Anyway back to Kenny. I asked him what he wanted for Christmas and he told me he wanted a whole bunch of fireworks. Well, I have to tell you when Kenny told me he wanted fireworks I have to admit that was the most unusual Christmas wish I have ever heard.

After Kenny told me that, I looked at him and asked, "Why do you want fireworks for Christmas?"

He looked at me and said, "Because the next time my mom's boyfriend starts beating up my mom, I'm going to blow him up. It makes me sad when I see my mom getting hurt and crying."

I couldn't believe what this little fellow just told me. I told Kenny, "Next time your mom's boyfriend tries to hurt your mom, call 911 and ask for help."

"We don't have a phone, that's why I need the fireworks."

I then gave him some other ideas that might help him if this ever happens again. I felt sorry for this little guy.

When we got to his school, he pulled out a little sack of change to pay me. The cab fare was $4.50. He started crying when he was counting his money.

"What's the matter Kenny?"

"I saved this money to buy my mom a Christmas present and after I pay you I won't have enough to buy my mom anything nice."

I decided to let him keep his money. He gave me a funny look like he didn't believe me or something. Then he said, "Are you sure I can keep my money?" I reassured him again that it was OK and he left with a big smile on his face.

So everyone, when you're sitting in your warm homes on Christmas all nice and cozy with your loved ones, with plenty to eat and lots of gifts to open, take a moment and look out your window.

Then think of people like Kenny and his mom and hope that their Christmas was just as special to them as your Christmas was to you.

A BIKE RODEO CURES RANDY'S WRITERS BLOCK

As a writer sometimes you experience what is known as writer's block. One week I was sitting at my computer with hundreds of ideas going through my head, but I just couldn't find one that I was interested in writing about.

I struggled for about an hour to the point that I wanted to shoot my computer. Then I thought maybe I shouldn't use the word shoot right now, because everybody's up in "arms" right now about all these school shootings. Let's see; I know. I will just spray paint the screen on my monitor, and go pour myself a Jack Daniel's on the rocks and think about how stupid it was for me to get so mad over nothing.

About the time I was getting up to go look for a can of paint, my son Zachary reminded me that he was going to Bloomfield School in a few minutes to help his Cub Scout group help set up for a bicycle rodeo. As Zachary, my wife Dannette and my other son Benjamin were leaving, I told them I would be down there in a few minutes.

I was thinking, "All right; I'll go and watch the bike rodeo and collect my thoughts for a while and hopefully when I get back home I will be able to finish writing a column for this week."

Zachary belongs to Den 12, Pack 95. His den is helping the Arcata Sunrise Rotary Club and General Mel Brown's Army, the A.P.D., which sponsors this great event, set up the bike rodeo as a service project for his den.

The reason for these bike rodeos is to promote bike safety, to teach the kids that bicyclists must follow the same rules as cars and they must wear the proper helmet.

When I got to the school the bike rodeo was in full swing. It was a beautiful day. There were a lot of parents and kids there. As I was walking onto the school grounds I noticed a few people I knew standing off to one side watching the bike rodeo, so I went over to talk and watch the rodeo with them.

I was only there for about five minutes when Lt. Randy Mendosa, General Mel Brown's right hand man at the police department and Sunrise Rotary member, wanted to talk to me. Since I didn't see him holding any handcuffs or anything, I went over to see what he wanted.

One thing about Randy is he's a great guy and is always smiling. Probably the only time he doesn't smile is when he's in his patrol car and sees someone coming through a broken window with a TV in his arms and running down the street.

Randy and I have a lot in common. We both have the same name, we both pick up people that need a ride. He takes his to jail, I take mine home. In some cases I take my customers to places where they get in trouble and they can get a ride from Randy, too.

Another thing we have in common is we are both big fans of each other's occupation. The A.P.D. has some of the nicest guys and gals protecting our city. They do an excellent job and are hardly ever given praise or appreciation for the potentially dangerous jobs they have.

Randy is a big Cab10 fan and is always telling me that I'm the best cab driver in Arcata. That's a nice compliment, Randy, but I'm the only cab driver stationed in Arcata.

When I got to where Randy was standing I asked him, "Randy what's up?"

"How about Cab10 helping us out?"

"Sure. What do you want me to do?"

"I need you to help with the kid's bike inspections."

"I would be glad to help."

Randy handed me a checkoff booklet and a pen and told me to go to the line of kids waiting to participate in the rodeo and start inspecting their bikes.

For the next fifteen minutes I helped a couple of other people inspect all the kid's bikes.

We had to make sure all the kids' bikes were safe to ride. Just a few things we checked for were their cables, seats, handlebars, chains, pedals, spokes, and reflectors.

A few of the bikes didn't pass our inspections. But Rich Miller, from Adventures Edge bicycle shop in Arcata, was volunteering his services by performing free safety checks and repairing the bikes that needed adjustments or repairs. Great job, Rich, and thanks to the Adventures Edge for the great community service.

After the kids' bikes passed inspection, they rode their bikes on a course which had stop signs and other obstacles. They were being graded by Jennifer Parrish, who was wearing an A.P.D. uniform. I asked Jennifer, "What is your rank?"

"What rank," she said laughing. I started laughing too.

"I'm a police service person," she said.

"That sounds pretty important." I said sarcastically. She gave me one of those looks which meant it was time for me to leave, which I did.

About that time I saw my son's scout leader, Scott Gourley. He's a great guy who puts in a lot of time and energy to help the kids in his cub scout den have fun and achieve their goals as scouts.

I talked to him for a few minutes; then Randy asked me to help again. He was standing at the end of the obstacle course handing out giant bubble gum jawbreakers to the finishers of the obstacle course. He wanted me to hand to him the kids graded booklets after Jennifer finished grading each participant.

I went over to Jennifer to tell her the good news. I tapped her on the shoulder and said, "I'm baaaack!"

"So, do I care! What do you want, Cab10?"

"I'm supposed to take the graded booklets from you and hand them to Randy."

She gave me a funny look and said, "OK."

Everything was going smoothly until someone would start talking to me and I would forget to grab the booklet from Jennifer. But I had good backup because Susan Patrick, who also works for the A.P.D., was there to get the booklet for me when I forgot.

If you have ever been to the A.P.D. and needed some information, you'll know it's Susan behind the counter waiting on you because she has a big smile and is very helpful.

After about the third time I forgot to get the booklet from Jennifer, she was getting a little frustrated with me and told me I was fired, jokingly of course.

Everyone got a kick out of that. But after a little begging she gave me back my job. About fifteen minutes later I had forgotten a few more times, but again Susan was always there to cover for me.

Then I noticed my son Benjamin was getting ready to take his turn on the course. So I went to Jennifer and told her the bad news. "Jennifer, I need some time off to watch my son."

"Take all the time you want. Matter of fact, get yourself some coffee and a donut and take the rest of the day off." As I was walking away everyone was laughing. It was fun.

On my way over to where my son was, I stopped and talked to Bloomfield's principal Lynda Yeoman. I was told that Lynda and her staff were the first ones to the school to set things up. I never meet to many people like Lynda. She is always doing whatever it takes to help children and to make Bloomfield school a great place to send your kids.

She was there handing out bicycle brochures on safety and other related things. She was also answering people's questions and selling bicycle helmets to kids that needed one. If a family couldn't afford to buy one, they got one for free.

After talking to Lynda I went over and watched my son Benjamin who is five years old, go through the course. As he was maneuvering his bike through the course, I was thinking that my little boy was growing up too fast. It was fun watching him and the other kids participate in such a fun and great event as this bike rodeo.

CHAPTER 7

Travels with Randy

MY GREATEST ADVENTURE

My greatest adventure was when I took 6 homeless people to Martinez, California. I got a call that I will never forget. So many things happened, and a lot of what happened I can't even put into words. But I will do the best I can to tell you about my greatest adventure in my luxurious yellow cruiser.

9 a.m. I picked up a fare at the Comfort Inn in Arcata. There were two guys. One was clean cut and the other looked like a mountain man. When they saw me they asked me where Steve was. Steve was one of our other drivers who had given them a ride the day before. I told them that Steve was working in Eureka today so they're stuck with me. They grumbled a bit, and then got in my cruiser.

The mountain man had long hair, a long bushy beard, and a big hat. He was about 45 years old. His name was Bob and the other guy was named Skip. Bob was the boss, he had the money. He told me he wanted to pick up a few friends, check on a car that he might buy in Eureka, and then drive to San Diego to see his dad.

Bob told me he has been homeless for sixteen years. The other day he went to the bank to get his monthly check (which was for a few hundred dollars) that his brother in New York deposits for him. He was in for a big surprise. The bank told him that he had a message from his family saying that he had inherited $10,000.

I probably don't have to tell you, but Bob was a high roller now-until the money was gone, which probably wouldn't take too long. Seeing a story in the making, I started taking notes.

9:05 a.m. Bob told me he wants to go to Redwood Park and pick up a couple of friends, and then go to Eureka. On our way there, Bob asked me what I thought about their new clothes. Both guys were wearing all new clothes that Bob bought for them at Kmart the day before. I told them they looked like a couple of millionaires. They liked that!

Before we got to Redwood Park, Bob gave Skip $300. "Here's the money I promised you until you can pay me back!" he said.

"Thanks!" said Skip. Bob told Skip, "If we go our own ways, remember that you owe me that money, because I will be back to get it." Skip said not to worry about it.

9:16 a.m We finally got to Redwood Park. "Where are your friends Bob?" I asked. "Skip will go get them; they are living in the forest," he said. Bob told Skip, "You go get them so we can get going."

About fifteen minutes later, here came Skip with two more homeless guys. They all got in and Bob told me to go to the 101 Mall in Eureka across from Montgomery Wards.

Bob was a big operator since he had money and was in control. He kept telling these guys he was taking them to San Diego for a few days then he was going to fly all of them to Hawaii where they will live in the forest for a couple of months.

Once in a while one of these other guys would be talking and Bob would tell him to shut up because he wanted to talk or listen to the radio. He treated his so-called friends like crap. He was very rude. Money seems to drive some people over the edge, like this wacko.

9:26 a.m We pulled up to the 101 Mall and Bob told me to park along the brush behind the mall. Then he told Skip to get his butt out and go and get Linda and Tony. So Skip went into the bushes and in about 10 minutes came back with who I assume were Linda and Tony. They looked pretty rough. They looked like they just woke up and hadn't seen a shower in a long time. As they walked up to my luxurious yellow cruiser, Bob cussed at them to hurry up and get in, it was costing him money.

9:42 a.m After everyone was in, Bob told me to go to Pine Street. He told his buddies that he was going to buy a car that he looked at last week. Then he's taking everyone to San Diego for a few days so he can visit his dad. Then he was going to buy airplane tickets for everyone to fly to Hawaii.

Tony interrupted Bob and told him the car he looked at last week was already sold.

"What do you mean, sold?" Bob said.

"The guy that owns the car told me he thought you weren't coming back so he sold it. I talked to the guy yesterday," Tony said. Well, Bob was real hot now! He was cussing up a storm. "Take me to Pine Street right now. I'm going to give that old man hell. He promised me that car!" Bob said.

The other guys tried to tell Bob to forget about the car, but he wasn't listening. He told them all to shut up, he's got the money, he's the boss. Everyone was getting a little edgy.

9:51 a.m All the way to Pine Street Bob was telling the others that he was going to give the guy that had the car a piece of his mind. They were all trying to tell Bob to forget about it, but he just kept telling them to shut up and cussed them out.

When we got to the house where the car was that he wanted to buy, Bob got out and went to the door. Some old man came out and Bob started chewing him out. I felt sorry for the old man. Bob was being a jerk, and his friends weren't happy with him either.

A few minutes later Bob jumped back in and told me to take him to Ebb Tide Trailer Park. One of the other guys asked Bob why we were going there, and I was wondering the same thing.

Tony told us that Bob wanted to buy a sailboat he saw there the other day. I would love to see this bunch trying to maneuver a sailboat.

10:02 a.m. When we get to Ebb Tide, Bob got out and went into the office to talk to the manager about the sailboat, which was parked on a trailer by the office. It was a nice boat. A couple of minutes later Bob came out, madder than hell.

Tony asked him what was wrong now. Bob told us the sailboat was sold the day before. I wanted to laugh, but I didn't. One of the guys told Bob, "You don't need a boat anyway." Well, that made Bob even madder, and he cussed him out again.

When Bob was done being rude to his friend, he told me to take them to Bank Of America. The end was near, I thought.

10:09 a.m. When we got to the bank, Bob told everyone that he was going to get some more money and then the cabbie would drop them off at Stanton's Restaurant. There they would wait for the Amtrak bus to take them to Martinez, where they'd catch the train to San Diego, and then in a few days they would fly to Hawaii for a couple of months.

Not all of his buddies sounded too excited about going with Bob, the way he was treating them. But as long as Bob was paying, I think they would put up with him.

While Bob was in the bank, Skip told us he wasn't going with Bob because he was tired of his crap.

In a few minutes Bob came out with over $2,000 in his hand. Skip told Bob he was staying in Eureka. Bob tried begging him to go, but Skip said no way.

"Get the hell out of the cab, and don't forget, I'll be back for my money," Bob told him. Skip said "OK," and walked away. Now there were only five.

Then Bob asked me how much it would cost him if I drove them to Martinez. I told him $500!

That's a lot of money, he said. I was hoping he would say that!

Then he got his money out and handed me five $100 bills, and said, "Take us there!" I told him we needed to go to my work and give them the money, then we can go.

"Let's do it; hurry up," Bob ordered.

10:20 a.m. I couldn't believe this was happening. Another six hours of this and I'll go nuts. When I get to Yellow Cab on 7th street, I pay the dispatcher the $500 plus another $50 that was on the meter driving Bob and friends around up to this point. Then I checked my oil and water and told Bob that I was ready whenever he was. He handed me $50 and said, "Here's your tip in advance. Lets go!"

10:31 a.m. As I was leaving Yellow Cab, Linda told Bob they had to go back to where we picked them up to get her belongings.

"Forget it, we're leaving now." Bob said.

"I have $150 worth of food stamps back there," Linda said.

"I don't care," Bob said.

He then handed her $300 and told her to shut up. Then one of the guys told Bob we had to stop at the Eureka Police Department because they had some personal belongings that they took from him a couple of days ago when he was arrested for being drunk in public. Bob was getting mad again. "All right, cabbie. Take us to the police station."

10:37 a.m. At the police station Bob told his friend to hurry up, it was costing him money.

10:42 a.m. We're on the road again! Linda told Bob she wanted to stop at Al's Truck Stop to get some beer and cigarettes. He told her OK. They all went into the truck stop and came back with all kinds of stuff. As soon as they closed the doors, they were popping beers.

11:10 a.m. We're just past Fortuna and Bob wanted me to pull over because he needs to go pee. So I pulled over and three of them got out and took care of business.

11:21 a.m. Bob told Linda she needed to get her hair done

before they got to the train, because she looked like hell.

"We're going to stop somewhere and you're going to get your hair done," he said. "You look like a man, and we're going to buy you a dress, too. I want you to look good." Her boyfriend agreed.

All along, Bob was harassing everyone, acting like he's a king and his friends are his slaves. There was a lot of tension in the air. Also, Bob and his buddies kept turning the radio up and down and changing the channels over and over.

11:32 a.m. One of the guys was rolling a joint in the back seat, so I pulled over and told them I can't have that in my cab. They all got out and smoked their pot and then got back in. What a bunch of fruitcakes!

11:41 a.m. Bob and the two guys we picked up at Redwood Park were having a pretty heated exchange, because Bob kept telling them to shut up, that they're going to do what he says because he has the money. Every other word was a cuss word. It was getting old listening to these guys. Also, the beer was starting to affect them.

12:20 p.m. We're almost to Laytonville and Bob told me to pull over. He told the two guys from Redwood Park to get out if they didn't want to go with him. So they did. Now there were three left! They were yelling at each other and calling each other names. It was a mess. Bob told me to get going, so I took off. Bob was laughing and told us, "I showed them who was boss." I wanted to show him a few things too, but I kept my cool.

12:55 p.m. We're almost to Willits when Tony told Bob that Linda and he were getting hungry. "Tough luck, we're not stopping," he told them. Tony asked me if I would stop, so I told Bob that I was hungry too. He didn't like that, but he gave in. He kept telling me he paid for the cab ride so we shouldn't stop, but I told him I was getting tired; I need to rest. He finally agreed, but he was grumpy.

1:15 p.m. We were halfway to Ukiah when Bob told me to pull over. Linda had to throw up, because she had had too many beers. I looked back and saw her rocking back and forth, so I pulled over right away and she got out just in time. Then all three went pee again. There were no trees, but they didn't care. Cars were going by honking their horns. What next?

1:30 p.m. We're almost to Ukiah when Bob told Tony, "We're going to take Linda to a beauty shop and get her hair done, because I don't want her looking like that around me." He had a lot of room to talk. Bob was treating these guys like crap again. They were getting drunker by the minute.

When we got into Ukiah, we took Linda to a beauty shop and dropped her off. Then Bob wanted to go get some more beer. So we went to a sporting goods store that sells beer. Tony told Bob that he'd buy the beer. So Tony and I went inside. I needed to use the restroom.

In this store, the door was at the far left and the counter ran the length of the building to the right about a hundred feet. Behind the counter at the far end were rifles and fishing poles. Tony went to get the beer and I went into the restroom.

When I came out, Tony was at the far end of the store with a shotgun aimed at the store owner. I couldn't believe it. I backed into the restroom and peeked around the corner. I was going to get the hell out of there. When I looked again, he had the shotgun down on the counter and was talking to the clerk. I found out that he was looking through the scope and checking out the shotgun. From where I was standing it looked like he had it aimed at the clerk, but the clerk was a couple of feet away. I was happy to get out of there.

2:05 p.m. We picked up Linda, and she looked a lot better. She was happy she got her hair done. Then we stopped at a big store and they went inside to buy Linda a dress. I stayed outside trying to get my nerves settled. What a nightmare this was. About 15 minutes later they were back.

3:12 p.m. They were getting really drunk and doing a lot of yelling over the dumbest things. Pretty soon Bob told Tony, "I'm going to kick your ass, because you're not doing what I tell you." Tony told me to pull over because he was tired of Bob's crap. So I pulled over and they got out. They could hardly stand up. They started arguing and then they started punching each other right alongside the freeway.

It didn't last too long. Bob fell down and couldn't get up. So Tony and I picked him up and put him back in the cab. Bob told Tony, "You think you're tough? You were just lucky that time."

That had to the best part of this journey, I was thinking.

3:25 p.m. As we passed Santa Rosa, Tony was in the front seat, moneybags was in the middle seat (sleeping, I hoped), and Linda was lying down in the back seat.

3:45 p.m. I happened to look in my rearview mirror and Bob was awake and leaning over the back seat messing around with Linda. Linda started yelling for help, so I pulled over and told Tony to take care of his girlfriend. Linda was crying and upset with Bob. They all started yelling again, but they calmed down and got back in, and we were on the road again.

4:01 p.m. Now they were all yelling at each other again. Bob told me to pull over. When I stopped, he got out and told Tony and Linda to get the hell out. I told Bob, "Hey you guys have had too much to drink. Why don't you just relax? We're almost to Martinez."

"I don't care," Bob said. He closed the door and told me to take off. I got out and asked Tony and Linda if they were going to be OK. They told me to go ahead and take off. I got back in and Bob was mad at me for caring about what his friends thought about getting kicked out. "This is my cab, and I'm the boss," I told the jerk, "So why don't you take a nap and leave me alone?"

4:16 p.m. Bob can hardly talk, but he's still trying to talk about everything. Then he said, "I paid you good money for this trip, can't you go faster than 70 m.p.h.?"

I told him to leave me alone again. "OK, OK," he said. Then he started laughing.

"Wasn't that funny when I kicked those two bums out?" Bob said. That made me mad, so I told Bob off in language he understood, and told him I would be glad to get rid of him.

4:49 p.m. When we got into Martinez, Bob told me he wanted to buy me a big dinner for putting up with him. I told him to forget it. "No, I want to buy you whatever you want for dinner," he insisted. I told him I was having dinner in Santa Rosa with Jerry Gregori, a good friend of mine on my way home. He then handed me a $50 bill and said, "Use this for your dinner." "OK." I was polite and told him thanks. When we pulled into the train station, Bob pulled out $1,000 and said, "The hell with the train; just drive me to San Diego." I told him to forget it. I couldn't stand another minute with this guy.

"You better hurry up, the train's boarding," I said.

He grabbed his bag and just as he was getting out, a Mercedes pulled up real close to us. When Bob got out he stumbled against the Mercedes. The driver started yelling at Bob and Bob was yelling back. I put my cruiser in gear and headed for Santa Rosa. I was happy to get out of there.

6:20 p.m. I was in Santa Rosa at a gas station filling up with gas, and a couple of people asked me if I brought a fare all the way from Eureka. I told them yes, I had. So for the next 10 minutes I told these guys what happened. I showed them the 51 empty beer cans in my cab and they got a kick out of my story, I hope you did, too.

FAMILY TROUBLES

Every so often in our profession we get involved in situations that can be dangerous and that we didn't plan on running into. Domestic fights are the worst and this next story is one of the worst kind. I have to go to Manila to pick up a young lady and her daughter. I was told that when I get there she wants me to honk once and be ready to go right away. I was thinking, "no problem."

When I got to Manila I had to take a back road to this lady's house. It was raining and it was dark, so it was hard to see any addresses, plus half the houses don't have any numbers on them anyway.

I was driving along real slow trying to figure out which house I was looking for, when I heard a lady's voice behind some trees yelling, "Open the door, open the door!" I could hear her running while she was yelling at me, but I couldn't see her for a second or two because it was raining and really dark out.

So, I opened the back door, and here comes this young lady holding a baby; running through the trees like someone was following her or something.

She's yelling at me again, "Hurry and take off, please will you hurry!" So I ran around and jumped into my cruiser while she and her baby were getting in. "Take off, take off; my husband will be coming any minute and he's drunk and really angry!" she yelled. I was thinking, "Oh great, here I go, putting my life on the line again."

I was driving off while she was trying to slide the door closed when out of the bushes came her husband. He reached through the door and grabbed her arm, trying to pull her out. He was yelling and screaming and calling her all kinds of names while he was running alongside the cab.

I reached back and grabbed her arm to help her so he couldn't pull her out, and I was trying to drive ahead at the same time. I finally got a good grip and gave a big tug. Her husband must have slipped in the mud, because he fell down.

We finally got the door closed and took off for Arcata. She was pretty shook up about what had just happened. I tried to calm her down, which she finally did after a few more minutes. Then she said, "Thank you for helping me get out of there. I was really scared my husband was going to beat me up again tonight."

"Has he beat you up before?" I asked.

"Yes, I warned him if he came home again drunk I was leaving him, because my husband, when he gets drunk—he's a whole different kind of person. One little thing and he gets mad and wants to hit me, so when he came home drunk again tonight I told him I was leaving him for good. He then went and got my keys so I couldn't leave; so when he was in the bathroom I called for a cab. Then I waited by the front door hoping a cab would be here while he was eating dinner so I could sneak out the door."

"He must have heard me honk my horn?" I asked.

"He must have, I just grabbed my daughter, opened the door and just started running!" she said.

She told me while she was running she could hear her husband yelling from the porch at her. I ask her where she wanted to go. She told me she wanted to go to her sister's house until she can figure out what she's going to do next. As I was driving she was comforting her daughter and was crying.

I felt sorry for her, but I was thinking, I bet in a couple days she will go back, I see it all the time. When we got to her sister's house she was happy to see her. I wished her good luck, and went on my way.

THE DARK SIDE

If you ever saw the movie Star Wars or any of the Star Trek shows you will find this next call out of this world.

In the original Star Trek TV show, before each episode you heard William Shatner (Captain Kirk) say, "Space, the Final Frontier..." After you read this story, you might think the space in my luxurious yellow cruiser could be the Final Frontier for some people.

If you aren't familiar with these sci-fi shows, you probably weren't born yet or you've been lost in your own space somewhere and to understand this story you will need some additional information. In the movie Star Wars there was an evil force which was led by Darth Vader. Darth Vader disguised himself in all black and wore a black mask over his head so no one would recognize him.

This call will take you to another world. So grab your phaser, strap yourself in your chair and beam up something to drink. I hope you enjoy your flight.

I won't forget this call for a while. My dispatcher told me a friend of mine named Steve who lives in Blue Lake called and requested my services. When I got to his house, I honked my horn and Steve came running out. The expression on his face was like he had seen a ghost or something!

"What's the matter, Steve? You look like you're all shook up!"

"Randy, do you remember my roommate, Ann?"

"Yeah, I think I remember who she is, what's the matter?"

"She's acting very weird and I think she needs to go to the hospital. I had to call for you because I figure you could help me get her there instead of calling for an ambulance!"

"Did you try calling her family?"

"Yeah, but nobody was home and I think her family has disowned her anyway."

"Is she in the house and does she know that we're going to take her to the hospital?"

"Randy, you're not going to believe this, but she thinks Darth Vader is after her."

I started laughing. "You've got to be kidding me. Why do you have her for a roommate? Sounds like she's an alien from another planet or something."

"She has never done this before. She does act a little strange once in a while, but don't we all?"

"You're right about that, Steve. Let's go get her so we can go."

As I was walking up to the door I was thinking about what was waiting for me inside. I followed Steve into the house. I could see his roommate sitting on the couch. She was all dressed in black and had a dark scarf covering her head.

As soon as she saw me she went nuts. She jumped on the top of the couch and started screaming at Steve telling him that I was Darth Vader and I was going to kill them. I started backing up towards the door because I wasn't sure what was going to happen next. She was making all kinds of noises and was acting like she was really terrified that I was going to harm her. I told Steve I was going to wait outside and if he could get her under control, I would take them to the hospital.

About 10 minutes later they came out and got into my luxurious yellow cruiser. We then headed for the hospital. Steve's roommate was calm, but still saying weird things. She was really paranoid about someone trying to harm her. I asked her why she was wearing all black clothes. She told me that Darth Vader is after her and by wearing all black he will think that she is one of his people and he won't harm her. I looked at Steve after she said that and we just shook our heads and chuckled.

When we were a couple miles from the hospital Ann asked us why we were taking her there. Steve tried telling her that he felt that she might need to see a doctor because she hasn't been feeling well lately. She yelled at us and told us that there was nothing wrong with her. As we drove up to the emergency room, she told us she wasn't getting out. I looked at Steve and he just shrugged his shoulders. I think he was confused about what to do next.

I decided to take over, because of all my experiences handling aliens from outer space that have ridden in my cab. Plus, I wanted this nut case out of my cab. So I told her, "Ann, let's go inside and see the doctor and make sure that he feels you're OK, because Steve is worried about you. Then we'll take you home as soon as he is finished talking to you."

She looked at me and said, "I'm not going in there even if you drag me." I told Steve that I didn't have time for this crap. He told me he didn't know what to do. I told him we should go inside and get some advice, and he agreed.

So we left Ann in my cruiser and we went inside to the emergency room. There were about five people in line, so we had to wait. After about 15 minutes a lady came running in yelling that some wild woman is in the parking lot harassing her and other cars in the parking lot. I looked at Steve and told him we had better go see if it's Ann.

We ran outside. Ann is talking to a guy and a lady in a van. As we walked up we could see the lady yelling at Ann, telling her to get lost or she is going to call the police.

When we got to the van I asked the guy in the van if there was a problem.

The lady jumped out and said, "Is that bitch with you guys?" I didn't want to say that she was, but I did. Then I asked her what she was so upset about. She then told Steve and me, "Your lady friend is harassing us and just asked my husband how big his manhood is!" I looked at Steve and we just shook our heads. We then told Ann that the doctor wanted to see her.

Surprisingly, she went with us. I asked her what the hell was she doing harassing people.

"It's fun," she said. I thought that if we didn't get her to the doctor soon, I might need to see a doctor myself.

After we walked into the emergency room I thought that was going to be the end of this space odyssey, but I was going to find out that I hadn't even hit warp speed yet.

After a couple of minutes a nurse told us to bring Ann into a room and wait for the doctor. So we went into the room and were sitting there for a few minutes when all of a sudden Ann got paranoid again and wanted to leave. So we grabbed her and she got really mad at us, yelling and screaming. It was embarrassing. About a minute later, a nurse walked in and told us to calm her down. I was thinking, "What the heck am I still here for?" But Steve needed help and the meter was running so I figured I better stick it out.

A couple of minutes later we had Ann calmed down again but we had to hold on to her, because she wanted to leave. I was wishing the doctor would hurry up and get here.

About that time a nurse walked in to take Ann's blood pressure. She was a large woman. When the nurse grabbed Ann's arm, Ann went nuts again. She started yelling at the nurse. "Who do you think you are, grabbing my arm?"

"I'm a nurse and I'm just going to take your blood pressure, so just relax."

Ann didn't like the nurse. She told her, "It looks like you haven't missed a meal in your life."

When Ann said that I was really embarrassed. Ann went on to say a lot more very mean things. I felt sorry for the nurse because she was really nice, but she acted like Ann didn't bother her. As the nurse left I apologized to her. She told me not to worry about it.

I told Steve, "I think you better get a new roommate."

He laughed and said, "Yeah, that will happen soon. I can't put up with this again."

"That's good, Steve, because if you call me again to take Ann to the hospital, I'm not coming."

A few minutes later the doctor came in and asked how things were going. We didn't get to answer him. Ann started calling him all kinds of names and told the doctor she was getting the hell out of there. The doctor called for assistance and told us to help keep her from leaving, so we did. A couple of male nurses came in and we were all holding Ann. She was freaking out.

After a few minutes she calmed down again, so we let go of her and were all standing there while the doctor was trying to figure out what to do with her next. Ann was talking really weird. Then all of a sudden she pulls off her blouse and says, "I know what you guys want, so get it over with." Then she started swinging her arms, trying to hit and scratch us while she was calling us every name in the book.

That was it for me. I just stood back while they finally got her strapped down. You had to feel sorry for Ann, because Steve said most of the time she is a nice person. The doctor told us that she probably was on drugs.

As I was leaving, I was thinking that most of us don't realize how lucky we are to have good health.

Well it's time for me to get back to earth and wait for my next ride into the Twilight Zone.

KOOKY CAMPER

What do you get when a skinny eccentric woman—who is a vegetarian that drinks bottled water, loves to go camping and loves to smoke cigars—hires a big, shy, meat eating, whiskey drinking cab driver, that hates camping, but also likes to smoke cigars? Two very strange people that spent six hours together, shopping, lunching, smoking, and being totally confused.

Now that I have confused you, here's the rest of the story. One day I picked up one of my regular customers in Sunny Brae who wanted to go to Kmart in McKinleyville to buy some camping gear. She's around 40 years old and is very eccentric.

Everytime I pick her up I know it's going to be an adventure. All my regular customers usually go to the same places every time, but this lady is different because I never know where she's going or what she's up too, and today was no exception.

On our way to Kmart, she asked me if I would help her shop for some camping gear, because she will probably have two or three full baskets. I told her I would be glad to help.

After a couple of hours of shopping, we had three full baskets of all the camping gear that one person could ever use. She had enough stuff to supply an army platoon. Some of the things she bought were a sleeping bag, stove, lantern, and a tent. The total bill was $260.

As GI Jane and I were heading out to my luxurious yellow camper she told me we needed to go to Cask and Flask liquor store so she could buy some tobacco. She loves to chew and smoke cigars. Like I said earlier, she's different.

Next she wanted to go to Safeway to get some groceries. About an hour later, here she comes with a basket that was overflowing. I asked her, "You sure bought a lot of groceries, are you having company or something?" She gives me a funny look and says, "What do you think I bought all the camping gear for, I'm going camping."

"You're going camping this time of year?"

"Yes, I want you to take me to Redway now, so I can camp for a couple of weeks." I was thinking that she was nuts. It's been raining and cold, but she's the customer, so wherever she wants to go, we'll go. I told her it will probably cost about $100 and she told me let's go. I didn't realize when I picked her up she was going camping today; but that's why I like my job, because everyday is a mystery or an adventure.

About a half hour into our journey we were getting close to Fortuna and I mentioned to GI Jane that I hadn't eaten anything for lunch and I was getting hungry. She's really skinny so she probably wasn't thinking about lunch. "Well we better stop so I can buy you lunch; otherwise you might start eating my groceries," she said.

I laughed and told her, "Yeah, because I'm pretty hungry."

Then she asked, "What kind of food do you like?"

"I like to eat almost anything, how about going to Burger King?"

"No, I'm a vegetarian."

"They have salads."

"OK, let's go there then, I'm sure you would prefer a burger over a salad."

"I like salads, too; I'm a Cab10 vegetarian."

She gives me a funny look and asks, "What is a Cab10 vegetarian?"

"I only eat meat from animals that are vegetarians such as cows, chickens and pigs. I can't eat meat from animals such as lions, tigers and bears, because they are meat eaters." She got a kick out of that.

After a boring lunch we continued on our great journey. When we got down by Pepperwood she wanted to know if she could smoke a cigar. I told her she could, but I wanted one too. About five minutes later were on our way again puffing on our cigars. It was crazy, but pretty funny really. People in cars passing me that noticed got a good laugh.

We finally got to Redway and went to a local campground where she wanted to stay. She got out and went into the office to get her camping space. About ten minutes later she came back out. She seemed upset about something. She then went looking around. A few minutes later she came back and said, "They want $16 per day. That's expensive, and they told me there are no taxis or buses, so that means I would be stranded here. Let's go back to Arcata."

I couldn't believe what she just said. I then told her, "Let's check out a couple of other campgrounds in the area. Maybe they will be cheaper." She thought that was a good idea, but after striking out at two more campgrounds, she wanted to head back to Arcata. Her cab fare was already at $175. On our way back we smoked a couple more cigars.

When we got to Eureka she told me she wanted to go to KOA Campground which is halfway between Arcata and Eureka. After 200 miles we finally got to KOA Campground, which is only four miles from her house where we started from six hours ago.

She went into the office and a few minutes later came out smiling. She rented a little camping area by a wooden fence. It was pretty boring to me. She could have rented my back yard for half price.

She told me to put all her stuff on a picnic table that was going to be her kitchen table for a couple of weeks. Before I got all her stuff on the table, the wind blew some of it off. It was cold and wet.

Just when I thought this camping adventure was over she asked if I could help her put up her tent because the wind was blowing so hard. I hate putting up tents, but I helped her out.

After we got her tent finished she paid me $285 for the fare and gave me a $20 tip. Not bad for six hours of hard labor. It was a camping trip I will never forget.

THE CAB10 ADVENTURES OF FIESTY, FORGETFUL, GENEROUS BEN

Last November I picked up a guy at a local hotel. He was all bandaged up and was in a lot of pain. He told me he used to live here, but after he retired from Humboldt State University he moved to Seattle.

His name is Ben. He's about 75 years old and loves to talk. Ben was on his way down here in November to see his kids who live here, and got into a big wreck, rolling his Blazer over several times. He told me he was lucky to survive the accident.

While he was recovering from his injuries he was a regular customer of mine for a couple of months going to doctors and therapy. Then in February he went back to Seattle to his home. Last Monday he was back in town. I had to pick him up at 7 a.m. at the Howard Johnson's Hotel in Arcata where he usually stays while he's in town visiting.

When I pulled up to the lobby I could see Ben inside waiting for me. I got out and went inside to see if Ben needed any help. He told me he wanted to go to three or four places and then to Henderson Center Camera Shop to drop off his camera and go see a friend of his.

On our way out to my luxurious yellow cruiser he's giving me hell for being late, like he always does. I could be an hour early to pick him up and he would still bitch at me, but that's Ok; he's cool and in this business you get use to it.

After Ben got in he said, "I'm hungry. Lets go to Toni's restaurant and eat; I'll buy you breakfast."

"That sounds good to me, Ben." I never turn down a free meal, so we head over to Toni's, which is located north of Arcata. They have the best breakfast in town. A lot of truckers, ranchers and business people eat there, so it's a good place to eat and to shoot the bull.

On our way there Ben said, "Don't you have a heater in this damn cab?" "Yeah, I'll turn it on. Where's your coat, Ben?" He always wears a coat.

"I don't know where it is. You won't believe what I have been through the last 12 hours."

"What happened?"

"After we order our breakfast, I'll tell you." Ben seemed to be a little edgy.

After we got to Toni's, we're at the counter ordering our food and a friend of mine, Steve Morias, a local rancher, asked me, "Randy, aren't you working today?"

"Yeah, Steve, I'm working hard. My customer is buying my breakfast."

He starts laughing and says, "You don't have your meter on, do you?"

"Of course I do, I'm working. My customer wants to eat before we go to Eureka, so I can't wait around for free. How am I going to pay for my three sons' college?" Steve and a few other people that were listening just shook their heads. They got a kick out of that.

Sharon Lampi, who works at Toni's, asked me, "You guys hiring at Yellow Cab? I want a job like yours, Randy." About that time Ben handed the waitress, Shirley Nunes, who is my Aunt, a check and yells, "Randy, get over here! Grab your coffee, let's get a table." Ben likes to be in control of everything, so I go along with it to keep him happy.

After we got our coffee we sat down with my dad, Tony, who was there having breakfast. After I introduced them to each other, Ben started telling us what happened to him. Here's his story.

Yesterday he wanted to come down here and see his kids, so he went to the airport to rent a car. He told us he always rents the same car, but this time the guy at the car rental agency talked him into renting a different car that was brand new and had only 2,000 miles on it. The clerk told him he would probably like it better than the one he normally rents. He really didn't want the car the clerk recommended, but gave in and said OK.

After a 100 miles or so the oil lights started flashing. So he pulled over and checked the oil. It was full of oil. So he jumped back in and kept going. About an hour later he was climbing a mountain when the car died. It was 4 a.m. and he was out in the middle of no where. He was madder than hell, he told us. He couldn't believe a new car's engine would blow up with less than 3000 miles on it.

He was lucky he had his cell phone with him. He called the car rental agency to tell them what happened. When he called, he got a recording telling him to call back during business hours. He was really mad now, he said.

He called for a tow truck. After three hours a tow truck finally showed up. He said he almost froze to death waiting.

After they got the car hooked up to the tow truck, they went to the nearest airport so Ben could fly down here. When they got to the airport he got hold of a guy who had his own plane and paid him $1,800 to fly him to Arcata.

About 20 minutes after taking off, he started feeling weak, and his injuries from a few months earlier were starting to hurt. He called for an ambulance to meet the plane at the Arcata-McKinleyville airport. Just before they landed he said he was feeling terrible, and was cold.

After they landed the ambulance was there waiting for him. The pilot opened the door and the medic came in to see how he's doing. Ben told us that the ambulance drivers are familiar with him and his medical problems. The medic was asking Ben different questions, but Ben felt like the medic wasn't listening to him when he was trying to explain to the medic what was bothering him. He told us he was getting very upset.

Then the medic asked Ben if he's feeling a little manic depression coming on. That did it, he said. He was really mad now and started yelling at the medic. The medic then went and called the police.

About 10 minutes later, up rolled two sheriffs' cars and News Channel 3 with their fancy news van with the big antenna on it. Ben couldn't believe it. All he wanted to do was go to the hospital for a while and then go to his hotel room. They were acting like they were dealing with a terrorist.

After talking to the sheriff deputies for a few minutes he calmed down and explained to them what had happened to him. They asked him what he wanted to do. He told the deputies he would like a ride to his hotel room so he could get some rest. They told him they would give him a ride.

After he got in the squad car, the deputy asked him where the Howard Johnson Hotel was, because he wasn't familiar with it's location. Ben told us he couldn't believe it. So he showed the rookie deputy where the Hotel was and finally went to bed. After he finished telling us about his nightmare we left Toni's and headed to his doctor's office in Arcata. He needed to get some medicine, because he forgot to bring back from Seattle the medicine that he needs to take every day.

When we got to the doctor's office, the nurse was concerned that Ben had just misplaced his pills. Ben didn't like that and started giving the poor nurse a bad time. A few minutes later he had the nurse convinced to order his pills. She told us Lima's Pharmacy in McKinleyville would have them ready whenever Ben wanted to pick them up. Ben told her thanks and we left.

We then went to his attorney's office in Bayside, where he dropped off some papers. He told me he is suing the car rental agency for all the trouble they put him through.

A few minutes later he came out and told me, "Let's go to Sunny Brae, I want to show you where my ex-wife lives." I started laughing I have never done that before.

When we get to his ex-wife's house, that used to be his house - he told me to pull into the driveway. That was sort of weird, but what's new?

After I turned off my turbo-charged cruiser I asked him, "Why did you get a divorce?" He told me that they were having problems and one night he came home from work and his wife was throwing their stuff out of the upstairs window. He told me that was the last straw and he divorced her. Ben's been married four times.

After a few minutes and a few laughs we headed for Eureka. We finally got to the camera shop in Henderson Center. As Ben was getting out he was looking through his stuff for his camera. A couple minutes later he told me, "I guess I left my camera back at the Hotel."

I couldn't help but laugh.

"What are you going to do now?"

"I'll bring the camera over tomorrow. How much do I owe you?" I pointed at the meter and told him $86. He went through his pockets and realized he had forgotten his wallet too. He always uses a credit card, because we don't take checks.

He got back in and closed his door. He then said, "I guess you better take me back to the Hotel. We'll try again tomorrow." I started laughing, and then he started laughing too.

"That's what happens when you get old Randy," he said.

So we head back to Arcata. About half way to Arcata Ben said, "Boy it's cold. I need a coat. Let's go get my wallet and go to Kmart in McKinleyville."

So we head to Howard Johnson's.

After Ben got his wallet, he came out of his room and said, "Let's go to Lima's Pharmacy first, I need my medicine." When we get to Lima's he went inside and I waited in my cab.

About 10 minutes later I could see Ben waving a cane at the clerk. I thought I better go check out what's going on.

When I got inside the pharmacy, Ben's mad at the clerk because he wanted to buy a cane, but the clerk won't let him charge it.

After a few minutes I calmed Ben down and we left. Ben was growling all the way to my cab, but he got over it. I told him, "Let's go to Kmart." When we got to Kmart he told me to come inside with him in case he gets weak and needs help back to my cab.

So we both went into the store's men's department and a few minutes later, Ben found a coat he wanted to buy. Then he said, "Randy, you better get one of these coats, too; they're on sale."

"I don't have enough money on me, Ben."

"Pick out the one you want, I'll buy you one."

So I tried on a few and found one I liked. I couldn't turn Ben's offer down. I needed a new coat. Plus, I didn't want to hurt his feelings by saying no.

A few minutes later we walked out of Kmart with our new coats on and headed back to the Howard Johnson's hotel. The cab fare was $140. And he gave me a $30 tip. I thanked Ben for the tip, the coat and the breakfast.

As Ben was getting out he said, "See you tomorrow morning, Randy, at 7 a.m. Maybe tomorrow I'll have better luck.

I was thinking, "I can't wait." Then I thought, hey I could use a new pair of shoes.

CHAPTER 8

Love in Motion

FLAVORS OF LOVE ON VALENTINE'S DAY

This chapter is about love, romance and what some of my customers did or didn't do for Valentine's Day.

Before I get to all that mushy stuff, I want to say that I wish we had a Valentine's Day once a month. I know Hallmark's cards and the florist shops do too. Our world needs more love, more romance and more friendship. Valentine's Day is not just for sweethearts either. It's for everyone. Yes, it's a good time to tell your sweetheart that you love them and treat them extra special, but what about the rest of the year. It's also a good time to tell your friends that you care about them and you enjoy their friendship.

If everyone would just practice a little Valentine's Day love and friendship every day in their lives we would live in a lot happier world.

Well, it's time to see if you measured up to all these people that couldn't wait to tell me their Valentines Day memories.

Garth, who is a student at Humboldt State University went to Los Angeles to see his girlfriend for Valentine's Day. When he got to L.A. his girlfriend picked him up and they went to the mall and bought each other gifts. That night his girlfriend took him to see a professional hockey game for Valentine's Day.

On Valentine's Day Garth took her to his Dad's rustic log cabin that is in the mountains outside of L.A. They spent the day there. That night he barbecued and after dinner they made love in front of the roaring fireplace. He told me it was awesome.

Melissa Phenix, who is Harold Phenix's (The real mayor of Blue Lake) daughter, told me her favorite part of Valentine's Day weekend was going to the Arcata Volunteer Firemen's ball at St. Mary's School with her friends and having a great time and getting to dance a dance with Cab10.

Page Fitting's boyfriend, Greg Noble of Shingletown, took her to San Francisco for Valentine's Day weekend. During the day they went sightseeing and then shopping at Jack London's Square. Greg bought Page some flowers and a teapot. They then visited with her son Christian who lives there, and later went out to a great Chinese Restaurant where you cook your own food.

She said it was a lot of fun. After dinner they went to their hotel, the Holiday Inn. "Then what happened?" I asked. She laughs and then said, "Well, we had champagne, some caviar and the rest of the story is up to you."

Anyone who has worked in journalism has probably heard the unfortunate phrase, "Not tonight, honey, I have a deadline." Such was the case on Valentine's Day for McKinleyville Press co-publishers Jack Durham and Sherilynn "CP" Silvernail, who instead of going to bed, put a paper to bed.

For the Press, Sunday is "deadline day." There's no time for hanky panky. While lovers strolled the beach or dined by candlelight, Jack and CP sat behind computers, editing Cab10, writing stories and laying out pages. But the evening did get a little hot and steamy when they shared lucious shrimp, red pepper and pesto pizza, taking care to not get crumbs on their keyboards.

Mitch took Dawn up to Trinity Lake and got a motel room in Weaverville the night before and went out to dinner in Weaverville. "We got up early in the morning and took my four wheel rig (Pathfinder) to the Lake and went out to check out the houseboat. It turned out to be a great day and we sat out on the deck of the boat and drank a bottle of champagne with the snow covered mountains as a backdrop."

Tom Gomes bought his lovely wife Shelly a very sexy nightgown and a weed eater. (I hope the weed eater was for the yard) Shelly bought Tom a large fudge heart. I asked Tom if there was any romance that night and he smiled and said, "We had a very romantic evening."

Reba Johnson from Los Angeles told me, "I know you think

all of us Orange County folks are strange. But you had to ask...For the first time in 10 years my husband Ron and I sat down 2 weeks before Valentine' Day to decide on what we could get as a mutual gift. No surprises this year. Wow! In one moment we decided...and agreed. (After 10 years that's pretty good.) We would get our fishing licenses together and take our new boat out for a day of fishing. Now it's not much for romance but when the fish aren't biting..you could pretty well guess what was.

Linda Rodgers from Tennessee tells me her husband always gets her a card and they stay home. "It's just another day to my husband. We ordered a pizza and watched TV. My husband drank a six pack of beer and smoked some cigarettes sitting in his shorts in front of the TV, burping once in awhile. Then we went to bed.

Dexter Wixson from Colorado told me that his wife Serena had to go to work early on Valentine's Day. When he woke up she had left him some balloons and yellow roses. When his wife got home from work, he gave her a red teddy. That night they went to the Comedy Works in downtown Denver. It was a blast. They got home at midnight and made good use of the teddy—surprisingly enough it held up (Barely).

Bill Cook took his lovely wife Chris out for a romantic dinner at the Samurai Restaurant in Eureka. They had an excellent meal. Chris tells me that Valentine's Day is very special to them, because 19 years ago they went to Sonoma for the weekend and got engaged. Bill took Chris downtown. He then blindfolded her and walked her into a jewelry store. He then took the blindfold off and told her to pick out any wedding ring she wanted. I thought that was neat. Chris bought Bill the Titanic Movie Sound Track CD. Bill bought Chris a heart shaped box full of goodies from Bubbles in Arcata. After dinner they went to see the movie *As good as it Gets*. When the movie was over they went home. Bill told me they got home rather early. He said Chris is going to Hawaii with some girlfriends and he wanted to make sure he got a lot of loving in before she left.

John McDonald took his girlfriend to a romantic dinner at Dennis and Geri's restaurant in Eureka. After eating a big prime rib dinner, they went home and John said he took care of business.

Veronica, a wild redhead bought her boyfriend some chocolates and a card. He bought her a ring and told her that should be enough for her, and that she shouldn't expect anything else the rest of the day. That night the redhead had a few drinks with her friend Rose while her boyfriend played darts all night with friends. She told me the dart board got more attention than she did. After a few boring hours of darts she went to bed alone.

The next guy who gets in I have known for along time. I asked him, "What did you do Valentine's Day?" "Not a damn thing," he said. I asked him did you take your wife anywhere? "Nope!" Did you buy her anything? "Nope!" Did she buy you anything? "Nope!" Nothing, I ask? "Nope!" What did you guys do all day, just watch TV? "Nope!" Can I use your name in my book? "Nope!"

Ray Christie told me that he went to Oregon on Saturday with some friends to bet on the rooster fights. He left his wife Jennifer at home. On the way home Sunday, Ray bought his wife a glass swan vase with a red rose. When Ray got home his wife had made him some oatmeal cookies and a chocolate cake.

Diane's boyfriend rented a suite at a motel with a king size bed and a hot tub. They went to Hunan's and got dinner to go, then picked up a bottle of wine and took it back to their room. Everything was going great. Then they got into an argument, and things took a turn for the worse. She got in bed, he got in the hot tub, they argued some more, she fell asleep, he got none.

Marci and Greg Davy went to their summer cabin in Trinity Village early Valentine's Day. They had a nice breakfast. After they had breakfast, Marci called her mom, Marilynn and her husband Gordon and wished them a Happy Valentine's Day. It was raining real hard on Saturday so Greg started a nice big fire in the fireplace. He then grabbed a bottle of wine and asked Marci to join him on their large, fluffy couch that's right in front of the fireplace. Marci told me it was very romantic, listening to the rain outside, and the crackling of the fire all cuddled up with her honey. She told me it was great, no kids—no TV, just holding, and loving each other.

That night they went to OH's Townhouse in Eureka and had an excellent dinner. They had a really special day. When they got home Marci gave Greg a T-shirt as a gift. I asked her, a T-shirt? Marci told me, "Yes, but it's a Nike shirt that said, `Just do it!' I didn't have to ask her what they did next.

Rachel is in town on business. She is a stock market analyst from New York. Her boyfriend sent a beautiful bouquet of flowers to her at home on Friday. That night they flew to Utah to go snow skiing for the weekend. Valentines night they had a very romantic dinner. After dinner they went back to the ski lodge to their room and took a two hour bubble bath.

Kevin the Arcata Eye's Editor, told me "I meddled around with the Eye's back pages till about 8:30 p.m., when some friends called to sing Happy Birthday to me over the phone. At that precise moment, Rick walked in the office door and placed a piece of birthday cake before me (it was his daughter's birthday, too). Then I went home and wrote the police log."

Laura received a dozen roses (half pink and half red) and some Godiva chocolates from her husband, Bert. They went to Bracco's and had a wonderful dinner. During dinner Bert gave her a tri - dinosaur bone necklace. After dinner, they went to the Eureka Inn where they had a room for the night. Laura gave Bert a bottle of Gewerztraminer. Bert gave her another half dozen roses and a bottle of champagne. Laura said, "That's all I am going to tell you."

Ginger Hernandez bought her sweetheart Steve Daly a box of Almond Rocha and a card. Ginger told me when Steve got home from work on Valentine's Day he woke her up with Roses. That night they watched That 70's show and The X-files while eating a very romantic dinner from McDonalds. I asked her what they did after they went to bed, she just smiled.

Shannon Aspinwall had to work during Valentine's Day. After work she picked up her boyfriend Kelly and went to his house. He gave her a card which said "Happy Valentines Day to a friend." She told me she would have preferred love instead of friend, but that's life. She also got some flowers and a chocolate heart. He then cooked her a spaghetti dinner, which she wasn't too thrilled about. I asked her, "Anything else exciting happen?" she growled and then said, "No, he had a headache!"

Jay Smolik from Portola Valley, Calif. took his family to Hawaii. Jay is a headhunter for the 3-Com Corporation and other large corporations. If you don't know what a headhunter is, they hire personnel for companies. He said all they did every day was lie around the pool drinking Mai Tais, swimming and enjoying every thing else Hawaii has to offer. He told me it was great to get away from the rain and enjoy the sunshine—even getting a tan.

Dave Simpson sent his lovely wife Sharon an electronic

Valentine's Card and a red pillow with white lace around it with the words "I love you" in the middle of the pillow done in white lace also. It was Dave's birthday two days earlier so Sharon bought Dave a card and several gifts. They also bought each other some chocoholic body frosting. (I'm getting hungry.) That night they had a very romantic dinner at Celestino's in Eureka with a bottle of wine. "What happened after you guys got home?" I asked. Dave laughed. Again I asked Dave, "Well, come on we need to know?" He laughed again and said, "Guess." "You tell me!" He knew he was losing the conversation and said, "Well, when Sharon saw the pillow I bought her on the bed, she smiled and she knew what to do next."

Monica Dixon of Sacramento had a nice Valentine's Day. "I got a nice card from my husband Greg and attached to it was a C.D. of the Dixie Chicks, a country group I like. I also received a nice card from my son, Tyler, along with a box of chocolates. It was really nice.

Randy Hendricks and his honey Tina Wheaton watched movies all night. "Anything exciting happen later in the evening?" I asked. "Hell no; the kids wouldn't go to sleep." Randy said.

Steve Nunes of Fallon, Nevada bought his wife Ruthie a dozen roses and Ruthie bought Steve a card and gave him some gifts she had made for him. They own and operate a large dairy in Fallon. That night they had a party with some friends. I asked Ruthie, "Did anything else happen after the party?" She laughed and said, "Let's just say it was a night to remember."

Jim Icenbice and his wife Heather from Oregon cleaned the house for the baby-sitter and then left their kid with her. He took his wife to see Blast from the Past. "Her idea, not mine. I wanted to see Payback. After the movie we went out for a drink, bought some take out Chinese food and then went home to do what married couples do; (wink, wink)."

FINDING LOVE IN THE BUSHES

Love is a wonderful thing. Love can be found everywhere—even in the bushes. Just ask JR of Arkansas and Suzanne Blackburn of Eureka.

Last Winter I got a call to go to a local gas station and pick up JR, whose car had broken down. He needed to go to the airport to catch a plane. The dispatcher told me to look for a Chevrolet Blazer.

When I got to the gas station, I could see the Blazer parked behind the building. There was oil running down the driveway from it. It was the biggest vehicle oil leak I had ever seen. I pulled over and honked my horn. After a couple of minutes I still didn't see anyone, so I decided to go look for my fare.

I walked to the back of the gas station towards the Blazer and I still didn't see anyone. Then I heard some bushes moving by the fence that surrounds the back of the gas station. I looked over to where the noise was coming from and I didn't see anyone at first. Then, under the bushes, I could see two sets of feet. At first I thought it was a couple of guys just taking a leak. I yelled, "Hey, did you call for a taxi?"

They acted a little startled when they heard me. Then a guy yells out that they will be right out.

As I was waiting I realized it was a guy and a gal having a little fun.

After a few minutes, they came out. The girl was carrying her bra and trying to get her sweater straightened out, and he was getting himself together too.

They were laughing and talking while they were coming towards me. The lady walked over to the Blazer and threw her bra in the front seat. Loverboy came over and told me he would be ready in a few minutes. He then walked back over to his lady friend and they started kissing and hugging each other like it would be the last time they ever saw each other.

After a few minutes of slobbering all over each other, they told each other good-bye. The guy then grabbed his luggage out of the Blazer and got into my luxurious yellow cruiser. He wanted to go to the airport.

As we're driving off, he's looking at the Blazer and waving good-bye to his lady friend. He then said, "I sure hate to leave her broke down like this, but I have to get back to Arkansas so I can go to work."

"Is that your wife?" I asked.

"No, I'm a long-haul trucker. I met her a few months ago, so I came out to see her for Christmas."

"I can't believe how much oil is leaking from her Blazer."

"Yeah, I know it. We were on our way to the airport and it was losing power so we decided to pull off and call for a cab. There was oil coming out everywhere. I feel bad I couldn't stay to help her, but I called her a tow truck."

I had to ask him, "So what was going on in the bushes back there? Getting some for the road?"

He laughed. "Something like that. We were hoping to stop at the beach up by the airport for an hour or so and go for a walk, if you know what I mean."

We're both laughing now. Then he said, "She's a wild one. While we were waiting for you, she got the big idea of playing around in the bushes. It was funny because a couple of people walked by just before you got here wondering what we were doing."

"Yeah, I thought it was funny too." I told him. As we pulled up to the airport he told me he would be back in a couple of months, but he figured his lady friend wouldn't be able to wait that long and would probably be coming back to Arkansas to see him.

I told him that I hope she waits until summer because the bushes in Arkansas are frozen now.

He laughed as he was getting out.

READ ALL ABOUT IT!
THE WEST COAST CABBIE LOVES HIS MOM

One of my favorite columns was not about cab driving, but about Mother's Day, and I want to share it with you. Every year in May we celebrate Mother's Day. Really, in my opinion every day should be Mother's Day. It's a day for us to honor our mothers, and the mothers of our children. They're the number one reason we're all here. They gave us life.

So every year in May it's a good time for us to show them that we love them, and to thank them for everything they have done for us.

I have two special ladies in my life I wish a Happy Mother's Day to and thank on Mother's day.

My wife Dannette is a great mother to our three sons. I'm proud of her also because besides working full time for Yakima Products in Arcata, she always makes sure our boys are well taken care of, are happy, and know that they are loved and are very special to us.

Taking care of them and me is also a full time job. She also volunteers for various events that our kids are involved in. Just a few other things I want to thank her for are: helping me publish my monthly newsletter, driving tractor and hauling hay on the weekends during the summer for our hay business, her love and affection, and of course putting up with me.

I also wish my mother LaVina Collenberg a very Happy Mother's Day! I will never be able to tell her enough how thankful I am for everything she has done for me. I do want to mention a few things, and I hope they bring back memories of some of the things that make your mom so special to you.

Here are fifteen reasons why my mom is so special to me that I want to share with you:

1.) I want to thank my mother for marrying my dad. They have been married for 47 years! He's the best dad anyone could have. Besides, I wouldn't be writing this book if it weren't for those two special people in my life.

2.) When I was little I had a bad habit of dumping my bowl of spaghetti over my head. I don't remember why I used to do that, but it must have been a mess. I want to thank my mom for always cleaning me up.

3.) After I got over my spaghetti habit, I found something new to get in trouble about. When my grandpa Otto would baby-sit, he would always fall asleep. I would then start little fires in all the ashtrays. One time my dad found out, and he was really upset with me. He was going to give me a spanking, but Mom had a talk with him and he calmed down.

4.) A couple of years later I was sleeping when I heard a noise in our front room. I went to see what the noise was, and the wall by the wood stove in the front room was on fire.(No, I didn't start it) I ran to my mom's room to tell her the house was on fire, but she didn't believe me. She told me to go back to bed. So I went back to bed. After about the 3rd time, she said, "OK, Let's go see!" When she saw the fire, she yelled at me to run over to the barn and tell my dad who was milking the cows. When I got back home, my mom told me to go outside in front of the house and flag down the fire trucks when they showed up. That was cool.

5.) When I was nine years old, my dad signed me up for 4-H. Then one day he took me to Dave Henry's ranch in McKinleyville to buy a beef cow for my 4-H project. When we got home I was all excited about our new family member. I was telling my mom all about my beef cow, when my dad walked in and handed me my savings book. It had $305 in it, which was given to me as gifts for my birthdays, and Christmas. I was wondering why my dad had it.

Well, I was in for a rude awakening. I thought my dad used his money to buy my beef cow, but he used my money. I started crying and told my dad that I didn't want that dumb cow. I wanted my money back. He told me, "By using your money, you'll learn how to invest your money to make more money to purchase bigger things someday. I didn't care; I wanted my money back. My mom finally stepped in and calmed me down and explained everything again to me. I felt better, but I didn't like the cow for quite awhile.

6.) About the time I got used to that cow, my mom took up golfing. One night we were going to have homemade sausage and macaroni for dinner, my favorite. I couldn't wait for dinner. My mother is an excellent cook.

While dinner was cooking, my mom wanted to show me how to hit a golf ball. So we went into the back yard. She showed me how to swing the golf club and a few other pointers. Then she told me to go ahead and try to hit the golf ball by myself. I said, "OK!" She was walking away, when I took a big swing. At that time she had looked back to see how I was doing, and I hit her square on the eye. I thought I killed her.

I was really scared and sad as my dad put her into the car so we could take her to the hospital. When she got home the next day, I told her I was sorry about 100 times. She said, "It was an accident, and it was my fault, too, for not getting out of the way in time!" She knew I felt really bad about what had happened. She then said, "Let me cook your favorite dinner, sausage and macaroni." I just smiled! Everything was going to be OK.

7.) While we're on the subject of food, I want to thank my mom for making my dad buy us dinner almost every Sunday night. It was a treat for the whole family. We would go to the Big 4 Inn, which used to be on L.K. Wood Boulevard, and get a big pot of ravioli. Then we would go to BIM's Restaurant just down the road and get a tub of chicken.

After we got home, we would eat dinner as we watched Walt Disney's Wonderful World of Color and My Favorite Martian. What great memories I have of those times together as a family.

8.) When I was in the 8th grade, I had my first steady girl-friend. Then one day, she dumped me. I went home from school and thought I was going to die! I wouldn't come out of my room, even when dinner was ready. My mom finally came in and told me that I was too young to worry about one girl so much. She told me that I will meet a lot of girls before I find the right one. My dad overheard my mom and said, "Randy, you need to find a cute Portuguese girl like your mom!" My mom laughed!

"Lets go eat," she says, (Our family likes to eat.)I was feeling a little better now. I guess mom was right, as always.

9.) I want to thank my mom for letting me have my friends over all the time. She always made them feel special, and feed them good, too.

10.) I played lots of different sports and my mom always made sure I got to my practices. She and my dad went to all my games, too.

11.) When it was time to buy my first car, my mom took me to the bank to get the money that I had been saving. Remember that dumb cow I bought?

Well, over the years she had calves, and I had built my herd up to quite a few. Every once in a while I would sell one and put the money in the bank. So that cow that I didn't want paid for my car. My dad was right. Of course he reminded me of that when I got home in my new car.

12.) I don't know if I want to thank my mom for this next once in a lifetime achievement. Every year in high school we had "crazy clothes day," where everyone dressed up.

One year, my mom talked my brother and me into dressing up for the contest. She dressed me up like a hooker, and my brother wore our sister's confirmation dress, bonnet, and a little purse. They handed out the awards for the best dressed in each class, and then the best dressed in the whole high school. There was a tie. The winners were the Collenberg "sisters!" Thanks mom.

13.) Next up was my first prom. I was really excited and very nervous. I wore a tuxedo, and all the stuff that goes with it. My mom helped me get ready; you know how some moms are. It was time to go, so I grabbed my dates corsage and headed out the door. I was getting into my car, when my mom hollered out, "Did you forget something." I was thinking, "No, I don't think so, mom!" I look at my mom, and she's laughing. She has my shoes in her hand. I didn't have any shoes on, and didn't even realize it. We laughed for a few years over that.

14.)When I was a Senior in high school, my mom would come to school to see me, or bring me something that I needed.

Once in a while, people that didn't know her would ask me if she was my girlfriend. She was and still is a very beautiful woman. We would tell them, "Yes, she's a senior at Humboldt State University." We fooled a lot of people. She would always go along with me. We had a lot of fun teasing people about that. She would hold my hand and give me a hug once in awhile to get everyone all stirred up. It was great!

15.)After I graduated from St. Bernard's High School my dad and mom helped me get into the dairy business with them. The money I used for a down payment, came from selling the rest of my cows that I had—that started with that very first one that I didn't want anything to do with. Dad always was right.

We were in business for about 15 years when my dad sold out to my brother. My mom was always there in the background doing the books for us and giving us advice. My mom was always there for our family, and still is today.

Well, now you know just a few reasons why I'm thankful for my mother.

Mom, thanks for everything! Thanks for the great memories, the love, hugs, support, and the generosity you have given me and my family.

Happy Mothers Day Mom! I love you.

LOOKING FOR LOVE

One day I picked up Mary, one of my regular customers. She lives in a seniors-only mobile home park.

Mary is probably about 75 years old. She's a character and is always very nice. I usually take Mary shopping or to the Post Office. But the other day when I picked her up she wanted to go to a senior lunch being served in town.

On our way there she told me, "Randy, I'm tired of living alone, it's time to look for a man again."

I smiled and said, "So you're going to check out the guys while you're having lunch today?"

She laughed, and said, "That's right; I still have a few good years left."

I told her that I thought that was neat and I hoped that someday she would find someone as nice as her to spend time with. As she was getting out I told her, "Good luck, and if you find found someone interesting, make sure he has a big bank account."

Mary smiled and told me to pick her up in a couple of hours. I told her OK.

A couple of hours later I picked Mary up and asked her, "Well, did you find the man of your dreams?"

She gave me a dirty look and said, "I can't believe it."

"What's that Mary?"

"Those guys were all old, really old. They looked like they were just dug up."

"That bad Mary?"

"Oh, I couldn't believe it. The women were nice and dressed nice too, but the men were terrible. Take me back home." She was all upset.

"What about where you live, Mary. There's a lot of retired single men living there." She gave me a dirty look and said, "You mean Tombstone City."

I started laughing. "Why do you call it that?"

"Because almost everyone that lives there is old and just waiting to die. Kids can't live there so you don't hear any kids playing or laughing, and I don't think the birds even come around there."

As Mary was getting out I told her to keep her chin up. Then I told her I would use my Cab10 love connection services to help her locate someone special.

She sort of smiled and said, "See you later, Randy; I'm going back to my tomb."

CHAPTER 9

Breaking News

CAB10 TRAVELS TO THE EDGES OF A LOST WORLD

In my travels I have met a lot of interesting people. When the Jurassic Park sequel, *The Lost World*, was being made here in Humboldt County I was lucky enough to meet Steven Spielberg, the director.

I had just dropped off somebody at the airport and I was talking to Joe Stover, an airport-shuttle employee, when I saw a large private jet coming in for a landing. I asked Joe if he knew who owned that jet that was landing. He told me that the plane belonged to Steven Spielberg, and it had been coming in the last few days quite often, bringing supplies and personnel for the movie.

Joe said he'd heard from a reliable source that Spielberg might be on this flight, but that the famous producer/director didn't want the press to know he was up here yet. I wondered where the people on the plane would be coming out, because usually the private planes use the side gates. Joe said they would be using the south gate. So I  jumped into my luxurious yellow cruiser, circled the airport parking lot and drove to the south gate where the rental cars are parked.

When I entered the parking lot, I saw five cars all parked in a row ready to go. In the middle of these cars was a fancy suburban with big tires and flashy wheels. It was then that I knew that Spielberg had to be one of the people that was on that plane. And I was hoping he might need a cab.

There was enough room for me to back my cruiser in front of these cars so I could park in front of the gate. Everyone who came through it would have to walk right by me.

About five minutes later, I saw about eight people coming towards me. It looked like a couple of guys who were probably body guards, a couple of good-looking women, a few guys in suits and, I couldn't believe it, there was Steven Speilberg. (In case you couldn't tell, I'm a big fan of his movies.)

So they were coming through the gate and I was telling all of them hello. They were being nice and doing the same. When Spielberg was right in front of me, I put out my hand and said, "Hi, Mr. Spielberg. How are you today?" He said he was doing great. I had to ask him if he needed a cab. He smiled and said that he already had a ride and thanks. Then he said that he was sure that his staff would be calling for rides in the next day or so because they need someone who knows the area and can deliver and pick up things that they need for filming *The Lost World*. I said that would be great, I told him make sure they request Cab10. He said OK and got in his Suburban and went on his way.

A couple of days went by and I got a call to go to the airport to pick up a large crate that needed to go to Eureka. When I got to the airport, a guy came out of the terminal and told me to go with him to get the crate. We went inside the ticket booth and there was a large, heavy wooden crate. We carried it outside and put it into my cab. As we put it down, I noticed the words "Lost World" on the lid.

I asked this guy what was in the crate and he said it was the film from the first day of filming the movie. He told me to take it to an address on Third Street in Eureka and not to let the crate out of my sight.

I jumped into my cruiser and headed for Eureka with a very valuable cargo of film that might be another blockbuster movie, right here in Cab10. Now I was thinking of all kinds of crazy things, which is normal for me. I stopped in Arcata for a minute because I had to call my wife, Dannette. When she answered the phone, I told her I had good news and bad news. She said, "You sound like you're up to something. What did you do now?"

I told her, "The good news is you are going to be rich, and the bad news, I'm going to jail. "She said, "I know you've lost your marbles now. What are you talking about?" I told her that I had the film from the first day of the filming from the movie The Lost World, and I was going to sell some of it to the rag magazines or Hard Copy, because they would love to get their hands on the film. She told me, Get back to work; all this movie stuff is going to your head." Women, they can't take a joke.

But I guess she's right. I had better go to Eureka. I went to a large Victorian on Third Street which Spielberg had converted into a film lab. Five guys there will get the film ready for shipment and prepare cameras for use at the movie sights. They told me it will take a couple hours and then they will have the film ready for me to take back to the airport so it can be flown to Santa Monica to be processed. While I waited I asked all kinds of questions and snooped around. It was an interesting place.

It was time to put the crate back into my cruiser and head to the airport. When I got there I took the crate, into the terminal and had it put on the next flight.

The next day I got a call to the airport. I'm supposed to pick up some boxes and take them to the third floor of the DoubleTree Hotel in Eureka. When I got there, I went up to the third floor. I'm supposed to take the boxes to room 308. Walking down the hallway, I noticed all the doors had signs on them such as supplies, makeup, parts, fax, mailroom, costumes, video, staff, etc. This was the command center for the movie that Steven Speilberg was making. It was a very busy place.

I gave the boxes to this guy in room 308. He said thanks, and wanted to know if I could pick up a couple of guys on Broadway and take them to Fieldbrook to the movie sight. I told him the meter is still going and I have all day.

On my way to Broadway I passed a semi truck carrying some dinosaurs. Now that was an interesting sight to see. On Broadway I picked up these two guys at a paint shop. They got in and we headed for Fieldbrook. I asked them all kinds of questions. I wanted to know what they had to do with the movie.

They said they were hired to paint some dinosaurs and were asked if they wanted to do a little part in the movie. They of course said yes. They were both going to drive a couple of army trucks for about five minutes in a scene and were getting paid $1000 each. Where's Mr. Speilberg? I thought. I would do it for maybe $800.

I was looking at my cab meter and it only had $133 for three hours of hard work and all the pressure I was going through to be efficient. I felt underpaid. I guess that's show business for you. When we arrived in Fieldbrook there was a lot going on. I stayed for a little while and watched, then it was time to go.

On several more occasions, I had to take more supplies and boxes to different locations for Mr. Speilberg. It was all very interesting and fun being involved in the background of making a movie as big as *The Lost World*.

RANDY IN FRONT OF THE TRINIDAD LIGHTHOUSE
TRINIDAD, CA

A CAB10 SPECIAL INVESTIGATION POTHOLES-ARCATA'S RENEWABLE RESOURCE

One day I was cruising down Janes Road towards the hospital in my luxurious yellow cruiser with a passenger aboard, when I hit a minefield of potholes.

It seems like the roads are getting worse everyday. I used to drive around the potholes, but now it's not worth the danger of getting into a wreck. If you dodge one hole, you're bound to hit another one. My passengers are always complaining about how rough the roads are.

It seems like whoever is responsible for keeping up the roads would be aware of their terrible condition and fix them. I don't see how they can't notice the roads on their way to work everyday—unless they come to work in a helicopter, or maybe a hot air balloon.

If I was the mayor or any city leader, I would be going ballistic on this issue. Maybe all these people responsible for the roads are members of the Alliance for Paving Moratorium.

I think they are just going to let the roads crumble to gravel, and eventually down to sand. Then we can all walk, ride our bikes or use skateboards around town.

I hate to tell you this, but Cab10 is fed up with these potholes. We have enough potholes running our country in the White House; we don't need them in our streets, too. I'm not going to point my finger at anyone; you know who you are!

I'm tired of picking up customers' false teeth off the floor of my cab. I'm tired of my customers complaining that all the bumps in the road hurt their backs, legs, or hips. I'm tired of putting new shocks and tires on more often than necessary.

I hate to admit it, but once in a while I do like the potholes. But only when I have a customer who won't shut up. I'll hit a pothole on purpose so they will have to stop talking.

Something has to be done about this dangerous situation on our streets. The other day I was following an ambulance that had its siren on going towards the hospital. It hit a few potholes and was bouncing around all over the place. I just knew the back door was going to pop open and a body would come rolling out in front of me. If the person in the ambulance that day made it alive to the hospital, he or she was lucky because our streets could beat you to death.

I was thinking maybe I'm the only one who thinks the roads around here are dangerous. So I thought I'd better see if anyone else feels the same as I do about our roads by launching a Cab10 investigation to see if I was the only one complaining.

In my very important duty of fact finding on the subject of potholes, I thought I should interview people that use the streets the most.

I saw Camellia Clark who drives a City of Arcata bus. I asked her, "What do you think of our roads here in Arcata?" She said, "They're terrible! It's embarrassing! It's humiliating to have to drive a City bus that's bumping and throwing people around. Sometimes when I hit one of our famous potholes with the ADA (disabled) people, I have to ask them if they were thrown from their seats and if they're OK!"

A lady at the hospital told me they stink! I saw a couple of Mel Brown's (A.P.D.) troopers and asked their opinions. They didn't want to comment because they didn't want a pothole in their paycheck.

I asked one of my regular customers, Hope Lindsay, what she thought about our roads. "They are the worst roads in the world," she said. "I have never seen anything like it before."

John Peterson of Arcata Muffler told me his "favorite" road is 11th Street going up to Fickle Hill Road. He said it's a great place to check your car for rattles.

Don Kolshinski (the hot dog man) told me the roads are a mess. That's why the sales tax revenues are down. It doesn't take a brain surgeon to figure it out. Don also told me that Paul Rex, director of Arcata Main Street, told him the other day that he hit a big pothole with his car and had to replace his tire. Isn't he the guy who is supposed to make our downtown appealing to outsiders?

A local fireman told me the roads have been really hard on the firetruck tires and equipment. He also told me that the public wants the fire department to respond as fast as they can to their calls. Sometimes the potholes slow them down.

Kelly Wilson, a paramedic with Arcata-Mad River Ambulance, said, "After about 10 years, they finally paved Spear Avenue. However, Janes Road, the major road to the hospital, is probably the worst. As a medic, I don't have to see were I'm going, I know I have about a two-minute ETA by the road conditions. People with broken hips are the worst. I feel really bad for the little old grandmas. I have hit my head a few times, but I just hold on and take care of my patient.

The other day I was parked by Murphy's Market when a lady parked next to me. It was Cindy Chandler and her daughter, Janice. I asked her what she thought of our road conditions. She said they're terrible. She told me that when her husband Frank is in the car with her, he makes her nervous. He always tells her to go around the potholes. Cindy tells me she used to try to avoid them, but you just run into another one.

These quotes are from a random selection of citizens. I have a lot more, but these give you a good idea of what the public thinks.

I bet my Cab10 survey would be 100 percent if I asked everyone else. I told a lot of people I was writing about our famous potholes, and they all asked me, "Why do you think the City won't fix these potholes?" I told them there are always two main reasons! They will always tell you that they don't have the manpower or the money to fix them. Maybe they can't find them? Another reason could be that I heard there was a shortage on standup shovels.

I have an idea. I think the City should have a pothole-a-thon like a run-a-thon. You can divide the streets up into groups and have different charities ask for donations for each hole their group fills up for their particular charity. Do it on a Saturday and have all the groups, when they are finished, meet at the Redwood Park, and the City can supply a big barbecue to celebrate a historic event. The first pothole-a-thon in the World—that would make me feel good to be an Arcatan.

You probably think by now that this cab driver is totally nuts. Well, maybe I am, but do you have a better idea?

Sometimes the citizens need to take charge. So I talked to a lot of business people about getting donations to help with fixing these potholes. You wouldn't believe the response I got.

Jack Nicholls, owner of Nicholls Trucking, would bring the asphalt; he will bring my dad, Tony Collenberg with him to supervise the filling of the potholes.

Alan Fusi and Sharon Suddult of Fusi and Suddult Flagging Company will flag the traffic.

John Phillips of Bayside Market will provide free hot-dogs to the workers. And I got hundreds of people that wanted to lean up against a stand-up shovel and watch one guy do all the work. Even Art and Tim Hooven of Hooven Trucking in McKinleyville offered their equipment.

Of course, we wouldn't be allowed to fix the potholes because we're not covered by the City's insurance. Even if we were allowed to fix the potholes, it would be years before we got all the permits.

But wait, the City seems it always wants to be an example for something, such as our recycling Center, our Marsh, and the other pothole, the Cannabis Center. How about our famous potholes?

I would rather Arcata be recognized for the great schools we have here in Arcata. I know lots of the teachers, and I think they are all great people, too.

How about having the best parks in America for families to have picnics, to play or just to spend quality time together? We have a beautiful area; lets take advantage of that.

We have one of the nicest Plazas in America. Let's clean it up! Let's turn the Plaza into a beautiful place for families to shop and have fun—a family place. These are the things that I think our city should be trying to accomplish.

But the one thing that we have now and can be proud of is

our potholes. We have one of the biggest tourist attraction; available, and the City isn't taking advantage of that! We probably have the best potholes in the whole USA.

Tourists are always coming here to see our Marsh and Wildlife Sanctuary, the hippies on the Plaza, the trees; how about the potholes?

The City could start an adopt a pothole program like Cal Trans adopt-a-freeway program. Almost everyone has a pothole in front of his house or business. I know a few of you will be upset because you don't have a pothole of your own, but maybe you can share one with your neighbor.

It would be a big responsibility to care for your own private pothole. You would have to keep it clean and neat for our visitors.

I was asked whether, if a program like this went into effect, one would be allowed to have a snack bar or a souvenir stand next to their pothole so they could make a little extra money. I told them it should be OK because according to the local newspaper, the Arcata Eye reports, the city's sales tax revenues are way down.

How will the tourist find your pothole? I made a map. It's called the Cab10's Guide to Arcata's World Famous Potholes.

It took me two weeks to log all the potholes in Arcata. Since I drive more miles in Arcata than anyone else, I figured it was my duty to take on this tremendous responsibility at no expense to you, the taxpayers.

After I did the first two roads, I wanted to quit. There were just too many. I had to make a plan. Then one day, Larry Walker was riding in my cab. He told me to get a seismograph, like they use for earthquakes, and install it in my cab. So I had a friend of mine in high places hook one up in my cab. My plan now was any pothole that registered a five or higher would be registered on my list.

I know some of you are going to be upset your pothole didn't make the list. Maybe next time. I ended up with 125 listings. A lot of these have more than one pothole. I have listed all the streets that made the list so you can locate them on the map to show all your friends and relatives when they come to town to visit.

To attract tourists to our famous potholes, I felt it necessary to change the names of all the streets and to name all the potholes. I even named one after me, I was so excited. I will be giving tours in my luxurious yellow cruiser. It will be called The Cab10 Tour of Arcata's World-famous Potholes. The tour takes two hours and consists of several stops.

Here's a schedule of my luxurious tour:

11 a.m. I will pick up your group on the Plaza. We will be able to see two of our town's favorite potholes on G Street: Hip pies and the Panhandler's potholes.

11:05 a.m. Clinton's pothole: We will go to 13th and J Streets and see Arcata's biggest pothole (Bill). At 11th and J streets, you will see Arcata's worse intersection (Hillary). At 609 is Chelsea's. A favorite place on my tour is 668 (Monica), 759 (Paula), and 956 (Jennifer). These are Bill Clinton's three favorite potholes, too. A Cab10 Picture spot!

11:15 a.m. Arcata Police Department potholes: Some of Mel Brown's Army are located on 14th Street. You will find your favorite police officers on this street.

11:25 a.m. Roughest railroad crossing: We will stop at 17th street and Alliance Road to see this bone crusher.

11:35 a.m. City Leaders: On Q street you will find our five coun cil members at 1140 (Jim), 1246 (Connie), 1320 (Bad Bob), 1565 (Jennifer), and 17th and Q (Jason). This is another Cab10 picture spot.

11:40 a.m. Arcata Eye: On 13th street, you will see the editors' pothole at 77 (Kevin), 120, the advertising pothole is at 130 (Terrance), the columnist pothole is 814 (Rick), the reporter's pothole is at 989 (Tom), and the cartoonist pot hole is at 1031 (Dave).

11:50 a.m. Killer Alley: We will be going to West End Road. The second worst railroad crossing is at Ericson. Some of our most famous potholes are located on Killer Alley.

Noon: Lunch at Toni's Restaurant. She will be serving her world famous pothole burgers.

12:30 p.m. Torture Alley: Janes Road will beat you to death. You will find three potholes that are brutal. They seem like they could be related. At 3146 you will see Melissa, then at 3289 you will find Krista and at 3956 is Connie's pothole. In front of the Quality Inn you will discover why this street was named Torture Alley.

12:45 p.m. Movie Star Lane: The most popular stop is saved for your last stop. You will want to take a lot of pictures on this street. I named all the potholes after famous movie stars. All the potholes on this street have beautiful curves and shapes. At 1957 we have Raquel Welch, 1972 Sharon Stone, 1994 Heather Locklear, and at 1999 is Cindy Crawford. Another Cab10 picture spot.

1p.m. Back to the Plaza. This is the end of your world famous tour of Arcata's famous potholes in the luxurious yellow cruiser. I will be available for pictures and autographs at this time. Thanks for coming.

CBS NEWS CORRESPONDENT JOHN BLACKSTONE AND CAB10

This next story was the first one I ever wrote. It was about a current news story and working for CBS National News Correspondent, John Blackstone. I received a call at 7a.m. to go to the McKinleyville Airport to pick up someone on a private plane that couldn't land at Murray Field because it was too foggy. (I love the fog because lots of times like this they have to fly to McKinleyville so they can land, and they almost always go to Eureka. That's a good fare, and usually it's an attorney. I love to do my own interrogation to see which case they're working on.)

Well, I was wrong. There were two people including the pilot. The passenger told me he was John Blackstone, Correspondent for CBS News, and he was doing a local story for Dan Rather. He asked if he could hire me for about three hours. Well, I had nothing else to do (of course I wanted a good fare too). This will be great! I thought to myself.

So I started loading our (remember, I'm working with CBS now) equipment into my yellow CBS van and Mr. Blackstone; I mean John, and Nelo the pilot get in and we're off. I asked John what our assignment was and he said we were covering the story about the use of pepper spray on the Headwaters demonstrators.

We had to go to the Sheriff's department at the courthouse to interview a certain officer about his views. This was exciting! But I had a job to do so I tried to control myself.

I decided I'd better ask John some questions about our assignment, just in case someone asked me any questions (that way I could inform them about our objectives and act like I know what the hell I was doing). John got me up to speed; I love this job.

When we finally arrived at the Sheriff's Department, there were no parking spaces for the public, but there was one Media space. It was full however with a Sheriff's car. (Can't they read)? So I went inside and asked an officer if I could park in the empty sheriff's spot since there was a Sheriff's car in the media spot. I told him I was with CBS and that I needed a place to park. He said go ahead, but I might get towed. Nice guy!

We finally went inside, and of course I was packing everything. A lady opened the security door for us to go through and two officers approached me and asked, "What's are in the bags?" John told them video equipment. The officers said, "I hope so."

They finally wind up interviewing Sheriff Lewis instead of the officer they were going to interview. After that they were going to interview Terry Farmer but the secretary said we were seven minutes late and he had other appointments (but I think he just didn't want to be interviewed).

So we packed up and went to the Eureka Police station to interview Police Chief Arnie Millsap. Sheriff Lewis felt the Chief of Police would tell us what we wanted to hear.

As I was unloading our equipment, I set the video camera on the ground next to the tripod along with the other equipment. A typical Humboldt County Tweaker walked up and told us we were stupid idiots because the camera goes on the tripod. I guess she thought we were going to video from the ground, She was all screwed up.

John asked me what her problem was and I told him that she was a tweaker. He asked what that meant. I explained to him (tweaked on meth-a cranker) and suggested he do a story on that someday. He just laughed.

It was a great interview with Chief Millsap (he said what he felt, and he stood up for the actions of his men).

John then asked me where a good place would be for a background for his closing thoughts on his interviews. So I took them down to the pier and they shot it there.

Our assignment was now over. On our way back to the airport, John asked if we wanted lunch (of course I said Yes). He asked if Burger King was Okay. I was hoping for something a little more fancy, but we had a deadline to meet.

I pulled into BK and ordered 3 meals. As we were on our way, John said his chips (fries) were good and asked if I had an extra tissue (napkin). I have a long way to go with all these out-of-town words.

John finished his lunch and called our producer. He explained to him our work was done and it shouldn't be any problem getting the story on Dan's desk in time for the 7p.m. CBS news broadcast.

We arrived back at the airport we had left three hours earlier. I unloaded our things into the airplane. The fare was over $150 and John gave me a $25 tip.

Of course, I did tell him during our ride to Eureka that I was writing a weekly newspaper column about my adventures driving a cab and that he would be one of my stories. He thought that was great and gave me his address so I could mail him a copy. (Which I did.)

It was a fun day! The plane is now out of sight; the one-time CBS crew member is just a cab driver again.

THE PLAZA - ARCATA, CA

THE FURBY AND THE BEANIE BABY PHENOMENA

First, I think the Furby is about the ugliest toy I have ever seen. The Beanie Babies are cute, I guess. I hear women, and even some men, talking about buying these two toys everywhere. I always ask them, "Why are you wasting your money on these items? It's just a another fad."

After you ask this question, they always look at you like you're stupid or something. Then they all tell you they are going to be worth a lot of money someday.

I'm stupid or something. I then tell them, "Wait until the year 2000; I bet they're going to be worth a fortune." They like it when I say that.

Anyway, not too long ago I found out my wife had been buying Beanie Babies. She didn't want to tell me how many she had, but she had the nerve to tell me that a store in the Arcata Hotel, the Natural Selection, which is a very nice store, was selling several dozen of them the next morning at 9 a.m. and she wanted me to get in line around 6 a.m. and buy her a few of them.

I looked at her like she was nuts. Then I heard the Beanie Baby story again. She told me, "They're going to be worth a lot of money. Some are already worth hundreds of dollars. Some are even retired already."

"Retired?" I asked.

"Yes, they don't make some of them anymore."

I started laughing, "The only thing that is retired when you buy those Beanie Babies is our money."

"Are you going to go and stand in line or not?" she demanded.

"I'm not going to stand in line, but I will drive by around 8:45 and if there is no line, I will go in at 9 a.m. and see if I can buy you a couple." (I had to give in a little or my love life might be retired, too.) She was happy; I was at least going to drive by.

So, the next morning I cruised up to the Plaza in my luxurious yellow cruiser and I couldn't believe what I saw. There must have been 150 people in line. I started laughing, I know we have a lot of crazy people in the world, but to stand in line for a toy is nuts.

I had to drive by the line to see if I knew anyone; I must have known at least 20 of them. I would like to mention their names, but it's not right to expose people that have an illness as serious as the Beanie Baby disease.

I then decided that I needed to go and check this out so I went and parked. I then walked over to the people that were in line and started walking by them like I didn't know what the heck was going on. I asked a few people I knew what they were standing in line for. In excited voices they all said they were in line to buy the Beanie Babies.

So I acted dumb and asked them in a loud voice, "What's that?" They looked at me like I hadn't been on earth for along time and then explained to me what a Beanie Baby is.

I told them that they were nuts. I then told them to call me next Christmas because I will be offering a quarter for every Beanie Baby they have, which will be more than they're worth. I will then donate the dolls to children for Christmas gifts. I got a lot of dirty looks, so I don't think they liked what I just said.

I decided I'd better leave and go home to tell my wife the bad news. She was upset and told me what I expected to hear, "See— I told you; you didn't believe me."

I didn't say anything. I just comforted her like a good husband would do in any other sad situation.

While I was writing this story, my wife called me from her work. She asked me what I was doing on my day off? "I'm writing a story about the Beanie Babies."

She laughed, "I hate to tell you honey, but I just bought another one today on my way to work."

"I thought you were done buying them."

"I had to buy 'Daisy the Cow.' She's retired too; plus I have 'Snort the Bull.' You have to have the pair."

So I thought I'd better ask the big question. "How many of these Beanie's do we own now?"

"Fourteen!" she said in an excited voice.

As a good husband I told her that I was glad that she got her new Beanie Baby. After she got off the phone, I thought I'd better look into a new security system for my home because I want to protect my million dollar investment.

Well, I hope this didn't bore you non-Beanie Baby fans. I do have inside information on the millennium's first new collector's item. It will be coming out in a few months and only I know what it is. Yes, that's right. I know you can't wait that long so I'm going to tell you now. That way you have time to sell your house or whatever you have so you can stock up on this new item that will be the talk of the next century.

Are you ready? It's called the Cab10 fuzzy wuzzie babies. Just a few that are in production that will sell out fast are Patch the Pirate, Randy the Cabbie (my wife's favorite), Pete the Ragman, Timber the Logger, and Squeeze the Dairyman.

So order today, because you don't want to be left out in the cold when you can hold and squeeze your new Millennium Cab10 fuzzy wuzzie babies.

CHAPTER 10

Learning Curve

HOW I BECAME CAB 10?

When a person first starts driving a cab, they assign you a call number that they use to call you on the cab radio. I had a choice between number 10 or 6. I asked for number 6.

Then the boss said that I better take number 10 because number 6 sometimes sounds like sex on the radio, and we don't want that. So I became driver number 10. When I first started driving cab, which I did for almost a year, I drove Cab17.

Then one day, my boss wanted to try to put everyone in a cab that matched their call number. He told me that since I drive Cab17 I would be driver number 17 from then on. Well, I never have to many complaints, but I didn't like the number 17. So I told my boss, and a couple days later when I went to work they changed my cab number to 10. I became Cab10 and the rest is history.

AND NOW FOR SOME CAB DRIVING LINGO

Fares always ask me how I can understand all the information the dispatcher is giving me out on my radio.

When the dispatcher says "Number 10," I know he's talking to me. He'll say something like, "No. 10, go to Food Mart in McKinleyville."All the other drivers know that it's for me and I know where my next fare is. I respond by saying, "10 check," letting the dispatcher know I heard him.

When I talk to the dispatcher I always say "Number 10," and then I tell him the total of my fare. Then after my fare gets out of my cab, I say I'm clear and on my way to my next call.

When we don't have any calls waiting, we go and park at certain places that are called stands. My stands are the Plaza and Valley West shopping center in Arcata and K-Mart and Safeway in McKinleyville. Once in a while, when we are driving to a stand, someone will try to flag us down for a ride. These kinds of calls, which are common in big cities, are called flags.

One day I picked up a flag that was walking along Central

Avenue. He got in and wanted to go to Toby and Jacks in Arcata. I tell my dispatcher I just picked up a flag going to Toby and Jacks. All of a sudden the guy started calling me a bunch of names and said, "Hey! I'm not a fag!" He thought I said I picked up a "fag," instead of a "flag." It took a few minutes for me to calm him down and explain to him what I said. By the time we arrived at his destination, we're both laughing.

SHANNON ASPINWALL & DAVE FRAZIER
OF YELLOW CAB COMPANY OF EUREKA, CA
SERVING HUMBOLDT COUNTY 24 HOURS A DAY.
AIRPORT SHUTTLE AVAILABLE 24 HOURS A DAY.
707.442.4551

WHERE DO CABBIE'S COME FROM?

One day I picked up a mother and daughter in Eureka. We were riding down 3rd Street when the daughter noticed some scantily clad women standing on a street corner. "Mommy," the little girl asked, "What are all those ladies doing?

"They're waiting for their husbands to come home from work," the mother replied. I gave her a funny look.

"C'mon, lady," I said, "tell her the truth. They're hookers!"

After a stunned silence, the daughter asked "Mommy, do hookers have children?"

I looked in my rear view mirror at the mother to see what she was going to say. The mother looked at me in the mirror and smiled. "Of course," the mother replied. "Where do you think cabbies come from?"

SEMESTER AT SEA

A floating University? I went to the airport to pick up a guy who wanted to go to Humboldt State University, a nice young man with lots of luggage. I asked him if he went to HSU, and he told me that this semester would be his first at HSU. He also told me he has never been here before.

I asked him where he went to college last semester and he said that he went through a special program at the University of Pittsburgh. He lives in Alaska and worked all summer fishing to pay his own way through college.

Last semester, through a program at the University of Pittsburgh, he got to go on a cruise ship that goes to 10 different countries and lasts 100 days. They have classes on the ship for a total of 50 days, and the other 50 days are divided up between the 10 countries. They take normal college classes on the ship, and when they arrive in a certain country, they have several days off to explore new customs, people and the scenery.

He said it was a lot of fun. There were 600 students on board. The 10 countries he went to were India, Vietnam, Africa, Egypt, Venezuela, Brazil, South America, Philippines, Hong Kong and Japan. I never heard of these kinds of floating universities before. Maybe it's because of the $14,000 cost for the 100-day cruise. If anyone is interested in going to school on this ship, you can get more information at www.pitt.edu and look up Semester at Sea.

SCAMMER TO THE SLAMMER

One day I picked up Mike, one of my regular customers, who was very upset about something. After he told me where he wanted to go, I asked him, "What's bothering you, Mike? You seem a little edgy today."

"I'm mad as hell at my bank."

"What's the problem?"

"It's a long story, but a few months ago a telemarketer called saying that he was representing my bank. He was trying to sell me a special service that would protect my credit cards if they're lost and pay my credit card bill if I lose my job. It sounded like something I might need, so I told him to mail me some information and after reviewing the material, I would decide if it's worth the $300 per year fee they wanted for it."

"Three hundred dollars!" I told Mike that I thought that was ridiculous; it sounds like a scam or a rip-off to me because most banks only charge about $30-$40 for those services. Mike said that when his credit card bill came, the $300 dollar fee was on his card and he never gave them permission to activate the service.

That made him really mad. He then called his bank and told them he was upset with them and wanted the fee removed. They told him it would be taken off his account and his next bill would show that he was credited the $300.

Well, yesterday he got this month's bill and the $300 fee is still on it. I told him he needed to go to his local bank and ask them to help him solve his problem. He thought that was a good idea. I told Mike that it seemed like every week someone calls trying to sell us more magazines, change our phone services or our insurance.

I told him next time someone tries selling you something that sounds like a scam; you need to use the Cab10 "scammer to the slammer technique."

"What's that Randy?" Mike asked.

A few years ago there were several different scams going around. One particular scam, which I had read about in the newspaper, tried to con me, too.

A telemarketer would call saying he represents the highway patrol and they were looking for donations for a special fund they have set up for the families of officers killed or injured in the line of duty. If I donated to their fund, they would send me a special sticker, which I could put on the window of my car so people would know that I had donated to the fund. He also told me that if a highway patrolmen pulled me over and saw the sticker, he might go easier on me. When I heard that, I knew it was probably a scam.

It was time to use the Cab10 scammer to the slammer technique. I told the telemarketer that I couldn't afford anything right now, but my brother-in-law and my uncle, who are rich, are always donating their money to worthwhile causes such as his. Then the telemarketer asked me if I would give him their names so he could contact them. Sure. "My uncle's name is Mel Brown (local police chief) and you can call him and ask for Uncle Mel, because everyone calls him that."

By this time the telemarketer is all excited that I'm helping him. I then put the frosting on the cake and give him my brother-in-law's name and phone number.

I want to help this salesman out so I tell him, "Call my brother-in-law, Terry Farmer (District Attorney).

After the telemarketer writes all this down, they always thank me, like I did them a big favor, and they hang up.

Mike laughed and said, "That's a great idea. I'm going to try that next time someone calls trying to sell me something."

I told Mike, "I wonder how many phone calls my uncle and brother-in-law have received in the last few years because of me."

Mike laughed again and said, "I bet they get a lot of hang ups!" When Mike got out he told me, "I can't wait for the next telemarketer to call so I can try out the Cab10 "scammer to the slammer" with my Uncle Mel and a brother-in-law Terry.

So if any of you out there get a lot of telemarketers calling you, make sure you have Uncle Mel and your brother-in-law Terry's phone numbers and addresses handy by your phone. For those of you who don't live here in Humboldt County just look up your police chief and District Attorney's phone numbers and have some fun with this.

I guarantee after you have done this once, you won't be able to sleep at night hoping another telemarketer will call you tomorrow so you can have some more fun using the Cab10 "scammer to the slammer technique."

THE DUDE WITH THE DOO-DOO HAIRCUT

Every once in a while I get a call that I wish I never got. I had to pick up someone at a bus stop in town. When I pulled up to the bus stop, there wasn't anyone there. Then some creepy-looking guy jumped out of the bushes and walked up to my cab. I get a little nervous when that happens and I always wonder if the person has any strange ideas up his sleeve.

When this guy got in, he's acting real nervous. He was in his early 20's and looked like he was probably homeless. He was wearing more earrings than an earring display at a jewelry store. His clothes had skulls and other strange emblems all over them.

He also has one of those haircuts I always dreamed about having. You know one of those fancy dog-doo haircuts that some

119

people call dreadlocks or something like that. You don't need to go to any expensive beauty parlor or buy any shampoo; all you need is a dog. Feed it a bunch of gross food, and after the dog has digested it, he will give it back to you in a nice round package on the sidewalk. Then you scoop it up, barehanded of course, and just start rubbing it through your hair. Keep doing it every day until you get to a point where your hair is solid like a rock. You will be the talk of all your friends sitting on the street corner. Also, everyone who has a beat-up old Volkswagen bus that drives by you and sees your dog-doo haircut will go around the block and beg you to ride around with them.

Another thing I always wonder about this classic haircut, and I'm sure some of you have wondered, is what it was like when two lovers that had the dog-doo haircut took a hot tub or a steam bath together and they started sweating, I bet the smell from their hair just drives them nuts. I can imagine the smiles on their faces, especially when their dog-doo starts running down their faces. Someday I will have to experience this just so I can tell all of you what you're missing.

Back to my story. I ask my fare, "Where do you want to go today?" "I'm new in town, is there a McDonald's around here?" After he said that, I was thinking I hope he eats and catches the next Volkswagen bus out of town.

Then I told him, "Yeah, we have a McDonald's in the Valley West Shopping Center."

"Oh good, take me there so I can eat."

As I was driving, I was checking out his clothes and his great looking earrings.

A few minutes later he asked me, "Where do all the kids hang out in this town?"

I didn't want to answer him, but it's my job to help my customers so I told him to go to the center of town, because that's where they all hang out. Then I was thinking, "Great, he's not leaving town. Just what we need, another guy with a beautiful dog-doo haircut in town on a street corner hanging out working hard at doing nothing." When we got to McDonald's, he thanked me, and I was thankful he got out.

CHAPTER 11

International Affairs

A PAPERWORK-DRENCHED DAY WITH ONE UNLUCKY AUSSIE

It's surprising how many visitors we get from foreign countries here in Humboldt County. I had to pick up a lady from Australia at the Quality Inn.

She needed to go to a local towing company and get her car. She told me that she has had nothing but bad luck since she came to America last week. She came to America to go to school and get away from the alligators and the kangaroos. She's a nice lady, but you wouldn't want to get on her bad side. She probably could give an alligator a good fight.

I asked her why they towed her car, and she told me that her dad gave her $1,000 to find an apartment. She bought a car from a friend who lives in Portland, Oregon and drove to Arcata.

After she got a motel and had dinner, she went to the Plaza to party. She had a few beeaas (beer's, in America). She then started to drive back to her motel and the police pulled her over. They told her the registration had expired, and it's illegal to drive until the fees are paid.

She tried to explain her situation—which was a big mistake since she had been drinking. The next thing she knew, she was being arrested on the suspicion of driving drunk. The police had her car towed and took her to the County Jail. She told me it was terrible.

After about 10 minutes at the towing company, they told her she couldn't have the car until the registration is paid. She wasn't happy!

We had to go to Eureka to the DMV office so she could pay the $300 to get all the paper work done.

Then we had to go to the Arcata Police station (Mel Browns Army headquarters) to prove to them that she had the proper paperwork so they would give her a release form to take to the towing company so she could get her car. (You would be surprised how many times I have taken people to do exactly what she had to do).

I went into the police station with her because she was a nervous wreck. I told her I would help her get the proper paperwork. It's a good thing I did, because they informed her that she owed them $125 for the towing; she got real upset. She thought the towing company's bill included the towing charge.

I finally got her back into my cab, and explained to her that the people at the police station are only doing their jobs. I told her that even though she has gone through hell with APD, they are in my opinion very professional, helpful, and are probably one of the best police forces in our country.

We went back to the towing company. She gave them all the paper work and finally got her car. It cost her another $110 for storage and $45 for the cab fare.

Just before she left I told her that she ought to send a bill to her friend, the one who sold her the car, and make him pay her back.

She thought that was a good idea, thanked me for my help and went on her way.

I didn't want to tell her that her DUI is probably going to cost another $2,000.

THUMBS DOWN

I pick up a lot of people that miss their bus and have no choice but call for the luxurious yellow cruiser. It's good business for me. I just hope they don't find out that I changed all the bus schedules so they have to call me. You just have to do whatever it takes nowadays to make a buck, you know! Here's what happened to one lucky guy from Greece.

I picked him up in McKinleyville he wanted to go to the bus station in Eureka. He was very upset he had to call for a cab because he had just missed the bus that would have taken him to Eureka. He was also upset because he tried to hitchhike, but nobody would give him a ride. He was about 25 years old, clean cut and seemed to be a very nice guy.

I asked him how come he missed the bus. He told me he just moved here from Greece with his wife, who is from McKinleyville, and he's not too familiar with the area yet. He lives on Ocean Drive so his wife told him to walk up Hiller Road which would take him to the bus stop on Central Avenue.

When he got to the intersection of Hiller and McKinleyville Avenue, he realized he probably wouldn't make it on time. He then decided he would just hitchhike. About that time a car pulled up to the stop sign; he walked up to the car to see if he could hitch a ride.

"You walked up to the car?" I asked.

"Yes, that's how I do it in Greece, and I always get a ride," he said.

"Nobody would give you a ride?"

"No, I would have been on time, but nobody would give me a ride. I think they were scared to pick me up. I went up to four cars, but everyone drove off!"

"What kind of reactions did you get when you walked up to those different cars?

"The first car I walked up to, the lady saw me walking towards her. She looked scared and made the tires spin really fast and took off."

I started laughing. "What else happened?"

"The next car was a woman driver too. She rolled down her window just enough so I could talk to her. She told me she had to go somewhere. So I asked her where she had to go. After she thought for a moment, she told me she was going to church, so I told her to pray for me!"

This guy was funny, especially telling me what happened in his European voice.

"The next car was a truck with two young guys in it. They gave me the finger and told me to get a job! You Americans are scared of getting murdered or raped, but I'm not going to hurt any one!"

I told him most Americans don't trust hitchhikers. Then I asked him about the fourth car.

Well, I thought the driver of this car was going to give me a ride. She was an older lady; she rolled down her window and I asked her if she was going towards Central Avenue on Hiller and she said yes. So I asked her if she could give me a ride to the bus, and she then said, 'I would but I forgot something at home, sorry;' and rolled up her window. She then makes a U-turn and heads back down Hiller. I think she was scared too!"

"So you gave up and decided to call for a cab?"

"That's right, I don't know if I'm going to like living in America!"

"You will like it here," I told him. "America has a lot of opportunities for people like you. After you get used to the American way of life, you will do fine."

He told me he already had a good job so he's planning on staying in America. But he's not going to try to hitchhike anymore.

HOSTESS WITH LEASTEST

This next story is about families that are hosting exchange students! I want to say it's a wonderful thing that these families do, opening their homes to these young kids from other countries. But if you're like this lady you're going to read about next, you had better straighten up. It's not fair to these young ambassadors who will go home some day after having had a bad experience because of their hosting family. We want these kids to go back to their countries bragging to their families and friends that America has great people and a lot to offer.

The other day I went to pick up a young man in Arcata who needed to go to McKinleyville High School. A lady came out to the cab with him. I thought she was probably his mom, but I was going to find out wasn't.

She handed me $5 and asked if I could take him to school. I told her I could, but I needed another $10. She told me that the dispatcher told her yesterday it would be only $5. I told her someone had made a mistake, and it wasn't me. She was a big grumpy old fart.

So I told her the bad news again; "It's going to be $15."

She got all hot and lathered up. She then turned around and marched into the house. In a couple of minutes she rolled back out with the money, still growling.

"Here's your money," she said. "Take him to school."

So we took off. Boy, was I was glad to get out of there. Then I told my passenger, "Your mom wasn't too happy!"

"That wasn't my mom," the boy said. "I'm an exchange student, and she is my host!"

"Is she always like that?"

"I hope not. I just got here two days ago, and I wish I had a different family to live with!"

"What grade are you in and why are you going to high school in McKinleyville when there is a high school here in Arcata?"

"I'm a senior. Arcata High School didn't have any room for me right now."

"It's going to be expensive if you have to take a cab everyday."

"I can't afford it if it's going to cost $15 everyday."

"You have to use your money? How come that lady you're staying with doesn't drive you to school?"

"She's lazy. The two days I have been here all she does is eat, watch TV and complain about everything."

"So do you think you're going to like it here in America?"

"I like everything so far except my host family!"

"I can understand why; that lady back at the house doesn't seem like a very nice person!"

He said he hopes things get better. I told him he should talk to the school and tell them he isn't happy with his host family. Maybe they can find somewhere else he can stay. He thought that was a good idea.

When I dropped him off, I told him that we have a lot of nice people in America so I hope he can find a nice family to live with. He smiled and told me thanks!

SADAMN'S NEIGHBOR

Almost everyday we hear or read something about Iraq in the news. I always wonder what the countries around Iraq really think about America's involvement over there. You hear all kinds of things in the news—that these countries think we're evil, and that they would prefer that we stay out of their business.

The other day I picked up a guy at the airport who was from Saudi Arabia. He was a really nice guy. He wanted to go to Humboldt State University where he will be going to school this semester. After he told me he was from Saudi Arabia, I asked him what he thought and other people in his country really think about America. He told me that the people in his country love America and think what we're doing in their part of the world is very important to everyone's safety.

I then asked him what he thought of Saddam Hussein and if he was ever invited for dinner. He gave me a funny look, and then told me the people in his country wish the Iraqi's would overthrow Saddam, but they're all scared of being executed.

I then asked him if he knew why the Iraqi Navy has glass bottoms boats. He gave me another funny look and asked why? I told him, "Because that way they can see their Air Force." He liked that, so I had to tell him one more Iraqi joke, "Why does it only cost half as much to train Iraqi fighter pilots?" He didn't know. So

I told him, "Because you only have to teach them to take off!

He liked that one too. When we got to the university, he told me thanks for the ride and told me he was going to share my jokes with his family back home.

A BAD ATTITUDE

One thing I learned about driving a cab is that you had better be a people person. You have to like people, and I mean the good, the bad, and the ugly.

The call I'm going to tell you about next makes you wonder how some people can be such jerks. I had to go to the airport to pick up a lady.

I pulled up to the terminal and saw a business-type lady standing by her luggage. She looked like she was one of those sophisticated better-than-you types.

I got out of my luxurious yellow cruiser and walked over to her and asked her if she had called for a cab. She put her hands on her hips and said, "Yes, I did. But I called for a cab, and this is not a cab." I looked at this lady, who still had her hands on her hips, and thought, "What the hell is her problem?"

I was thinking she was one of those people who can get on your nerves quick. You feel like walking up behind them, give them a good boot you-know-where and say, "Get a life."

Well, I was trying to be polite and nice (that is my job). I told her this is a cab. She again said, "No, it's not; it looks like a small bus to me." I had to turn around and look; maybe she was seeing something I wasn't. Then I told her the bad news; if she didn't want to get in, she could walk.

She went off again, "I want a cab that is a car, not a bus."

"It's going to be a long day," I thought, I told her, "This is it; do you want a ride or not?" "Fine," she said, "Get my luggage. I need to be at a meeting." So I put her luggage in and opened the front door so she could get in.

Just when I thought we were getting somewhere, she said, "I'm not riding in the front seat with a cab driver, I want to ride in the back seat." Biting my tongue, I said OK. I was glad to get her to her meeting.

CHAPTER 12

Real People

A WANNABE BUSINESS MAN

Having a job is important in order to live a comfortable life; but to have a job and enjoy your work is even better. I enjoy driving a taxi because of all the interesting people I meet and never knowing where my next call will take me. This next call is about a wannabe businessman. He wasn't wearing a suit, but he had an expensive briefcase. He walked up to the cab like he was really important. He got in and wanted to go to his job, but he needed to go to an ATM at his bank and then go to a store.

We stopped at a bank along the way so he could withdraw some cash. Next we went to a grocery store and he was in there for about 15 minutes. He came out carrying a bag full food. We're on our way again and he reached down and grabbed his fancy briefcase. He opened it up, and of course I'm looking to see what this important businessman has in his briefcase.

You're not going to believe this-neither did I. I started laughing to myself. There was nothing in it. He started taking the food out of his grocery bag—candy bars, chips, peanuts, sodas, burritos, gum, a cookie—and putting all this stuff into his fancy briefcase, or should I say lunch pail.

His briefcase or lunch pail or whatever it is now full. He must work for a junk food company. Now he's ready for work and it's time for me to take this big shot to his job. We arrived at this big business building in Eureka. I asked him if he was the head honcho or something. "No, I'm the janitor," he said. Then I thought this guy was all right. At least he has a job and he was proud of it. I know one thing; he's got the fanciest lunch pail I've ever seen.

SHAKE, RATTLE AND ROLL

As most of you know here in Humboldt County is a very active earthquake area. It's a wonder we haven't had a big earthquake here in Northern California for several years. But if you ask Dorothy Riley of McKinleyville she will tell you a different story. I

127

call her the earthquake lady.

I pick up Dorothy three times a week and take her and several other people to Mad River Adult Day program at Mad River Community Hospital. She's from Minnesota, and now lives in McKinleyville in a large travel trailer that's parked next door to her daughter Jill and her son-in-law Rich's house. Dorothy is a very nice lady and loves to be teased and joked around with, as I can do well.

One beautiful morning I pulled up in Dorothy's driveway. I had four people in my cab and I usually park behind her trailer so that I can see if she is coming out after I have honked my horn. Most of the time she comes right out.

Well, this time it was taking her a long time, so I walked up to her trailer and got a crazy idea (which is normal for me). I started pushing and shaking Dorothy's' trailer to see if she would feel it. As soon as I got it rocking pretty good I ran around my cruiser and stood by the door. Just about that time Dorothy came running out of her trailer hollering, "Did you feel that earthquake? It was a big one!" I look at my passengers and we all started laughing. I told Dorothy it sure was a big one. She then went to get her coat. She finally came out and got into my cruiser and asked everyone what they thought of that big earthquake. Of course, I had prepared everyone to tell her it was unbelievable, but not to tell her what really happened!

So, about once a month I do that to Dorothy and every time she comes out asking if we felt an earthquake. Lots of times when she comes out I start rocking back and forth as I'm standing by Cab10 (like the ground is still shaking) and she just gives me a funny look, but she still believes it was the real thing.

The other passengers always got a good laugh out of it and that's my job to make sure my guest have a safe and enjoyable ride to their destination. I always wonder when Dorothy is going to figure out that when Cab10 pulls up, an earthquake is only seconds away. Dorothy's a lot of fun and if I have any new customers on board another earthquake is sure to happen.

WORLD TRAVELER

Do you ever dream that someday you could travel around the world? I think a lot of us do at one time or another. This next story is about a lady that is living that dream.

I picked her up in McKinleyville and she wanted to go to Fortuna and get a motel. She's carrying a sleeping bag and wearing a large backpack. She told me she is hitchhiking around the world. At this time, all kinds of things are going through my mind. This lady is up there in age. I had to ask her how old she was; she was 81 years old.

I couldn't believe it. She was about 6 feet tall, very spunky, and had a tough look about her, but she was very nice and very intelligent. I asked her why she was hitchhiking at her age. She told me that she's from Virginia and retired as a school teacher after 40 years.

She was an only child and never married, doesn't have any family left and most of her friends have died too. So, it was time for her to see the world. She sold everything she had, put the money into her school retirement fund and is traveling all over the world before she dies.

She said she just got back from hitchhiking in Europe for two years. She usually hitchhikes and on occasion, such as this will take a cab, or a train.

I asked her if she ever got scared about getting robbed. She said that there better be two or three of them or they'd be asking for trouble. I laughed and I believe she could take care of herself.

She told me a lot of very interesting things. Just before we got to Fortuna, she told me that she would never stop traveling. Her dream was to travel the world until one night she gets in her sleeping bag along the road somewhere, happy with where she has been and die peacefully in her sleep.

I had a tear in my eye when she got out; it was like saying good-bye to an old friend.

TRAVELS WITH JOHNNY

This next story is about one of my more colorful customers Johnny Antonioli. I bet almost every town in America has a character that stands out from the regular crowd like Johnny. Almost every day you will see Johnny hitchhiking to Orick to see his hometown. He has a lot of colorful nicknames. Under all his scruffy looks is an interesting person, but most people have never talked to him. Every once in awhile nobody sees Johnny for awhile. Then people start asking me if I have seen Johnny around because he's

The Place to Eat in North Arcata!

The BEST breakfast in town!
Home-style cooking – burgers, shakes
and homemade pies.

Open 24 Hours!

1901 Heindon Road
Arcata

(707) 822-0091

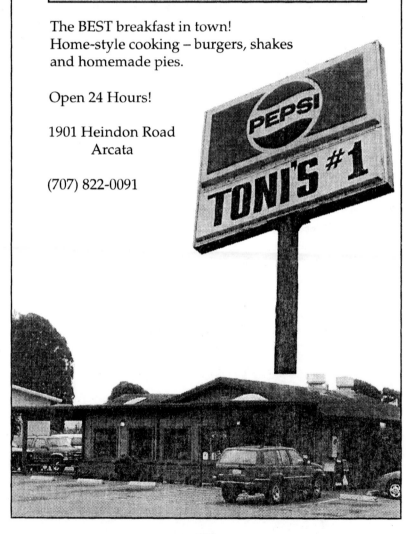

a regular Cab10 customer. I usually give him a ride home from Toni's Restaurant or the grocery store almost everyday.

One day I had to go to Toni's and pick up Johnny and take him home. When I got to Toni's, Johnny wasn't quite ready. So, I sat down with my dad, who happened to be there, and had a cup of coffee.

Shirley Stonebarger, the manager, poured my coffee. I asked her what Johnny usually orders because we need to know. She told me he usually orders pancakes, eggs and a cup of coffee.

A couple of minutes later, Dudley and Stacey Sacchi walked in. They meet a bunch of their friends here everyday around 3:30 p.m. I have known them since I was a kid. Dudley is Bill (The Barber) Sacchi's dad. Dudley and Stacey owned the Alliance Store when I was growing up.

My dad would take me there all the time, because he was friends with the Sacchi's. Stacey was the butcher at the store. I always tried to talk him into giving me a hot dog out of the meat case; they were so good.

Dudley always gave me a bad time about my newspaper columns. When I first started writing, he saw me one day at Toni's and hollered out, "Here comes one of the biggest B.S.'ers in town, and now he writes it in the newspaper and we have to buy it."

Everyone laughed. I told him, "You don't have to buy the paper." He said, "I have to, so I know what's going on in Cab10."

Johnny now tells me that he is ready to go. As Johnny and I were walking out the door, Al Toste, John Sherman, Ron Brown, Wally Turner, Herb Frazer, and Gary Nickolson were coming in to have coffee with the Sacchi's. I was thinking they had better get their hip boots on and a shovel—it's going to get deep in there.

THE MYSTERY OF THE DISAPPEARING PURSE!

The other night I was at my night job, and my wife Dannette called me. She told me that she has Hope Lindsay on the phone. Hope is one of my very special customers who rides with me a couple of times a week.

Earlier in the day I took her home from town. My wife told me that Hope can't find her purse, and wanted to know if I could look in my cruiser and see if it was under the seat or anywhere else because she is sure she had it with her in my cruiser.

So I went outside and looked in my cruiser and I didn't see her purse anywhere. I told my wife to tell Hope that she must have lost it somewhere else. She told Hope the bad news. After I got off the phone, I felt bad that I couldn't help Hope find her purse, especially since she told me she had cashed a check, and I'm sure she had other valuable things in her purse that can't be replaced.

About a week went by and I got a call to pick up Hope and take her to the Plaza. On our way there she was telling me about how bad she has felt about losing her purse last week. She told me it was the first time in her life that she ever has lost her purse. She also told me that she had $80 in her purse, but she's not going to blame or accuse anyone. Her mom had told her when she was growing up that if you do, it's just as bad a sin as the one the person who stole her purse had committed.

After I dropped her off, I went on to other calls that were waiting for me. Three hours later I had to go back to Safeway to pick up Hope and take her home.

After Mrs. Lindsay got in, I closed the door for her and went around and jumped into my cruiser.

Mrs. Lindsay is a dial-a-ride (dial-a-ride customers pay with tickets) customer. As she hands me her tickets for her cab fare, she drops them between her seat and the console that is between the seats.

We both leaned over at the same time to get the tickets, almost hitting our heads. We are both looking down, and we couldn't believe what we saw. There was her billfold.

She grabbed it and was so excited that she found it. I couldn't believe it was there the whole time.

I know what you're thinking. Doesn't that cab driver ever clean his cab? I know when my boss reads this, that's probably what he's going to think, and he will want to inspect my cab.

Well, here's the rest of the story. The night I went to look for her purse I was looking for the purse that she normally carries, which is rather large. It's the kind most ladies have; they can carry everything plus the kitchen sink in it. But her purse, in this case her billfold which a lot of ladies call a purse, fell down between my maps and other things I need for my everyday business.

Every morning I reach over and put my newspaper there on top of my maps and things. It's a really tight area. At night when it's dark, I reach over and grab my paper and go home, so I hardly ever use my maps.

So when I looked for her purse that night, my newspaper was there, and I didn't figure her purse could have fallen down there, so I never looked there. Don't believe me, do ya?

Well, it's true, and if you're wondering, Mrs. Lindsay's money and other personal belongings were still in her purse. When I got to Mrs. Lindsay's house, she was so happy she had her purse back that she couldn't wait to call her daughters and tell them what happened. She had told me earlier that she didn't want to tell them or they might get upset with her. Now she said they will all be able to laugh about what happened. I told her to tell them that I knew where it was the whole time I was just waiting for a reward to be offered for her purse. She laughed and went happily on her way.

WHAT WOULD YOU DO IF YOU EVER WON A FEW MILLION DOLLARS IN THE LOTTO?

A lot of my customers buy tickets for the lotto every week. Once in a while I ask them what would they do with all that money. Most of them give the same answers—buy a new house or a car, quit their job and a lot of other things too numerous to mention.

One guy told me he would call his boss and tell him he's retiring. Then he would call all his friends and have a big party. The next day he would buy a case of champagne and then hire a fancy stretch limousine to take him and his wife to Sacramento, California to claim his prize. I was thinking that a fancy stretch limousine can't compare to my luxurious yellow cruiser and my excellent hospitality, but that's his business.

Most of you have probably had dreams similar to these peoples. But I bet you have never had the same dream as this next lady about her transportation to Sacramento.

The other day I stopped at Cask and Flask Liquor store in McKinleyville. No, I wasn't buying any Jack Daniels or cigars. I was buying a newspaper. Anyway, on my way out the door I heard Jerry Richardson, the store's owner, yell at me. "Hey Randy, come back in here for a minute. I have something I want to tell you!" So I went back into the store.

"What's up, Jerry?"

"I have to tell you what happened the other day, because it involves you!"

"Oh really, what happened?"

"Well, one day a lady, who is one of my regular customers, came in to buy some lotto tickets. That week the lotto was over $40 million! I told her good luck and that I hope she won because I would win a large sum also since she purchased her ticket here. Then I told her if she won, I would supply the champagne and rent us a fancy stretch limousine (There's that fancy thing again.) to take us down to Sacramento to get our money!"

I was starting to wonder what this was all about. "That's nice of you Jerry; can I go, too?"

Jerry smiled. Then he told me the lady told him that if she wins the lotto she's not riding in a stretch limousine. She's going to call for Cab10 and ride in the luxurious yellow cruiser. I told you there was a big difference between fancy and luxurious. This lady knows!

So if any of you win the lotto and want to ride in luxury, drink free champagne, smoke cigars and be entertained, call for Cab10! I'll even supply moneybags to carry your money home.

CHAPTER 13

Extra Curricular

A NIGHT OUT ON THE TOWN WITH CAB10

One thing about driving a cab is that people are always asking me for information about everything. Sometimes I feel like the Chamber of Commerce ought to hire me because of all the work I do for them.

Our out-of-the-area guest asks me all kinds of questions. Some of the things they ask me about are where's a good place to eat, best tourist sights, a good place to go dancing, where they can buy some Humboldt County pot, where's a good place to stay, is there a gay bar in town, where can I get my car fixed, where's a good place to party, or which beauty shop do I recommend, etc, etc.

Then there are times I have heard my customers discussing things that they want to do, or a place where they want to go, but they can't make up their minds and are probably too shy to ask me. If I feel that I can help them, I will volunteer my ideas. I tell them I couldn't help but overhear their conversation, and that as their cab driver, it's my job to satisfy my customers, so if they want a suggestion, I would be happy to share it with them!

Then there are times when I have people that I know I can give a bad time to, so I just butt right in and take over the conversation. That's what happened when I picked up three couples at the Holiday Express in Eureka. They seemed like really nice people. They had a few beers and were laughing and teasing each other. They were giving me a bad time, too. I like people like this. They are the kind of people who get out and enjoy life and don't sit home wondering why their life is so boring, like some people do.

I asked them, "Where do you guys want to go tonight?" One of the guys, Don, hollers out the name of a popular restaurant which I don't (I'm an expert on food) feel is good enough for this group. I told them, "I know of a place that you guys will like better, the Sea Grill!" A couple of the ladies wanted to know more about my suggestion. They told me Don's idea wasn't that good last time they were here, and that this time they would rather try somewhere else. I told them the Sea Grill is a very nice place, has excellent meals, a great salad bar, great cocktails (that's important), and the hostess, Holly, who is also the owner, and her staff will make sure they have great service and a delicious meal.

Don gave in, and they all agreed on my idea. The ladies thanked me for changing Don's plans. Before we left the hotel, one of the guys handed everyone a beer, then jumped in and we we're off.

Don wanted me to drive by the Carson Mansion and down Third Street to the Sea Grill. As we're driving down Third Street, we pass a couple of drunks, some other street people, a couple of hookers, and some regular people too. My fun-loving fares were making all kinds of funny remarks. They were having a good time laughing about everything.

We pulled up to the Sea Grill and Don said, "What's so special about this place?" The ladies told him to shutup; they all laughed again. I told them that I will go inside, reserve a table for them, and have Holly come out and greet them.

They told me they never had a cab driver reserve a table for them before. I told them when you ride in the luxurious yellow cruiser you get luxurious service too.

I went inside and told Holly to reserve a table for six, and asked her if she had a minute to greet these nice folks. She came with me. When we got into the bar, the three couples were already ordering drinks.

I told them their table was reserved and Holly will take care of everything. They told me thanks for everything, and gave me a $10 tip for being a great tour guide.

A ONE-WAY TRIP TO A PLACE OF NUKED SHORTS

Driving a taxi you experience something new almost everyday. But putting out fires is something else, especially when it's someone's shorts. I got a call to pick up Carole and Duke, who are regulars; they wanted to go to the grocery store. I pulled up to their house and honked my horn. I saw that the door was open, but nobody was coming out. So I walked up to the door which was open, and I heard Caroline screaming. I walked into the house to see if everything's OK.

I asked Carole, who's running into the kitchen, "What's the matter?" She yelled back at me that her husband's shorts were on fire. I started laughing and said, "Need more time? Want me to leave?"

"No, help me put the fire out!" she said.

I went into the kitchen scratching my head, and I about died laughing. There's a fire in her microwave oven. I grabbed a pan of water and threw it on an overcooked pair of shorts.

This is what had happened. They were running late getting ready, and she realized her husband didn't have any clean shorts. She grabbed a pair, washed them in the sink, and then put them into the microwave oven to dry.

After a couple of minutes she checked them, and they weren't dry yet. She then turned the oven on a little longer than needed. That's when I pulled up in my luxurious yellow one-man water brigade cruiser. Another mission accomplished by Cab10, putting out fires.

DRIVE-THRU CROONER

As a cab driver we perform a lot of duties. When I first started driving, I thought all that cab drivers do is take people from one place to another. But as you have read, we do it all; I even had to sing live on the radio. It wasn't my idea.

One morning about 8 a.m. I was driving through town when my wife Dannette called me on my cell phone. She told me that on her way to work earlier, she was listening to KRED Radio and Rollin Trehearne, the morning DJ.

He was saying that it was the anniversary of the first drive-up restaurant back in the 1950s, and they were having a contest where you could win a trip for four people to Konocti Harbor to attend the Mary Chapin Carpenter concert. So, what about it? I asked Dannette. (Now if it were a Shania Twain concert, that would be a different story.)

She told me that the first person in a car with a cell phone who goes to a fast food restaurant drive-up window and calls KRED will be given instructions on how to win this fabulous vacation. I told Dannette that by the time I drive to Valley West to McDonald's, someone would probably already have won.

She wasn't listening to me. She told me to hurry up and get going. So I fired up my turbocharged cruiser and headed to McDonald's. I still had no idea for sure what was going on.

When I got to McDonald's, I dialed KRED radio. Rollin answered the phone. I asked him, "Has anyone won the trip to the

Mary Chapin Carpenter concert yet?" He said, "No." Then he asked me if I'm in a drive through at a fast food restaurant. I told him, "Yes, I am, I'm driving my taxi!" He then asked, "Who am I talking to?" I told him my name and that I'm Cab10.

He said, "Oh you're the guy who writes about your adventures as a taxi driver here locally for different newspapers." "That's me!" I told him.

"What do I have to do to win this trip to the concert?" I asked.

"Drive up to the menu board where you order your food," he instructed me. "Then when the waitress asks you for your order, start singing Old McDonald had a farm over and over until she sings back e-i-e-i-o."

I started laughing! I wanted to squeeze my wife's neck about now. Here I am live on the radio, and I'm supposed to sing. How did I get myself into this one? But I'm a good sport.

About a minute went by, then the waitress asked me what I wanted to order. Then in my deep Swiss, Italian, German and Portuguese voice, I started singing "Old McDonald had a farm."

The girl again asked me what I wanted to order, I kept singing, and suddenly she sang back, "e-i-e-i-o!"

Then Rollin yelled out, "Congratulations, you just won a trip for four to Konocti Harbor."

I couldn't believe it! Then the girl asked me again if I wanted to order something. So I ordered an orange juice to soothe my throat after all the singing I'd done. I then drove up to get my orange juice and told the young lady thanks. And I gave her a tip too.

So my wife and I and two of our sons spent a nice weekend at the lakes—thanks to my singing talent. We had a great time.

I tell ya, this cab-driving job is more demanding than I ever dreamed of.

CAB10 VOTES

What do voting and cab driving have in common, nothing right? Well, that's what I thought until Election Day came. Last November, we're all supposed to have gone to the polls and voted. It's our American right to vote or not to vote. It's really sad that less than half of the American people vote. Almost everyone at one time or another complains about a certain elected official, or a law they don't approve of. A lot of these people complain, but don't vote.

It's time for these people who complain all the time to get off their lazy asses, do something about those complaints and make their vote count.

I decided to conduct a Cab10 election poll. My question to my customers was: "Did you vote, and if not why?"

Some of the answers were:

"I could care less!"

"The President breaks all the laws, gets away with it, and nobody cares!"

"Whoever we vote for won't be any better!"

"My vote won't make a difference!"

"They're all crooks!"

"I forgot, and my car broke down." (He could have called for Cab10.)

Most of these answers, I'm sure you have heard before, or you feel the same frustration as these people. Well, by now you're probably wondering what the importance of voting has to do with the luxurious yellow cruiser.

I always vote, but to tell you the truth, I almost forgot to vote this time. I had to vote at St. Mary's School. I got there just in time, about five minutes before the polls closed. When I went into the room to vote, there were five people sitting at a table processing the ballots and several people voting.

I was in for a big surprise. It's a good thing I made it in time. One of the guys at the table looked up and saw me, and yelled out, "It's about time Cab10 showed up!" I smiled, sort of confused. He then said, "We were all talking about you a few minutes ago."

"About what," I asked?

Another guy told me, "If you're going to write for the newspapers, and be in the public eye, you better vote."

The other guy told me, "We were going to call the newspaper and tell them that Cab10 didn't vote!" Then a lady said, "Cab10 is a city treasure; you have to vote. What would some of your readers think if they knew the driver of the luxurious yellow cruiser didn't make time to vote?"

I was speechless (hard to believe that I was speechless huh?). I laughed, and they were all smiling. I voted, and before I left I told them, "Next time I will vote earlier."

A PEANUT FREE ZONE

While I'm on the subject of elections, I'm sure all of you are sad when the elections are over, too. I just know you miss all the election stuff that was on TV, or on the radio.

My favorite part of the elections is all the election junk mail we get in our mailboxes. I keep all of my election mail. I have boxes full of election materials. You're probably thinking that this taxi driver has lost it again, but I haven't. There is a reason I keep all those boxes of mailers; I don't have to buy toilet paper until the next elections.

One last thing about the elections is I never heard one thing from any of the candidates about one of the most important issues facing America today. This issue was in the news all last summer. No, it's not education, or crime prevention, or hiring male interns only, or the taxpayers paying for truckloads of WD-40 to keep President Clinton's zipper oiled; it's the issue of establishing peanut free zones on airplanes.

This nutty story has been in the news several different times. It's about people who are allergic to peanuts and the allergic reaction these people have when exposed to peanuts, such as on an airplane where peanuts are served. There is a group of these people who are trying to get the airlines to designate the first three rows on every airplane in America as a peanut-free area. Sounds nutty, doesn't it; but this is true.

This is a serious problem for those people who are allergic to peanuts. The only problem I see with setting aside seats for these nuts is that everyone with an allergy would come forward to try to get some rows designated for their allergy. Other possible allergic reactions on an airplane could be caused by the aroma of coffee, or people that wear strong perfume, or the disinfectant in the bathroom on an airplane. Probably the worst allergy problem that I suffer from is called the "smelly feet" allergy, which comes from people who take off their shoes next to me on an airplane. If these peanut people get three rows for their allergy, I might want some rows designated for my serious allergy problem also. But if that happens, the next thing you know, there won't be any seats left for the normal people.

You're probably wondering what the hell all this talk about

peanuts has to do with Cab10. Well, I feel sorry for these nuts that have these legitimate allergies. If they get the airlines to designate three rows for them, great, I want you to know that I will do whatever I can to help these people out when I pick any of them up at the airport. I will make sure their trip from the airport to their final destination is also peanut free.

So I have designated the passenger seat in the front of my cab as a peanut free zone. The only exception is if former President Jimmy Carter, a retired peanut farmer, comes to Humboldt County and wants my services. I am the only taxi in the world that has taken this large step to help out humanity in this serious and growing national crisis that is only now coming to our attention.

MACAROON MECHANIC

One day I was on the freeway and I could see ahead of me that there was a truck pulled off at the side of the road with its flashers on. It looked like a delivery truck of some kind. So I thought I'd better stop and see if the driver needed any kind of help.

My boss likes us to stop and help people who are in need of assistance or are involved in an accident to make sure people are safe or if they need emergency care, we can call for help for them.

When I stopped behind the truck, the driver saw me and started walking towards me. I knew the driver—it was John Williams of McKinleyville. He drives a Williams bread truck in the Arcata and McKinleyville areas. He's a great guy and has a nice family. He's always smiling or laughing when you see him around town, and today was no exception.

"What's wrong with your truck?" I asked. With this big grin and laugh he said, "My steering wheel fell off!"

"I'm glad I wasn't driving next to you when that happened!"

"I don't think you're the only one; you should have seen a friend of mine who was driving by me. I started to wave at him and I discovered I was waving the steering wheel at him. I was lucky I got off the road with no steering wheel without getting into a wreck!"

We were both laughing now.

John then asked me, "Do you have any wrenches?" I told him I would get them.

So for about 10 minutes I was fastening his steering wheel

back on so he could get back to work. We finally got it back on, laughing the whole time.

John was pretty happy that I stopped by to help him. He asked me if he could give me some money for my services and I told him no. Then I thought about that for a moment, and asked John, "Hey, do you have any of those large containers of Chocolate Coconut Macaroons in your truck?"

"I sure do!" he said.

"I'll take one of those for my hard work!"

"I'll get you one!"

After he handed it to me and thanked me again, he asked me, "You're not going to write about this, are you Randy?"

"No, I wouldn't do that to ya!" I lied.

So if you see John driving next to you someday in his bread truck and he's waving at you with his steering wheel in his hands, don't hang around hoping for a macaroon get the hell out of there!

AN ARMED GOVERNMENT AGENT TURNS TO A HALF-EATEN DOG'S DINNER FOR PROTECTION

I picked up a businesswoman at the airport who wanted to go to her home in Westhaven. As we're loading her luggage, I was thinking this was going to be just another routine call, but I was going to find out different. This lady had lots of luggage and even helped me load all of it into my luxurious yellow cruiser.

As she was reaching down to grab the last suitcase, I noticed her coat opened up and I could see she was carrying a gun. I didn't say anything, but I was curious as to why she was carrying heat.

As we're leaving the airport I asked her, "Have you been on vacation?"

"No, I have been in Washington, D.C, for a couple of months on business."

"That's a long time. Do you go there often on business?"

"Yes, most of my work is on the East Coast, but I love to come back here to get away from the rat race."

"What kind of work do you do?"

"I work for the government, but I can't tell you specifically what I do because it's confidential."

The next few minutes I tried to trick her into telling me what she does, but I had no luck. I hate that; I needed to know.

On our way to her house we talked about a lot of other things, but she still wouldn't tell me about her job. She was very interesting, but there was something strange about her. I just couldn't put my finger on it.

When we got to Westhaven, we turned off the main road and went about two miles up a gravel road. It was a nice little drive because of all the trees and shrubbery.

As I was driving we came to a fork in the road and she told me to take the road to the right. A couple of minutes later she told me to turn right again on the next road because it was the road to her house.

As I was turning I could see a steel gate across the main road about 500 feet in front of us. Just as I turned onto her road there was a van parked in the middle of the road.

As I was stopping she said, "I wonder whose van that is parked in the middle of the road."

"Is your house the only one up this road?" I asked.

"Yes, it is. This sort of worries me though because I have been gone for so long," she said.

"I'll get out and see if anyone is sleeping in the van. Maybe the doors are unlocked. If so I can move it off the road enough so we can get by."

She thought that was a good idea. As I'm walking towards the van I could tell it had been there for several days. There were leaves and things on the windshield too that made me think the van could have been there possibly for weeks.

After looking through the van windows I didn't see anyone inside and the doors were locked. I walked back to my cab and told the lady the bad news. She wasn't too happy.

Then I told her, "Maybe we should go ask your neighbors up the road if they know anything about the van or the whereabouts of its owner."

The lady gave me a funny look and said, "I'm not asking them anything. The people that live up there are very strange and mysterious. They always give me dirty looks when I pass them on the road."

I was wondering what she was scared of, since she had a gun under her coat. I then told her to wait in my cab and I would walk up to her neighbor's house to see if I could find someone who might help us solve this problem.

As I approached the locked steel gate I noticed there were

signs everywhere warning people to keep out and no trespassing. I didn't see anyone on the other side of the gate, but there was a house in the distance, which was hidden in some trees. I decided to climb over the gate and go see if I could find someone to help us. Hopefully I wouldn't get shot by some lunatic or marijuana farmer protecting his garden.

Just as I was almost over the gate I heard some dogs barking. I looked up and there were three large hungry rottwiellers running towards me. Before I could climb back over the gate one of the dogs had his teeth buried in my leg and another dog started biting my pant leg on my other leg, trying to tear my pants off. The third dog was probably waiting to see what would be left for him.

After a lot of yelling and kicking I managed to free myself and got back over the gate. I sat there for a couple of minutes, relieved that I was still in one piece. The three dogs were still barking and growling at me. I never did see any humans. I guess next time I better do what the signs say.

I then got up and started limping back to my cab. About halfway back my customer was walking towards me and asked me, "Are you OK? I heard a lot of noise and I thought you might have been hurt or something."

"I'm OK. I think I went over your neighbor's gate at his dogs' dinnertime, because his dogs were trying to take my legs off."

"Are you going to be all right?"

"Yeah, I'm OK."

When we got back to my cab I wanted to tell her thanks for an exciting afternoon and that I was leaving but I knew she still wanted my help.

"What do you think I should do now about that van?" she asked. I told her to call the sheriff's department and have them come out. They will have the van towed off. She thought that was a good idea. I thought my mission was finally over, so I told her how much she owed me.

She looked at me funny and said, "You can't leave me out here all alone. What if the people that own the van are murderers or thieves and are in my house?"

At this point I didn't really care; it was her problem. But I couldn't let something happen to this lady. So we gathered up her luggage and we started walking towards her house. About 10 minutes later I still couldn't see her house and my half-eaten leg was starting to hurt. I asked her, "How much farther is your house, because I don't even see it yet?"

"We're almost there." When we finally got to her house, which was about 2 miles, I could hardly walk. I told her, "You wait by your garage while I go look around your house to see if anyone has broken into it."

She told me she was too scared to wait by herself and she was going with me. Again, I don't know what she was scared of since she has a gun. After a few minutes we determined that everything looked OK.

She then says, "Would you mind if we check inside the house, too?" I was thinking why not; maybe I'll clean it too while I'm here. I told her I would. About 15 minutes later she was finally confident that her house was safe. I then asked her if she could give me a ride back to my cab because my leg was swollen.

After we got back to my cab, she paid me and gave me a good tip. I was happy to be leaving there.

As I was closing my door to leave, I see the lady running over to me. What now? "Could you do me one more favor before you go? Could you turn my car around for me; the road is awful narrow and I'm afraid I might back into the ditch?"

So I got back out and turned her car around for her. She smiled and told me thanks again. She then got into her car and started driving back to her house.

I went and got into my cab and took off. I never looked back. I was afraid she might have backed up and was standing by the road wanting me to do something else for her.

CAB10 GETS HIS EARS CLEANED OUT AT THE CAR WASH

One day last week I was in Valley West dropping someone off at the Best Western Motel. As I was closing my sliding door, I noticed it was time to vacuum out my luxurious yellow cruiser. It was losing its luxurious feeling. Since the car wash was in the same general area of the motel I decided to go there to use their vacuum.

When I got to the turn lane in front of the car wash I had to wait a few minutes, because of all the traffic. As I was waiting to turn into the car wash, I noticed an older couple washing their pickup and their RV. Their RV was huge—it looked like a Holiday Inn on wheels. They were using the outdoor wash rack. In front of them was the vacuum site I was going to use.

When I finally got to turn into the car wash, I had noticed the man with the pickup and the RV hand the hose with the water sprayer to his wife so she could keep washing while he pulled ahead a little. As most of you know, the hose and water sprayer are attached to an overhead pipe that swivels around so you can wash your vehicle on both sides.

As the wife was washing, her husband started pulling ahead slowly. I then noticed the hose on top of the RV got stuck between something on top of the RV, and if her husband kept driving ahead, he'd tear down the whole mechanism. His wife finally realized the hose was caught too, and what would happen if her husband kept going. So she started yelling at her husband to stop. He couldn't hear or see her in his truck.

Since I was right in front of the ladies husband who was driving, I tried to get his attention to stop before he broke everything. He didn't pay any attention to me. So I decided to drive right up in front of him so he would have to stop. When I did, he slammed his brakes. I must have scared him.

Before I could get out to go explain to him why I pulled up in front of him like I did, he was out of his truck. He was walking towards me cussing up a storm waving his arms and calling me all kinds of names. As he was asking me why my brains were in my ass, I pointed to the top of his RV to try to explain to him what was going on but he kept on screaming at me. It wasn't bothering me what he was saying because I knew he still had no clue about what was going on.

Finally, his wife talked some sense into her husband and he realized he made a big mistake. He then turned around with his head sort of hanging low and came over to me and apologized for his behavior. I told him not to worry about it; I probably would have done the same thing. He must have apologized to me about five or six times.

When he was finished asking me for my forgiveness, I told him to back up his truck because the hose was really tight and might brake any minute. I was surprised it hadn't broken yet.

After he backed up, I climbed up on top of his RV and got the hose loose for him. When I got back down on the ground, the couple thanked me again and told me they were sorry again. I told them to have a nice vacation, and thanked the old man for all the nice compliments. He gave me a funny look and then we all laughed.

CHAPTER 14

On the Job

"So, WHAT DO YOU DO?" ASKED THE FRIENDLY CAB DRIVER

As you know I have a lot of interesting customers. Here are a few stories about people, and their occupations, who have ridden in my luxurious yellow cruiser. I asked them all the same questions, and of course I got a lot of different responses. So I hope you all enjoy your jobs. And if you don't, well, maybe you'll see a job in this chapter you might like to try. So let's get to work!

Tracey J. Borowski is from Newport Beach, California. She attended San Diego State for three years. Tracey works for Executive Aviation Logistics out of Chino, California, which is a charter plane service that who will fly you anywhere you want to go. Tracey is a flight attendant, and has been working for Executive for 5 months now. The best part of her job, she tells me, is meeting all the interesting people that fly on their planes. The worse thing about her job is the "takeoffs and landings". I asked her for a comment about her boss. "Watchful, very watchful," she said. I thought that was interesting. She wanted me to add a motto, which is her personal motto, "Life's too short not to be tall!" She's probably about 5-foot, 11 inches. I don't think she liked being so tall.

Marion Costello was born in Detroit, Michigan, but lived most of her life in Queens, New York. She is retired now. She used to work for a big distributor that sold air conditioners, TVs and other appliances. Marion worked in the billing and bookkeeping department. She worked at her job for 24 years. She made $160 per week working 35 hours per week. The best part of the job was the money, and the worse part was that it was very hectic work, always busy, she tells me.

Page Fitting has lived in Humboldt County since 1957. She graduated from College of the Redwoods nursing school in 1971. She is a registered nurse and currently works for the Mad River Hospital's Adult Day Health Care which is located behind the hospital. She has been there for 10 years. She also had worked for the hospital for 13 years. One of the best aspects of her job is caring for people on a long-term basis. They become family. The worse part of her job is when they lose participants. Right now her patients range from 28-98 years old.

Jerry Atlansky is from New York, and has lived in Florida, Los Angeles and now Arcata. He graduated from Junior College in Los Angeles. Jerry is self-employed and owns "Airport Services" at the Arcata Airport in McKinleyville. He's Humboldt County's only skycap who will help you with your luggage or cargo freight. Most all of you who have been to the airport have seen or met this very nice gentleman. He's always smiling and is always willing to help you if you have any questions at the airport. His pay is determined by how many hours he wants to work. Jerry likes everything about his job; he loves people and the world of aviation. The worse part of his job is going home; just kidding he tells me. I asked him about his boss? "God" is great to me, he tells me. He also added that he offers 1,001 travel tips and important information on how to work in the travel industry. So next time you're at the airport and your plane is delayed, go talk to Jerry; he will brighten up your day.

Jeff Spencer lives in Beverly Hills, California and is a college professor teaching Theatre Arts—mostly rich kids he tells me. He's been teaching for 12 years. He said teaching Theatre Arts close to Hollywood is very exciting, because lots of times he takes his classes to different studios to watch real actors do their work. And the actors talk to his students. The worse part of teaching rich kids is that all the kids' parents expect their kids to be like Steven Speilberg when they graduate.

Robert Magee lives in Redding and is a EMS pilot for Mercy Air Ambulance Service. He flies the Air-Med team to different locations to pick up patients that need surgery in Redding. He's been a pilot for 15 years. He likes helping patients and their families who fly on his plane or that he comes in contact with at the different hospitals. The worse part of his job is the pay.

SINGING THE BLUES

Every once in a while I pick up someone who is a celebrity. On Monday, the day after the Blues by the Bay, I got a call to pick up someone at the Carson House Inn. When I got there, there were five people that wanted to go to the airport.

After we were on our way the guy in the front seat told me his name was Dave Drapen and he's from Seattle. He is the tour manager for the Robert Cray Band. Robert Cray was sitting behind me. The other guys were members of his band.

Dave told me they have to be in Las Vegas by 8 p.m. for their next show. It was about 8 a.m. and very foggy. I told them the odds were not good for getting out of Humboldt County on a plane on time.

Dave's other responsibilities were logistics and accounting for the band, which he has been doing for 20 years. The best part of his job he told me was the travel, camaraderie, and meeting new people.

On the down side of his job are the long hours and high stress; all that traveling can get you down at times. He enjoys his job and likes his boss.

When we got to the airport it was really foggy. I helped them with their luggage to the ticket counter, and the girl at the counter told them the bad news—the first five flights were canceled. They were upset. It's a good thing they sing the blues because it's going to be that kind of day here at the airport.

INQUISITIVE CABBIE DARES TO QUESTION MALE PROSTITUTE

The other day I picked up a guy at the Golden Harvest Restaurant. He was wearing all black leather and carrying a backpack.

He looked like a Hells Angel rider without a motorcycle. He was a scary looking dude, the kind of person that you wouldn't want to meet in a dark alley. When he came out of the restaurant, a waitress was running behind him, telling him that he didn't pay for his breakfast. That was a bad sign, too!

He gave her some kind of excuse; then he fiddled around and finally paid her.

He told me that he wanted to go to the airport because he's flying to Mexico. Boy, are they going to love this guy down there, I thought. I was in for a big surprise.

"Do you live down there in Mexico?"

"No, I'm going down there to work," he tells me.

"What kind of work do you do?"

"I'm a male prostitute!"

Well, I've got to tell you folks, it was a good thing my door was latched, or I would have fallen out leaning on it.

After I unstuck my cheek from my window and got myself

together, I decided I needed to get some more information. All kinds of questions were going through my nosey head of mine. Not every day do I get a male prostitute in my pimpmobile, I mean my luxurious yellow cruiser.

"Where were you working before you decided to go to Mexico?"

"I was working in San Francisco."

"Taking a vacation?"

"No, it was time to move on. I got tired of all the crap I had to put up with!"

"I hope you don't mind, but like what?"

He told me that in his line of work you really find out that a lot of people are strange, weird, and have twisted mines.

"You can't believe what some of my customers wanted me to do," he said.

I asked him if he could give me an example, and tell me what kind of people took advantage of his services, and anything else he wanted to tell me.

"Well, most of my customers were businessmen in expensive suits who have a lot of money. In some cases, they were men with power," he explained.

"Most of them treated me like I was a dog, or I was supposed to be their slave or something."

" Isn't that part of your job description, to satisfy peoples' fantasies?"

"Well, yeah, I didn't mind it, most of the time, because I needed the money to live on, or to buy more drugs. I was just getting tired of being tied up and whipped. And sometimes they even wanted to urinate on me. I just decided it was time for some new scenery."

"Did you ever have any female customers?"

"Not very often, usually only when a couple would hire me. You would be surprised how many husbands like to watch their wife have sex with someone else."

"That's disgusting."

"Not to them it wasn't. There were even some women who wanted to watch me and their husband do different things."

"Did you ever have any very important people who wanted your services?"

"Yes, once in awhile, but I can't tell you who."

"So why are you moving to Mexico?"

"I just wanted a change. I heard Mexico is nice, so I'm going down there to work some of the fancy hotels. It's got to be better down there. San Francisco has too many freaks."

I was laughing to myself, and thinking that I had one in my cab, too!

When we get to the airport he told me, "Hey, if I you ever get to Mexico and see me, say hi and maybe we can have a beer or something."

I don't think so, I was thinking. What a life. What a world. In case you're wondering, folks, yes, he told me a lot more graphic and detailed stories. Of course you could always buy me lunch; and then I would tell you the rest of the story.

CHOPPER CHICK

Every once in a while you need to take your vehicle in for an overhaul, how about your helicopter? The other day I picked up a young lady at a local motel who needed to go to the airport.

She was the quiet type. I tried talking to her, but she was sort of shy like me so I wasn't getting anywhere. It took a few minutes, but I finally got her to open up. I asked her "Where are you from?"

"I'm from British Columbia," she told me.

"Are you flying home today?"

"No, I'm flying to Torrance, California."

"Taking a United flight."

"No, I'm flying myself."

"You fly your own plane, how old are you?"

I'm 21 and I don't fly an airplane, I fly a helicopter."

I looked at her and I couldn't believe it because she didn't look like she was over 18. I was thinking of all kinds of questions now.

"Are you in the military?"

"No, I work for a commercial contractor in Canada; we have 10 helicopters of different sizes that can do different kinds of jobs."

"What kind of jobs do you guys do?"

"The three main things we do are tours, haul loggers around logging sites in the high country, and I just finished working in a few remote oil fields in Canada cutting down weeds and brush around the oil derricks and checking for oil leaks in the pipeline."

I thought that was very interesting. She also told me she has seen a lot of beautiful country flying around in her Robinson 22 helicopter.

"So why are you flying to Torrance?"

"That's where the helicopter I'm flying is built, so my boss wanted me to take it down for it's annual overhaul."

This girl amazed me with the different things she told me about her unusual occupation.

When we got to the airport I drove her around the terminal to her helicopter. She let me look in it before she took off. It was cool. She asked me if I ever flew in a helicopter before, and I told her I rode in one when I was in the service during the Vietnam War. A few minutes later she was in the air and out of my sight.

MOUNTAIN CLIMBERS

I went to the Super 8 Motel in Valley West to pick up some people who wanted to go to the airport to rent a car because they burned up the engine in the car they were driving. There were four young adults waiting there with a lot of baggage and equipment that looked like it could be used for mountain climbing.

While I was loading up their stuff, I asked them if their equipment was used for mountain climbing. They told me they just came from Washington where they had climbed Mt. Rainier the week before.

On our way to the airport, they told me they are on the coast doing research for the Rocky Mountain Research Station, which they work for. It's a division of the United States Forest Service located in Pinedale, Wyoming.

They climbed Mt. Rainier to do research on different types of vegetation that grow at different elevations. Then after they finished there, they drove down the coast to look at other plant life along the coastline. When they get back home they will take all the information and data they have collected and share their results with other researchers.

They told me that their job is a lot of fun and very interesting--going to different locations and doing all kinds of research. Before we got to the airport, I asked them when they were going to climb Mount Everest. They told me probably never. They asked me if I ever thought about mountain climbing. I told them no way; I'm scared to get on a footstool.

152

CHAPTER 15

Special Deliveries

A COSTLY CUP

I know a lot of people that complain about the price of almost everything they buy. They just don't realize what it costs to make or produce a certain item. Then there are people who will pay any price for something if they are desperate, such as this next call.

This call is for all of you who think that you're a serious coffee drinker. Are you one of those people who have to have a cup of your favorite brew? Would you pay $13 for one cup? Come on now, you thought you were a serious coffee drinker.

I got a call from a man in Manila who wanted a large coffee delivered. I'm thinking this guy must be nuts. I asked Randy Hendricks, our dispatcher, "Are you serious? Does this guy know it's going to be expensive?" He said that the guy doesn't care, so just hurry up.

So I jumped in my luxurious yellow cruiser and headed for a local coffee shop on the Plaza. I purchased a large coffee and headed for Manila. Sure enough the guy is happy to see me. He told me I'm a lifesaver and that I wouldn't believe how bad he needs this coffee. I wanted to say something but thought I'd better keep my mouth shut.

He asked me how much he owes, and I told him it's $1 for the coffee and $11 for the cab fare. He said OK, and gave me the $12 and a $1 tip. $13 for one coffee, now that's a serious coffee drinker.

'60'S RELIC DEADBEATS A PATH TO THE HOSPITAL

This next story involves two of my co-workers at Yellow Cab of Eureka, Theresa Helms and Barry Hart.

One morning, my boss, Skip Arnold (also the owner of Yellow Cab), called to tell me to come to work early. Usually that means they have a big call waiting, such as going to Crescent City which is about 75 miles. He then told me the bad news, to hurry up and go over to Mad River Community Hospital and help out Theresa Helms, Cab20.

He told me that Theresa just took a guy to the hospital, and he refused to pay her and just disappeared into the hospital.

"See if you can help her find him," Skip said.

On my way there, my boss gave me a description, including what the customer was wearing, in case I saw him when I got to the hospital. On my way to the hospital, I was thinking that Theresa doesn't normally drive a cab. She drives a dial-a-ride lift van and doesn't pick up cash fares. We have three drivers that just do dial-a-riders only, and Theresa is one of them. So I thought that it was odd that she was driving a regular cab.

When I got to the hospital, I saw Theresa parked by the Emergency Room. I drove over where she was parked so I could get up to speed on what the heck was going on.

She told me when she came to work, our boss asked her to take a regular taxi and pick up a guy at Safeway in Eureka, because all the cabs were very busy. She said, OK.

This is her first time driving a cab, and probably will be her last, she told me. When she got to Safeway, she picked up her fare. He wanted to go to Mad River Community Hospital. On their way there, the fare told her he needed some drugs right away.

"Why go to Arcata, when there are two hospitals here in Eureka?" she asked.

"I already went to both of them, and they refused to help me," he said.

After just a couple minutes Theresa realized this guy was a couple of sandwiches shy of a picnic. He then told her that he flew in last night from San Jose (I bet it wasn't on an airplane) and he's staying at a local motel. He is supposed to receive a check today for $1,000 from his public guardian.

Theresa told me that he was talking about all kinds of strange things, such as living back in the '60s, and that he's still upset with his father because when he was little, he and his brother were sent to a special school which they hated, especially because one of their teachers was really weird.

She was always putting weird stuff into a coffee can and telling him they could use it to blow things up.

They finally arrived at the hospital, and Theresa told him he owed her $22.50.

"You're going to have to trust me," he told her.

"You don't have any money?" she asked.

"You're just going to have to trust me."

Theresa informed him that she will have to tell her boss, and that he will call the police and have him arrested.

The guy just stared at her, and told her again, "You're going to have to trust me!" Then he got out and walked into the hospital.

So Theresa called Skip, who told her to keep an eye out for the guy in case he walked out of the hospital.

It was then that Skip called me and told me to go and help Theresa. There was another Cab nearby driven by Barry Hart, Cab No. 7; he was told to help out also. In about five minutes we had three cabs and three of Mel Brown's Army (A.P.D.) squad cars on the scene. It looked like a war zone.

When I pulled in, I saw Barry walking into the hospital to see if he can locate our loony toon. So I decided to go around back. I put my coat on over my cab shirt and walked into the hospital, acting like I don't know what's going on, to see if I could locate our brainless wonder.

As I go into the hospital, I hear the dispatcher on my radio confirming with Barry that our freeloading fugitive had been caught.

So I jumped back into my cruiser and drove around to where Theresa was parked. One of Mel Brown's troopers came out of the hospital and had Theresa go inside to identify the guy. When she came back out she told me it was the guy. Then she filed a report with the police. I went inside the hospital to see what happened.

The emergency room had the guy on a stretcher, tied down. I asked what happened, but they couldn't tell me. So I found someone in the waiting room, and they gave me the rest of the story.

When the guy came in, he went to the nurse's window and

told them he needed some drugs right away. After a few minutes they realized this guy had a problem, so they strapped him down. He will be going to Sempervirens for observation. In the morning he will be booked and fined for not paying his cab fare.

Before I left, I asked Theresa, "Are you going to drive a cab on a regular basis, now that you see how exciting a job it can be?" She got in her cab, and told me that it was her first and last time driving a regular cab.

TURKEY EATING WITH SOMEONE'S MOM
WHILE THE METER RUNS

Do you want to do something special for someone that you care about who lives out of the area, or even here?

I received a call last year on Thanksgiving Day to make a food delivery. I do all kinds of deliveries such as food, parts, supplies, donuts, groceries, etc. I want to share with you one of my favorite deliveries. It's about special things that people will do for others. I got to help make last Thanksgiving Day special for this old lady in Arcata.

My dispatcher told me to go to a local restaurant to pick up a full course turkey dinner that was ordered, and deliver it to someone who lives on llth Street in Arcata. A man from Chicago had called and wanted me to deliver a meal to his mother in Arcata because he couldn't be with her, and he wanted to do something special for her.

My dispatcher said that guy had already ordered the meal and paid for it with his credit card that we have the card number for the cab fare, so when I finish the delivery, call it in and it will be taken care of. I said, "Ok." I fired up my engine and went to the restaurant and picked up the turkey feast (itsmelled gooood) and then headed for llth street.

I knocked and knocked and finally a lady about 80 asked me what I wanted. I told her that I had a surprise for her. She told me to, "Go away." Then I explained to her that it's from her son Jim in Chicago. She finally let me in. She asked me what her surprise was and I told her that her son loves her very much and was sorry that he couldn't be here, but he wanted her to enjoy a nice turkey dinner for Thanksgiving. She couldn't believe it and started crying.

She asked me if I could help her put her dinner on a couple of plates (did I hear 2 plates?) I said, "You bet!" Then she sat down and asked if I could stay and keep her company while she ate. I told her that the meter in my cab was running. She said her son wouldn't mind.

So I sat and watched this sweet old lady eat the whole thing and listened to her life history for about 20 minutes. Then I told her that I really needed to get going. She gave me a hug and said thanks for listening and to have a nice Thanksgiving. So there you are.

I have experienced a lot of good things driving a cab, and making people happy while doing my job is very rewarding. Sharing this idea with you might make someone thankful and happy that you care. Well, isn't that what Thanksgiving is all about?

MRS. DOUBTFIRE

Another call I received on Thanksgiving was to pick up eight full course turkey dinners that had been ordered and to take them to a house on Alliance Road in Arcata. When I got to the house I was supposed to pull up in the alley in back of the house and wait until the lady that ordered the food sees me. She requested that I not honk my horn or knock on the door (which I thought was sort of strange), but what's new in this line of work?

After a few minutes an older lady came out of the house wearing an apron, like she's been cooking all day. She told me to bring the food into the kitchen. This was a large and beautiful house. I went into the kitchen, and her table was covered with fancy silverware and dishes.

I had an idea what was going on now. I asked her why she was being so sneaky about me coming in the back door. She told me she hadn't cooked a turkey dinner in several years, and her husband had invited some important business associates and their wives over for dinner. She was afraid that she might screw it up, so her husband told her that if she wanted, she could just order it, then serve it in the dining room, while he kept the guests busy watching football and serving them cocktails. They will never know the difference.

She asked me if I could help her get the food ready. I told her, "The meter is running-I have plenty of time, I'll even serve the wine if you want."

"That's a thought," she said, then laughed.

It took us about 10 minutes, and her feast was ready for her guests. She then paid me and told me thanks. As I headed out the back door, she started carrying all the dishes of food into the dining room.

This lady reminded me of Robin Williams in the movie Mrs. Doubtfire, where he ordered out and served dinner, and Sally Fields and his kids weren't aware of what was going on. Another Thanksgiving Day when someone can be thankful for Cab10.

A LIFE SAVING DELIVERY

I had to go to the airport to pick up an important package that needed to go to one of the Eureka hospitals. After I got the package on board, the dispatcher told me when I got to the hospital to go to the cardiology department and to make sure the package went to the person addressed on the box.

He then told me it was a life and death situation, and to hurry, because the package was late getting to the airport. So I pumped on the throttle of my luxurious yellow cruiser and headed over to the hospital as fast as I could. When I got to the hospital, I asked for directions to the cardiology department.

When I got there I told the lady at the window that I had a very important package for the doctor listed on the package. She told me she didn't know who he was, but to go ahead and leave the package with her and she would find out where it goes.

I thought about that for a minute, and then I told her that I was told it was a life and death situation. Someone should know who the doctor listed on the package was. She called someone else, but that person didn't know the doctor listed on the package either.

I told these two ladies to take me to the surgery room - it has to go there, I thought. When we got to the surgery room a nurse told me the package goes to the doctor who's in surgery. She gave me a surgery mask to put on and told me to follow her into the surgery room. I have never delivered to a surgery room before. When we got inside, I noticed that a surgery was being performed. There were eight people working on the patient. The nurse took me over to where the surgery was being performed and told a doctor that I had his package.

"Just a minute," the doctor said. Then he turned around, covered in blood, and told me thanks a lot for getting the package to him. "You just saved this guy's life," he said. He took off one of his bloody gloves and signed the paper work I had, and then gave me a $5 tip. While he was signing my paper work, I could see the patient and where they had him opened up. It wasn't a pretty sight. The doctor put new gloves on and told the nurse to hurry and open the box, and get everything ready for him. I told them goodbye and left on another important mission.

CRUCIAL CORPUSCLES

When I first started driving a cab, I thought all cab drivers did was take people from one place to another. I'm sure that most of you think that's all we do, too.

I do about every kind of delivery you can think of. But when I'm delivering containers of blood for shipment to other states for people that have life threatening surgeries, it makes my job more important than I ever dreamed of.

I had to go to Arcata and pick up someone's blood that needed to be flown to Arizona and take it to the airport.

A young man answered the door. He wants me to go the airport and ship a container of blood. He has donated blood to the blood bank in Eureka for several years. His dad, who lives in Kentucky, is having surgery and needs a lot of blood during the operation. They both have a rare type. So he went to the blood bank and got what his dad will need for the surgery and is having it shipped to Kentucky.

I took the container to the airport and took care of the freight cost and made sure all of the flights to Kentucky were correct. Then the airline will put it on an airplane that will take it to Kentucky.

Another important mission accomplished by Cab10.

A NAKED LADY

Deliveries can always be an interesting experience as in this next story. I had to pick up a case of beer and four meals at Denny's and deliver them to one of our regular customers.

This guy is a really strange dude. He's overweight, worthless a lowdown kind of guy.

He likes to take pictures and videos of women doing all kinds of things. He has pictures everywhere. Everytime you go to his house there are different women and men there.

On the streets these women know if they need a fix of some kind, he will provide it in trade for sex or being photographed. It's hard to believe what goes on there.

When I go to his house, I always have to go around to the back bedroom window. You're never know what your going to see next. This time was no exception.

I tapped on the window frame while I was trying to see if anyone was in the house. I saw two couples in bed. I didn't want to disturb them, but I had to let them know I had their order. Finally one of the ladies got up and started walking over towards me; she was totally naked. I couldn't believe it. Then she asked, "How are you today, sir?"

I didn't know what to say at first because I'm such a shy kind of guy. She was talking to me like it was normal to be standing naked in front of a total stranger. I then handed her the food and beer and she asked me, "How much do we owe you for the food and the cab fare?"

I was still speechless, but then I remembered and told her what they owed me.

The naked lady then turned around and asked one of the guys in bed, "How much of a tip do you want me to give the cab driver?"

"The cab driver seeing you naked is enough," one of the guys said laughing.

Then he told her to give me $5. As she was paying me, she popped open a beer and started talking to me like we were old friends. I told her I would like to stay and visit, but I had to get back to work.

CHAPTER 16

Feminine Mystique

THE MYSTERIOUS BAG

This call is about one of our "ladies of the night." In her case, though, I think it's more of a sexual nightmare. She's not very attractive and she's usually high on drugs. I had given her and her "Johns" rides on several occasions. A lot of times I took them to a motel, or picked her up when she was finished with a job for some lucky guy (so he thinks) and take her home or back to a bar for her next trick. It must be her false teeth or that greasy hair that they like.

This time I picked her up at a trailer court. She got out carrying a couple of radio cassette players and a mysterious bag. She wanted to go back to the bar where she usually hangs out to wait for another lucky customer. I never had any problems with her paying her fare except the last time she was a dollar short.

We were on our way when I thought I better make sure she has enough money to pay the cab fare. I told her it was going to be about $10. She said she only has $5, but the bartender will cover the difference when we get to the bar. (Sometimes the bartender will cover the girls fares, but I don't want to take any chances).

I pulled over and told her to get out, and she said she really needed to get back to the bar at a certain time. I told her she was going to have to walk. She said, "Maybe we can work this out," as she puts her hand on my leg and asks me if I would give her a free ride in exchange for sex. "You mean you want to make a trade?" I asked. "Yeah," she said, "Let's go somewhere and have sex, then you can take me back to the bar."

I told her no way. She started bragging about what I would be missing out on. (Now she had me thinking-let's see. I could get AIDS, or just some other variety of sexually transmitted disease; get caught by the police and get fired; or a divorce.)

I still had to refuse. By now she is looking at the two cassette players and asked me, "How about if I give you these two cassette players, and you pay the fare?"

They were like new. They were both worth about 50-60 dol-

161

lars, so I said, "Okay." I will
pay the fare and keep the two
cassette players. (Now, that
was a good trade.) I dropped
her off and went on my way.
"But before I left," I asked her.
"What's in the mysterious
bag?" (I thought you would
want to know).

It contained about two
dozen rings from different "Johns" that were given to her as payment for her services.

SISSY

I had to go to a local motel and pick up a young lady around
25 years old. She was walking towards me when some guy about
60 years old in a business suit standing in the motel room she just
came from said, "Bye, bye, Sissy. See you next trip." The young
lady turned around and said, "Bye, Daddy. See you later."

I opened the door for her and she got in. We started driving
and I asked her, "Was that your dad?" She smiles and said no.

"Oh, a business deal."

"Yeah," she said, then laughed a little. I asked her, "Why did
you call him Daddy and he call you Sissy?" She said that he would
give her a $50 tip if she called him Daddy while they're having sex.

"Sounds like he's pretty kinky," I told her. She said it was
worth the extra $50. Then I asked (I'm pretty nosy, but we need to
know), "How much did you charge for your trick?" She told me
$100. I told her that was pretty good, because most of the girls
charge under $50. She smiled.

Then I noticed she was wearing a wedding band, and I asked
her if she was married. She said, "Yes I am."

"Does your husband know about this work you do?" I asked.
She laughed. "He's my pimp. He's going to be really happy because I made an extra $50 tip."

I just shook my head. She then said, "My husband owns a local business and if an out of town customer buys a lot of product,
from my husband and is looking for a good time before he leaves
town, my husband will offer them my services for $100," she said.

"That's a clever way to get repeat business," I said. She smiled and said, "Well, if you sell a good product and show your customers a good time while they're in town, they'll come back again and again. It works out good for them and for my me and my husband's business too." What a world!

DO YOU MIND IF I TAKE MY PANTS OFF?

One day I picked up an attractive young lady who wanted to go to her boyfriend's house.

As I was driving, we were talking about different things and I reached down and took a big sip of my soda. Out of the blue the young lady said, "Do you mind if I take my pants off?"

Well, you know what happened next. I sprayed the windshield and almost choked on my soda that I hadn't completely swallowed yet.

I finally got myself together, sort of embarrassed. She then said, "I guess I said that wrong."

"What do you mean by that?" I asked, She said, " I wanted to get my hash pipe. I keep it under my garter and I need to take my pants off to get it. Do you mine? It will only take a minute."

I told her the meter was running; go ahead. I was trying to keep my eyes on the road. She pulled down her pants and was sitting there in just her panties. She had a blue garter on with a pipe under it. I had to look because maybe she had a pistol or maybe a knife.

She grabbed the pipe and slid her pants back on. Thank God that's over with. She wanted to know if it was okay with me if she loaded her pipe so it would be ready to smoke when she got to her boyfriend's house. I told her to go ahead; I'm learning something new all the time. We got to her destination and she told me to have a nice day. I just smiled.

LEFT TO THEIR OWN DEVICES

One time I picked up a couple of lesbians who needed a ride to the bus station. They had a lot of luggage for two girls. While I was loading up their stuff, another young lady came running out of the apartment building. "I'm glad you guys haven't left yet," she said. "You almost forgot Tommy." One of the ladies told her, "I could care less if we take Tommy."

I felt sorry for whoever Tommy was. The other lady got out of my cruiser and told the other lady in my cab, "I don't know why you only like big Bob; I think Tommy is more fun, so I'm going to get Tommy."

They were now arguing pretty loud. I told them whoever is going, could you please go get him so we can get going; I have other calls waiting.

All three girls stopped arguing and looked at each other and then started laughing. I was wondering what I said that was so funny. Then I realized that big Bob and Tommy were not their boyfriends, but probably their sex toys. Then I started laughing, too! One of the girls told me she would be right back.

So a couple minutes went by, and she came back carrying a bag that probably contained Tommy. All three girls kissed and hugged each other good-bye. The one girl that was staying was walking away when one of the girls in my luxurious yellow cruiser told me to stop.

She rolled down the window and yelled, "Diane, what are you going to do without Big Bob or Tommy while we're gone?" "I have the Bazooka Kid," she yelled back. I couldn't help it, but I was dying laughing after I heard that.

On our way to the bus stop, the two ladies in my cab were talking about the Bazooka Kid. I think they were jealous because Diane never told them about the Bazooka Kid before. I thought a couple times they wanted to turn around and go back because they wanted to know more about the Bazooka Kid.

I have to admit; I had never heard about the kid before either. We finally got to the bus stop, and the two girls, Tommy, and Big Bob go on their way.

A RAVENOUS, TOOTHLESS, TATTOOED FARE

The other day a guy called and wanted me to pick up a horse racing card at the Turf Room at Redwood Acres, and then go pick up his date at a downtown bar. The guy wanted me to take his lady friend to a few places, so she could pick up a few things. He wanted me to pay for them. He would then reimburse me when he paid the cab fare.

When I got downtown, I went into one of the local pubs to look for his squeeze for the day. After I finally locate this beautiful creature, she told me to take her to the mall so she could pick up a dress she has on lay-away. She wanted to surprise this guy. Boy, what a surprise that will be; more like a living nightmare if you ask me.

She ought to look pretty good in that dress with half her teeth missing, and tattoos all over her legs. After we left the mall we headed for a grocery store so she could buy some food and a case of beer. When she got back into my cruiser, she popped open a beer, pulled a sandwich out of one of the grocery bags, and started eating it. I wanted to laugh because she made a lot of noise while she was eating. I don't think she had eaten for awhile; she sounded like a bunch of hogs eating. We finally got to the guy's house. She had just finished eating her sandwich. Before she got out, she wiped the food and beer off her face with the sleeve of her shirt. She was a real class act. The guy paid me and they walked off, happy to see each other. I hope he leaves the lights off!

AN UNFULFILLED ROMANTIC

When you pick up a date at a bar, you never know what will happen. A businessman from Chico found out the hard way. I went to a motel in Northtown to pick him up so he could go to the airport. While we were putting his stuff in my cab, he was bitching and griping about some girl.

"Are you having a bad day?" I asked. About that time, I heard a lady from the second floor yell, "Randy, get that jerk out of here!" The guy looked at me. "Do you know that slut?" he asked. "Yeah, I have given her and her boyfriend lots of rides. They're heavy drug users."

"Well, she's a whore!" he said.

"What happened? She rip you off?" I asked.

He told me he met her at a local bar and took her to dinner. Afterwards she agreed to go to his motel room. When they got back to the motel, they had a few more drinks and then got in bed. She then told him that she would have sex with him but needed $50 to buy some drugs.

He got really angry but agreed and gave her the money. Then, a few minutes later, she passed out. Now he was mad again but figured he would wait until the morning to claim his reward. When he woke up, she was getting dressed. "What about our deal?" he asked. "The party's over," she said.

He demanded his money back, and she told him to call the police if he had a problem. So he told me he tried and tried to get his $50 back from her but realized it wasn't worth the trouble. I was wondering if it had anything to do with the fact he was wearing a wedding ring.

DETECTIVE COLLENBERG HERE TO CHECK YOUR BRA SIZE, MA'AM

One thing about driving a taxi for a living is that it's never a dull moment when I get calls like this next one.

I picked up a lady about 45 years old at a motel in Arcata who wanted to go to Eureka. After she got in I asked her, "Where in Eureka do you want to go?"

"I need to go to Old Town to look for my luggage and then have you bring me back here to the motel."

"What do you mean, go look for your luggage? You don't know where it is?"

"This is embarrassing. I have no idea where it is."

"How are we going to find it if you don't know where it is?" She then told me what happened.

She's moving up here from San Diego to be close to her daughter who lives in Arcata. She came in on the bus last night in Eureka. Her daughter, who works in Eureka, was going to pick her up after she got off work, which was about two hours after she arrived on the bus.

As she was waiting for her daughter at the bus station, she started a conversation with a couple of homeless guys that were there panhandling. After about 15 minutes she said she was getting hungry.

She felt sorry for the two bums so she asked them if they would watch her luggage for $10 for about an hour while she walked to a restaurant to eat. Of course they happily said yes.

She had nine suitcases and there was no way she could take them with her to the restaurant.

Well, you can guess what happened. When she got back the bums and her luggage had disappeared. When her daughter came to pick her up, she told her what had happened, and of course she couldn't believe her mom would do something so dumb. They then drove up and down the streets near the bus station looking for the two thieves who stole her stuff. They didn't have any luck so they went to Arcata to a motel where she was going to stay for a couple of days before moving into her daughter's house.

After she told me that, she said, "I hope we can find my things today." I told her we would be lucky if we did. When we got into Eureka, she wanted to go by the bus station first to see if her two friends were there trying to rip-off someone else, but there wasn't anybody there.

We then started driving up and down Old Town to see if we could locate these guys or find someone who might know what had happened to her belongings.

After about 30 minutes we saw a guy walking on the sidewalk with a suitcase. She told me to pull over so she could talk to this guy because the suitcase looked like one of hers.

I stopped right next to this guy who looked a little out of place with a big fancy suitcase. She jumped out and told the guy, "That's my suitcase that you're carrying. Someone stole it from me last night."

He gave us a dirty look and said, "If you think this is your suitcase lady, what's in it?" So she told him what should have been in it. He started laughing and opened it up.

There was nothing in it. "See, lady, it's not yours." She was confused and didn't know what to do next. Then I noticed a name tag hanging from the handle. I asked her if she had her name on her suitcases and she said yes.

I then told the guy, "Hey, buddy, her name is on the suitcase." He laughed again and showed us an empty tag. He must have removed her name the same time he took the contents out. I then told this guy the suitcase belonged to the lady and she would like it back. He told me to stick my head where the sun doesn't shine, and then he yelled at us, "I bought this suitcase for a dollar at a rummage sale about ten  blocks down there," as he points towards Montgomery Wards.

"If you guys want a suitcase like this one, go buy one; they have a bunch of them." He then walked off. When we got back into my luxurious yellow cruiser, I told my fare that we just got a big clue about where her other suitcases might be. She was excited about the possibility of finding her things.

We then drove in the direction where our bargain shopper told us to go. We went up and down all the streets in that vicinity but still no luck in finding the rummage sale. I then decided we had better check the alleys also.

A few minutes later we were about halfway down our third alley when she told me to stop again. As she was getting out she said, "See that clothes line over there?" I looked over at the clothesline and there were clothes hanging on it drying.

"What about it?" I asked.

"You see those three sets of underwear over there?"

"You mean those three bras and panties?"

"Yes. Those are mine." I didn't know what to think. This was getting crazier by the minute.

There was a run-down apartment complex next to it. I got out and we knocked on one of the doors to see if we could locate the person who was so nice to wash her underwear for her. A few minutes later, a lady answered the door. Lady might be the wrong word for her because she was pretty tough looking. Matter of fact, if I was a peeping Tom and looked into her window and saw her, I would have to reach in and close the curtains and go on to the next house. "What do you guys want?" she asked, rubbing her eyes. She must have just waked up from her beauty sleep. As I was pointing at the clothesline, I said, "Some of those clothes on your clothes line belong to this lady here." She gave us a funny look, like we were nuts and said, "Sorry, but those are mine."

My fare started telling her that that underwear on the clothesline was stolen from her and she wanted it back. They then started yelling at each other. It was a mess.

As this was going on, a few more ladies and a couple guys come out of the other apartments wondering what's going on. They all looked like a bunch of druggies. One of the guys told us to leave or he was going to call the police.

I was getting tired of this craziness so I had decided I better step in and try to get this mess straightened out. As I was watching this circus performance, I noticed that my customer was smaller than the babe from the apartment was so I told my fare I wanted to talk to her.

When she came over, I asked her, "What size bra do you wear?"

"What?" she said, sort of embarrassed.

"Tell me what size bra do you wear. If that's your underwear, I bet the lady from the apartment doesn't know what size it is. She's 20 or 30 pounds bigger than you."

"That's a great idea." She then told me what size she wore and I walked over to the clothesline to check it out.

As I was walking over there, the other lady asked, "Where are you going?"

I turned around and said, "If that is your underwear, what size bra do you wear?"

"None of your damn business."

"If you're not going to tell us what we need to know, I will call the police and have them figure it out."

She was hot now. As I was standing by the clothesline, I noticed two ladies a couple of houses down. They were sitting behind a couple of tables. I told my fare I found the rummage sale we were looking for. As she was walking down there to check it out, I told our new friends that we would be right back. After my fare looked through all the junk for her belongings, she couldn't find anything that belonged to her.

I then asked the two businesswomen if they had any suitcases for sale. One of them said, "Yes, we do; they're inside the house. Do you want to buy one?"

"We would like to look at them first if that's OK." I said.

"Sure I'll get them for you." When she got up to go get the suitcases, my fare said, "Where did you get those pants you're wearing? Those were stolen from me yesterday."

The lady gave her a dirty look and told her that her boyfriend gave them to her a long time ago. I think she was lying, but I wasn't going to argue. I told my fare to forget about it, let's check out the luggage. A few minutes later the lady came out with a couple of suitcases, my fare told me they were hers. She looked in them, but there wasn't anything in them either. She was disappointed and asked the sales lady, "Where did you get these suitcases, and where are the things that were in them?" "I don't have any idea, lady. Everyone in the neighborhood trades things back and forth. I can't help you."

My fare questioned the two ladies for a few more minutes but got no where. I decided I had enough of this so I called the police. About 15 minutes later a Eureka Police officer showed up. After he got out of his car he started questioning my fare. By this time there were about eight or nine people watching, wondering what was going to happen next.

A couple of minutes later another officer shows up. He asked me what was going on. I explained to him the situation. He started laughing and said, "You could write a book." I just smiled as he walked over to talk to the other people about what had happened.

About an hour, later after we filed a police report, we had three empty suitcases in my luxurious yellow cruiser, heading back to my customers motel. She was upset about the fact that she will probably never get her things back but admitted it was her own fault.

When I dropped off my fare, she told me thanks for helping. I told her, "No! Thank you for a very interesting afternoon.

And if you're wondering about her underwear, we left it behind.

CHAPTER 17

Friends and Fans

I SAY MY GOOD MAN, ARE YOU THE WEST COAST CABBIE?

When I started writing I never dreamed that I would be writing a book some day. I also never realized that my stories would be as popular as they have become, and because of that I have fans all over the world. I would like to share with you a few stories about some of these special people that I have met.

I was going into the Post Office one day and this guy hollers out, "Are you the cabbie that writes the newspaper column?" I told him, "Yes I am."

He told me he was from London and reads my column every week. I asked him how he reads my column every week if he lives in England. He told me he was searching on the Internet for a nice place in California to move to and discovered Arcata. He then found the Arcata Eye newspaper web page and has been reading it every week to learn about the people and the area—which includes my column.

He told me he really enjoys my column and all the interesting articles in the Eye. He was a real nice guy. He told me if he does move here he will be calling me, because he will need a cab to get around for a while. I told him when he gets to town to call me, and I will help him get situated. He thought that was great. I told him we have a very nice town and he would like it here a lot. He told me thanks, and went on his way.

PLAYING NICE PEOPLE AGAINST EACH OTHER TO MAXIMIZE SNACKAGE

The best part of driving a taxi for a living is all the interesting people I meet, and all the new friendships I have made. I would like to share with you three of those friendships that I have made which have made my work more enjoyable. They are Deana Hendricks from Simpson Timber Company and Karen Peterson and Sandra Sundell of Arcata Redwood.

Every week, besides taking people places, I also make a lot of deliveries. My favorite weekly delivery is to Arcata Redwood Company and Simpson Timber Company in Korbel.

Every week the two mills have packages flown to the Arcata Airport from their corporate office in Portland Oregon. I pick up the packages and deliver them to the two mills. I always deliver to Simpson first and then continue on to Arcata Redwood, which is located on Highway 101 between Arcata and Eureka.

After doing that several times I was at Arcata Redwood one day when Karen and Sandra, who sign for the packages, asked me, "How come you don't bring our package first and then go to Simpson in Korbel?" I thought about that for a minute, because they're always giving me a bad time about going there first.

Then I said, "I always go to Simpson first, because Deana always gives me hot chocolate or coffee and donuts!"(I made that up, but Deana has given me candy and other treats).

"You're kidding," Karen said.

Laughing to myself I said, "No, I'm not; Deana's very nice and always has treats for me when I go there." Karen and Sandra just shook their heads.

A couple of months later I was at Arcata Redwood and Karen asked me, "Are you still going to Korbel first?"

"Yes, I am," I said.

"Is Deana still giving you treats?"

"Yes, she appreciates my good service."

"I can't believe it," said Karen. Then she offered me a soda and a cookie, and said, "Now next week, you come here first!" I laughed.

So the next few weeks I kept telling Karen and Sandra that Deana just kept out-doing them.

Of course I told Karen and Sandra I was getting a lot more than I was, so they would try harder to outdo Deana. It was a lot of fun.

Then, the Thursday before Valentine's Day weekend Sandra said, "Randy, we have a package coming in tomorrow with Simpson's. Could you please bring our package to us first tomorrow?"

Laughing to myself again, I told Sandra, "I will probably go see Deana first because she told me she has a little gift for me for Valentine's Day."

Sandra gave me a funny look and then said, "Randy, would you like a cranberry muffin?" I refused the offer since I hate cranberry muffins.

Then Sandra offered me a banana and I laughed. I told her, "That's for skinny people; I'm a fat person."

When I said that, all the girls in the office laughed and told Sandra she had better do better than that. Then Sandra said, "Randy, if you bring our package first tomorrow, I will have a few treats for you."

I laughed out loud this time and told Sandra, "OK, I will come here first tomorrow."

So, on Friday I went to Arcata Redwood first and Karen and Sandra were all smiles. After they signed for their package, they handed me a card they made on their computer which showed a box of candy and a big heart shaped box full of chocolates. They both gave me a hug. Then Sandra said, "I bet Deana can't beat that!"

We all laughed. Sandra, Karen and Deana are very special people and I'm glad I got to meet them. They make my job a lot more fun.

VIVA LAS VEGAS

One of my biggest fans, Stan Smith lives in Las Vegas. He loves my columns and e-mailed me to tell me that he will be in town soon to visit his mom and will be calling me to pick him up.

Well, a few weeks later I got a call to pick up Stan at the airport. After we introduced ourselves, we got into my luxurious yellow cruiser and we headed to Stan's mom's house in McKinleyville.

On our way there he told me that he was born and raised in Orick and has been living in Las Vegas for the past 16 years.

I asked him, "How did you end up living in Las Vegas?"

Stan laughed and then told me after he graduated from the police academy at College of the Redwoods he worked for the Humboldt County Sheriff department as a reserve officer from 1980-1983. Then he worked for the National Park System in security from 1983-1984. After that, he was off to Las Vegas.

Today he works for The Boyd Gaming Corporation, which owns 11 different casino properties. Stan is in charge of risk management for all 11 properties. His responsibilities include guest liability, security, safety, insurance and state comp. He is currently President of the Nevada Chapter of Risk Insurance Management Society. He was just awarded the Risk Manager of the year award for the state of Nevada. Not bad for a guy from Orick, California.

But Stan's biggest achievement was implementing the Automated External Defibrillator in Casinos all over Nevada. This has saved many peoples' lives. When we got to his mom's house, we talked for a few more minutes. I really enjoyed talking to him. He was a very interesting guy.

Just before I left he told me, "Randy, anytime you come to Las Vegas I, will set you up in one of our hotels."

"Hey that sounds great, Stan, thanks a lot; don't be surprised if I call in the next few months."

"That would be great, Randy. We'll have a good time when you come down."

As I was driving off, I was thinking how good it feels to meet new people from different places who are interested in my stories as much as I am interested in who they are and what they do.

The best part is I gained a new friend and that's a great feeling.

A BIRTHDAY DREAM COMES TRUE

When I decided to write a weekly newspaper column about my experiences driving around in my luxurious yellow cruiser I had set a few goals that I wanted to accomplish.

Some of my goals were:

To give people an inside look into the profession of a taxi driver here in Humboldt County.

To hopefully entertain people and make them laugh or just smile.

And to appeal to all age groups.

This next call accomplishes these goals.

One day I received an e-mail from Nancy Peacock of Sunny Brae. She wrote that her son Robin who will be 14 years old, is a big Cab10 fan.

She wanted to surprise him for his birthday by having me pick him up after school at the Veteran's building in Arcata. He is a freshman at Arcata High School.

Then she wanted me to take him to Burger King in McKinleyville and buy him whatever he wanted to eat, and then bring him back home to Sunny Brae. So I called Nancy back and we made the arrangements for Robin's birthday. On his birthday I went to pick up Robin at the Veteran's building. She had told me what he would be wearing, so I wouldn't have to guess who Robin was.

When I pulled up in front of the Veteran's building there were a few students hanging out talking. One of them was Robin.

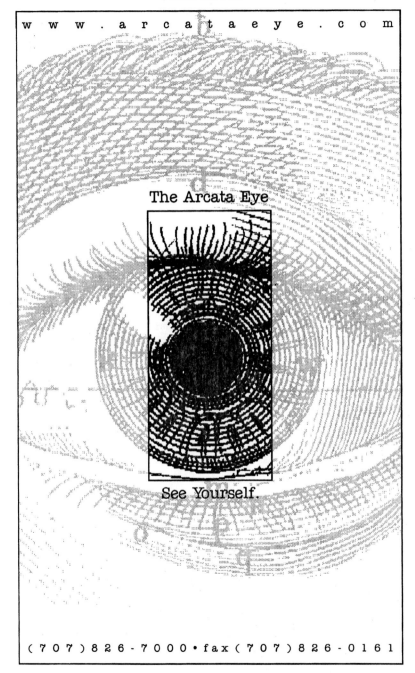

I told him, "Your mom told me it was your birthday and that you enjoy my column. She thought you might get a kick out of me picking you up." He smiled, and then looked at his best friend Brandon Lynch; then both looked at me, and then Robin got in. I told Robin that his mom wanted me to take him to Burger King to get whatever he wanted to eat, and then take him back home. He smiled and liked that idea. On our way to McKinleyville I asked him, "What do you think of your mom hiring me to pick you up?"

"Not a surprise; she's always doing something like this!" he said.

Then I asked Robin, "Why do you like my column?"

"Because I'm sure all cabdrivers have very interesting stories, and this area provides some very interesting ones which make your column very interesting to me to read!"

I asked my big fan a few more questions.

"In the world of sports who is your favorite team?"

"The San Francisco 49ers!"

"Who is your favorite sport hero?"

"Will Clark of the Baltimore Orioles!"

"Who is your favorite teacher at Arcata High School?'

"My concert Band teacher, Mr. David Bayes!'

"Which instrument do you play?"

"I will be playing the clarinet in Arcata High's Marching Band!"

We are now at Burger King and after we got his order we headed back to Arcata. When we got to Arcata, I told Robin we were going to the office of the Arcata Eye so we can get a picture of him for my column. He thought that was cool.

As we're driving through the Plaza, I asked him what he thought about the hippies that hang out on the plaza. "They're cool, they don't bother me!" he said.

After the Editor took our picture, we headed for Sunny Brae to his home. When we got to his house, his family came out to greet us—his little sister Mica, age seven, his mom Nancy who is a professional field trip driver, his dad Jeff who is chief financial officer for Yakima in Arcata, and his nana (grandma) from Palo Alto.

I stayed for a few minutes for pictures. While I was standing there, his grandmother told me she enjoys my columns, too. So I gave all of them some copies of my newsletters, wished Robin a Happy Birthday, told them thank you and went on my way.

It's very rewarding to do your job and make people happy at the same time. It's also very rewarding in today's world to meet a nice young man like Robin who has loving and caring parents.

TOURING ARCATA, CAB10 STYLE

This next call is about one of my fans that lives in Palo Alto, California. I was shopping in Arcata when a lady walked up to me and asked, "Are you Cab10?"

"Yes I am."

The lady then said, "My name is Janet Stradley. I live here in Arcata. I wanted to tell you that my sister Judith Dvorak who lives in Palo Alto is a big fan of yours. She will becoming to Arcata around Christmas time and I wanted to surprise her by hiring you to pick us up, give us a tour of Arcata and then go have coffee with us. Is that possible?"

"Sounds like fun to me. When your sister gets to town, just call and request Cab10 to pick you up, then we can do whatever you have planned."

"That's great; see you then," she said.

So just after Christmas I got a call to pick up someone in Arcata that needed my services for an extended period of time. When I got to the address I was given, I honked my horn. A lady came out and told me they'd be right out.

A few minutes later, a couple of ladies and a young girl came out of the house. One lady saw me and kept saying, "Oh my God, oh my God, it's Cab10. I can't believe it!"

I didn't know it, but it was Janet and her sister Judith from Palo Alto, and Janet's daughter Sara Stradley. They wanted me to take them around town.

Before we left, they wanted to know if they could take some pictures of my luxurious yellow cruiser. Of course, I told them to go right ahead and take all the pictures they wanted. After they were done, they jumped in and we took off.

"Where do you girls want to go?" I asked. Judith said, "First we want to go to the cemetery up by the high school and see our grandparents' graves and pay our respects."

After she said that, I looked at her in my rear view mirror to see if she was serious. I thought she was joking, but she wasn't. "That's a first; I have never taken anyone to a cemetery before," I told them.

As I was driving I asked Judith, "What do you do for a living?"

"I'm retired, but I used to work as a marketing manager for the Scott Foresman Company in Palo Alto. They publish children's textbooks." She also told me it was a good place to work.

When we got to the cemetery, they wanted me to drive through to where their grandparents are buried. Cemeteries give me the creeps, because I know someday I will be there too, so I was hoping they wouldn't want to stay too long. Plus there were a couple of guys there preparing a grave site.

After a few minutes, we left the cemetery. I decided when it was my time to go to that big taxi stand in the sky, I'm going to be buried at the Bayshore Mall because that way I know my wife will come and see me.

Our next stop was to Coldwell Banker Sellers Realty to meet Janet's husband, Jay Stradley.

They visited for a few minutes and then we headed towards the Plaza.

When we passed by the Jambalaya cocktail lounge, Judith told me that the Jambalaya was called Dan and Jerry's Western Bar over 30 years ago. She even told me that they had a 25 cent porno machine. I wanted to ask her if she ever spent any quarters on the machine, but I figured it wasn't any of my business.

As I was driving, the sisters told me they always cruise town when they get together to talk about old times. They also told me they always use different cars so no one recognizes them.

Our tour continued to A Street to their Aunt and Uncle's house, where they had big Christmas parties which were always a lot of fun. After we left there we headed for an apartment in Bayside where they talk about more of their memories.

Every place we went, they explained to me why it was a special place to them. It was interesting. We then headed up Shirley Boulevard, which is one of the steepest roads in Arcata. Just before we started climbing up Shirley, Judith said, "Can this thing make it up the hill?" In all of excitement of riding in Cab10, I think she forgot that she was riding in the luxurious yellow cruiser, and not in a "thing." I told her, "Don't worry; I'll make it up the hill."

After we get to the top up the hill, we headed for 14th Street to the Warren House and on to the College Elementary School where both sisters went to school. I asked them if they learned anything there and they laughed. Janet then told me that she is a teacher at McKinleyville High School, teaching health and physical education.

Next stop was Humboldt State University's Forestry Building, where their grandma's house use to be. After we left there, we went by the building at 14th and C streets where the Trinity Hospital used to be. They told me they were both born there. The sisters were talking and decided they had seen enough and asked me to take them to the Eureka Baking Company.

Judith asked me, "We're going to buy you an eggnog latte. How's that sound?" I don't like being rude or disrespectful, so I of course accepted the offer. Besides, not everyday does one get treated to a latte by two attractive women.

As I was waiting for my latte, I asked Sara, "Where do you go to school?" "I go to Pacific Union." "Who's your teacher and what grade are you in?"

"I'm in the 5th grade and my teacher is Mrs. Allen." I told her that my niece Molly Simas is in her class. She thought that was cool.

After drinking our lattes we headed back to Janet and Judith's mom's and dad's house. Their parents are Grant and Ruth Ferguson, who live in Arcata in a house that Grant built 47 years ago.

When we got to the house, Judith's husband Chuck was waiting for us. Judith asked him if he would take some pictures of all of us standing in front of my luxurious yellow cruiser. After he finished we said our good-byes, and I headed for my next call. As I was driving away, I was thinking, "Man, this is hard work. Oh well, somebody has to do it."

LIGHTS, CAMERA, ACTION!

Every once in a while, someone wants to interview me, take pictures or videotape my luxurious yellow cruiser and me. Such is this next call.

I picked up Andrea Jain of Arcata. I asked her where she wanted to go, and she told me that she wanted to hire me to be part of a video she's making for her husband Pete's 40th birthday. I asked her what she had in mind.

She told me that she is making a video of some of her husband's friends doing all kinds of crazy things. I asked her why Cab10 and me? She told me she and Pete are big Cab10 fans, and he would get a kick out of it if Cab10 and I were in the video.

In that case I turned on the meter and I said, "Andrea, let's go to work!"

I asked her what she wanted me to do. She told me that she has a script for us to play out while she videotapes me in Cab10 parked in front of the old Steward School on 16th Street. So we took a few minutes and went over the script, and we are now ready to start.

This is my first acting job, and I'm getting paid, too. I like this kind of work. Andrea walked across the street and told me she was ready!

Camera! Action! She started videotaping the school! She is now narrating! "This is the old Steward school where my husband Pete went to grammar school," she said.

She videotapes the school going past me, then back towards me and pretends like she doesn't know why I was parked here. She then said, "Hey there's Cab10." She walked towards me, taping me, and said, "What is Cab10 doing here?"

"I'm waiting for a customer! Why are you video taping me?"

"I'm doing a video for my husband Pete's 40th birthday! Do you remember my husband Pete Jain ,when you guys went to grammar school here together?"

"How could I forget him! He's your husband?"

"Yes, he is; do you have any special memories of him that you can recall?"

"Well, that's easy, he was always up to something. I remember one time Pete and his brother Ben took five cases of ice cream sandwiches out of the walk in freezer and ran home with their arms full. I asked if I could have a couple, and they never even turned around." Andrea laughed, "You're kidding."

"No, I'm not; that husband of yours was a wild and crazy guy. We called him the ice cream bandit after that day. What's he up to nowadays?"

"He's a music teacher, and vice-principle at South Bay Elementary."

"You're kidding! I wonder if you know whether he put down on his resume that he was the famous leader of the ice cream bandits."

Cut! That's a wrap! Andrea thanked me and I took her back home. She paid me for my acting services and gave me a nice tip.

I told Andrea thanks a lot, and hope that Pete enjoys his video.

CHAPTER 18

Distinguished Service Awards

A BUMPER CROP OF BOZOS WIN A CAB10 LUXURIOUS CRUISER AWARD

What's bigger than the Oscars, more talked about than the Emmys, and more prestigious than the Globe Awards?

It's the Cab10 Luxurious Cruiser Awards. The solid gold Luxurious Cruiser Awards go to a few lucky people that worked so hard to qualify for these prestigious honors. I created the awards to reward the Cab10 customers who deserve recognition.

I know a lot of you are going to be upset because you didn't win an award. But if you didn't ride in the mighty Cab10, you can't qualify. But there's always next time, so good luck, everyone.

BIGGEST PASSENGER TO RIDE IN CAB10

I had to go to the airport to pick someone up. I drove up to the terminal and I see this mountain, or I should say, this man walking up to me. He was bigggg. I was wondering, "How am I going to get him into the cab?" He told me he needed to go to Eureka. I opened the door for this guy and he squeezes in—barely. I'm a pretty good-sized guy, too, but I felt pretty small with my girlish figure next to this big guy. On our way to Eureka, I asked him how tall he was, and he told me that he is 6-foot-8 and weighs 575 pounds. Congratulations to this champion of food. I hope my shocks aren't broke.

GROSSEST PERSON

The grossest person award goes to a hippie I picked up by the U-haul office in Arcata. This guy was living in a Volkswagen bus. He needed to go to Eureka to the DMV office. He walked really slow, but finally got in.

I started driving, and the smell about killed me—worse than an old skunk. It was going to be a long day with this guy in my cruiser. We got to the DMV office, and he decided that he wanted me to wait and take him back to Arcata. I was so thrilled about the idea of spending more time with this guy.

When he went into the DMV, I had to get out of my cruiser for some fresh air. While I was standing there, I was watching him walk into the DMV office. I noticed that his pants are stained from going to the bathroom in his shorts. I bet it had been several days since he had seen a bathroom. When we got back to Arcata, I was glad to see him go; even his money smelled. He was one rotten dude.

THE BEAUTY AND THE BEAST AWARD

What an honor for someone to win two of my beautiful cruiser awards. I had to go to the Hotel Carter and pick up someone at 8:45 a.m. I arrived there a little early so I waited until 8:45 and then I turned my meter on. I waited for about five more minutes and still no one showed up. I decided I had better go inside to the front desk and ask the clerk if she knew if someone had called for a cab. She said, "Yes, I'll call her and tell her you're here!" I told the clerk that I would be outside waiting.

About 15 more minutes go by and I'm reading my newspaper when I noticed in my rear view mirror someone coming out of the front door of the hotel. I saw a very attractive young lady about 30 wearing a green miniskirt with high heels coming towards me. So I jumped out of my cab to help this young lady into my luxurious yellow cruiser.

After she got in she told me that she needed to go to a local business for a meeting. She was from New York. I don't get too many women all dressed up like this lady in my cab. But I was about to find out that in her case, beauty is only skin deep.

She noticed that the meter had a large amount on it because I had to wait for her at the Hotel Carter. "Is the amount on the meter correct?" she asked.

"You requested an 8:45 a.m. pickup, and you weren't ready for 20 minutes," I told her. "I have to turn the meter on at the time you requested my services. It's your fault for being late."

She was upset. "Too bad," I thought.

She then asked me if we take credit cards, and I said, "Yes, we do!" Then she quieted down, and didn't say too much the rest of the way. When we got to her meeting, she handed me a credit card that we don't take. I told her, "Sorry, but we can't take that card."

She's really mad now. It's a good thing I lived on a ranch all my life so I could understand the language she was using. I didn't know that someone with her looks could be so ugly and rude. She finally gave me another card that we do take. Why she didn't give that one to me in the first place instead of being so rude is beyond me.

When she was getting out, she didn't realize that she had won two awards while riding in my luxurious yellow cruiser—the beauty and the beast awards.

The Dumbest

The dumbest person to ride in Cab10 was a guy in Arcata. I picked up a guy at one of the University dorms. He was mad at his girlfriend. He told me that he tried calling her all morning, but she wasn't home.

He told me that he wanted to go look for her. He thinks she has been sleeping around, and he can't trust her anymore. I asked him if it wouldn't be smarter to find another woman. He told me that he doesn't want anyone else because he loves her.

"How dumb can you get?" I thought. He wanted me to take him to look for the love of his life. We went to about eight different houses in Arcata, Mckinleyville, and all over Eureka, but we couldn't find her.

After about an hour he told me to take him to his work. He's pretty upset. When we got to his work, some girl saw us and came running out It's his girlfriend, and they work together.

"Why are you late for work?" she yells. He told her, "I've been looking all over hell for you!" "Don't you remember?" she said, "I told you last night I had to go to work early today!" He's embarrassed. His cab fare was $58.

My Biggest Tip

The biggest tip I ever received was from a man who calls himself "Dr. Z" from Florida. He tipped me $150. I hope this record is broken soon. If you want to break this record, call for Cab10. I will even buy you lunch.

Most Eccentric

This award is always the hardest to pick a winner for, because there is so much competition. But one lady from Paris stood above all the rest of the field. I had to pick her up in Trinidad. When I pulled up to the house, there was a lady standing in the front yard waiting.

I had a hunch she was going to be an interesting fare. She looked like a very eccentric type of person dressed in all black like she was going to a funeral or something.

When I got out I opened the front door for her, she said that she doesn't ride in front and wanted to get in the back seat. I told her, "OK." When I opened the back door for her, she backed up to the seat and told me to look the other way. She had a long dress on, but was afraid I might look up her dress like all the limo drivers do in Europe. I was thinking she should be happy they look, because even if I was drunk I wouldn't want to look. I finally got her in and she told me she wants to go to Safeway in McKinleyville to get some groceries. "This is the first time I have bought my own groceries since I became an actress," she said. She then asked me if we have any limo's or towncars because she's embarrassed to ride in a taxi.

"What's wrong with taxis?" I asked. (I should have never asked her anything.)

"Well, young man, I'm an actress and an entertainer in Europe and over there I get treated better than your American movie stars. I'm used to being pampered and catered to. I'm always provided with a limo or a towncar where ever I go," she said.

I asked her why she is over here going through all this torture. She told me that her agent wanted her to take a month off from her busy schedule, so he arranged for her to come to America and stay at a friend's summer home in Trinidad for a month so she can kick back and relax.

On our way to Safeway, she told me her life history and I don't think she even breathed while she talked. I went all the way to McKinleyville without saying another word, because she would never shut up.

After I dropped her off the dispatcher asked me why I never told him where I was for half an hour. I told him I had an actress in my cab and she was practicing for her next movie about a lady that drove her husband to kill himself because she would never shut up.

"That's a good reason," he said laughing, "How about another call?"

So the actress with the fake French accent wins the Most Eccentric Award.

BIGGEST SHOPPER

This award goes to the biggest grocery shopper I ever picked up. Not in weight, but in the amount of groceries she bought. I went to Ray's Food place, a local grocery store, to pick up someone that had groceries and wanted to go home.

When I got to the store, the lady was out front waving me down. She had a big basket full of groceries next to her. After I got out and got ready to load her groceries, she told me that she has more groceries in the store. She told me that a couple of box boys were bringing them out now. I looked back at the store and I saw the two guys coming with two more big baskets full. I had never seen so many groceries packed into three baskets before.

I was almost done loading the three baskets into my luxurious yellow cruiser when I saw the two guys coming again with two more baskets. I asked the lady who had gotten into my cab, "How many baskets do you have?"

She told me there were thirteen in all together. I couldn't believe it, but it was true. She told me her bill was $980 and I can tell you it felt like a lot more than that. The lady told me she buys groceries only once a month. My cab was stuffed full. On our way to her house I asked her if there was going to be anyone there to help. She told me her son will be there to help.

Her son did help me, but he was lazy and slow. I was glad to get out of there.

BEST MATCHING PURSE AND SHOES

I know a lot of you ladies that have ridden in my cab are going to be upset because you didn't win this award for the best looking purse and shoes. But this lady won by a landslide.

I got a call to pick up a lady that is hiding in some bushes by an apartment building. Sounds strange, but in this business that's not unusual. I asked the dispatcher why she was hiding in the bushes.

He started laughing, and then said, "You'll see." I was thinking, "Oh great, another space case."

When I got to the apartment building, I saw a bunch of bushes off to one side. I drove over to the bushes and honked my horn. Then I heard a lady's voice asking me to come over towards the bushes; she needed to talk to me. I didn't want to get too close to where she was because I might be getting set up to get robbed or something. I still couldn't see her, but she could see me because she told me why she was hiding in the bushes.

As she was talking to me she walked out a little where I could see her. I couldn't believe what I saw. This lady had the neatest looking purse I ever saw. Her purse even matched her high heels. You ladies would be jealous of her.

You're probably wondering why I noticed her purse and shoes since I'm a guy.

Well, that's all she was wearing. That's right, she was naked; but all I could see was this beautiful purse and matching shoes. I couldn't keep my eyes off of them.

All right, you want to know more about why this lady was naked; I guess I better tell you.

After I gave her my coat she got into my cab. Of course, she was very embarrassed by all of this, and I could tell she had been crying. I then asked her, "How did you get yourself into this situation?"

She was really upset. After a couple of minutes she told me that she and this guy had just finished having sex in the guy's van by the Marina when they got into an argument about her seeing other guys. The next thing she knew, he threw her clothes out the van window and started driving towards town calling her names. She told me she was really scared because this guy can get violent.

When they got into town, he opened her door and pushed her out. She yelled at him, because she didn't have any clothes and he told her she didn't need any, because she's like an animal and animals don't wear clothes. Then he drove off.

She started crying again. Then she told me that she was lucky she had her purse, because she had her cell phone in it. She called a friend of hers, but nobody was home, so she called for a cab.

When we got to her house she handed me my coat and thanked me for helping me home. As she walked into the house all I could see was that beautiful purse and those matching high heels.

BIGGEST MOUTH

The person with the biggest mouth award goes to someone who has an even bigger mouth than I do! That's hard to do, but there is someone that qualified.

The lucky winner of this award is a lady from Oregon. I picked up six people at the airport who had to go to Crescent City. One of the passengers was a big lady that sat right behind me. All of the people seemed really nice. We had gone about two miles when this lady started talking. She works for a county office and she knows everything.

For the next 70 miles it was a living hell. She talked and talked and talked. When she laughed (she was the only one laughing), which was often, she rocked the cab. Every time someone said something, she had to butt in. All the way to Crescent City she would tell us about every little town, tree, stream, elk, or whatever she could think of. She knew it all. She thought she was my tour director or something.

I tried to ignore her, but it was hard to do with her booming voice. I wish I had a box of crackers or something to give her. Anyway, after about an hour and a half she rolled out, and I knew she was the winner because she has a bigger mouth than I do.

THE BIGGEST TIGHTWAD

This award is for the biggest tightwad. But I had a problem making the selection, since three guys tied for this award at the same time.

I picked up the three guys who had just flown in on their private plane at Murray Field Airport. They were all around 35 years old wearing suits and carrying briefcases. They seemed like nice guys, but were rather quiet. They wanted to go to an apartment complex in Arcata to take care of some business.

When we got to the apartment complex, one of the guys told me, "We're only going to be here for a few minutes, then we want you to take us to Eureka. Is that OK?"

"Sure, I'll wait for you guys."

They were walking off, when one of them came back and asked me, "It doesn't cost anything to wait for us does it?"

"Yes, waiting time is only thirty cents per minute. How long are you going to be?"

"About five minutes."

"Five minutes will only be $1.50 extra!"

He then walked over and talked to his buddies; a couple of seconds later one of the other guys asked me, "Can't you leave the meter off for a few minutes?"

I couldn't believe these guys in $500 suits couldn't afford an extra $1.50.

"No, I don't get paid when the meters off."

They talked some more, then they decided to pay me, and while they're paying me one guy tells me $1.50 is highway robbery.

I didn't want to tell them what I thought about them, except that they were the three biggest tightwads I ever met.

CHAPTER 19

Thanks, I guess...

ODD GIFTS

Driving a taxi you run into a lot of different people from all over the world. And in some cases I think a few of them come from another world. That goes for tipping too. Most of the time you get the usual 10 or 15 per cent and other times they're a little strange, but very much appreciated. Just to give you an idea of some of the tips I receive, I took a normal month and kept track so you could see what you are missing by not being a taxi driver.

One lady gave me 5 lbs. of potatoes, because she bought a bag that was to big for her to use. One lady gave me a dozen fresh eggs from her chickens. I got six pieces of cake, one fruit cup, two bottles of beer, one wine cooler, a bag of beef jerky, one dime from a lady who told me to keep the change. Two boxes of crackers, six candy bars, eight sodas, three apples, a banana, a bag of candy, four donuts, three mochas, four newspapers, a taco, a religious pamphlet, a book, some flowers, a piece of pizza, a partially drunk, half-gallon of whiskey, a sandwich with a small bite out of it (yummy!); a pair of washed, but used socks (how generous to wash them); a pair of old shoes; melted candy bars; three pennies; worthless foreign coins, and a few old sweaters, here and there.

This is a very rewarding job as you can tell.

CAB10 LOVES HOTDOGS!

This next call I had to go to Bayside Market. I like going there, because I love to get a couple of their famous hot dogs for lunch. If you haven't had one, you better go out there and have John Phillips fix one up for you. You'll love it. Plus they have lots of other good stuff there too in their deli. They'll even barbecue you a hamburger if you want. So if you ever see Cab10 parked out there, come on in and say hi.

Oh, back to my story.

I had to pick up a guy there that needed to go to North Bay Auto to pick up his car. I said to him, "If it's all right with you I would like to grab a couple of hot dogs for my lunch." He told me to get two for him too, and he would buy them. "That'll be your tip," he said. You don't have to ask me twice. So, I had lunch with a stranger and gained a new friend.

A BOGUS TIP

I picked up a man and a woman in Arcata who wanted to go to Eureka. They were good friends. He wanted to go to the mall and she wanted to get dropped off at the courthouse on the way to the mall.

On our way to Eureka, the lady asked me how much it will cost for the total cab fare because she would be paying for both of them. I told her it would be about $20. So she hands the guy a 20 and a 5, and tells him here's $20 for the cab fare and $5 for his tip. The guy tells her, "OK."

When we got to the courthouse we dropped her off and continued on to the mall. The guy in my cab was talking about all kinds of strange things on our way there. I was glad to get to the mall.

The guy asked me how much the fare was, so I told him it was $19.90. So I assumed I was going to get the $20 for the fare and the $5 for a tip, but boy was I in for a surprise.

The guy got out and handed me the $20 for the cab fare and put the $5 (my $5) in his pocket. Then he started to walk away. (I don't want to tell you what I was thinking.) He stopped, turned around, and came back, opened the passenger door and in a loud voice said, "Oh, I'm supposed to give you a tip too, huh?" (I was thinking to myself, yeah, the $5 he put in his pocket.)

Then, in a loud voice, he said, "Here's your tip for the day don't ever drive this cab when you have bald tires!" Then he closed the door and walked off with my $5 still in his pocket.

Well, I have to tell you I sat there for a minute, then I just shook my head and laughed. That's one tip that I will never forget.

A CABBIE ON THE RUN!!

One of the nicest gifts I have ever received from my customers was from Jean Knapp (my dad's bingo buddy). She wrote a poem about my luxurious yellow cruiser and me.

Arcata's blessed with this newcomer
A yellow cruiser with so much humor
A gentle fellow you'll love to meet

Attractive too and very neat.
They call him Cruiser Cab #10
Go once with him and he's your friend.
Cry on his shoulder and he'll cheer you up
His friendly smile is what he's got.
Friendly Randy is his name
Cruising Cab #10 is his game
He'll take you to your destinations
and he'll answer all your questions
So Cab #10 you need to know
Call him again and you're on the go.
He's the one and only kind
A person could ever find
So long Cab #10— I'm off to bingo
I'll see you later with your lingo.

YOU TRY TO BE A NICE GUY, AND THIS IS THE THANKS YOU GET

Were you ever in a big city and took a cab somewhere and it seemed like the taxi driver took you the longest possible route to your destination, so he could make more money? It's probably happened to all of us at one time or another.

Well, I have good news for you here locally; we don't do that, unless we're not familiar with a certain road or area.

The other day I was accused of taking the long way, but it was a very small mistake on my part. The other day I picked up a lady at Winco in Eureka. She had about 10 bags of groceries. She wanted to go home, but needed to go to a couple of other places first.

After Miss Tightwad got in, she told me she wanted to go to Eureka Market first, which is located a block off Broadway Street on Clark Street. So, I got on Henderson Street and headed for Broadway so I could go to Clark Street. Just before Broadway there is a street called Little Fairfield which ends up running into Broadway a few blocks from Clark Street.

After I passed Little Fairfield I was thinking I probably should have taken it, instead of going another couple blocks out of the way to Broadway. But I didn't think it would turn out to be such a big deal.

After I got on Broadway, my customer let me have it with

both barrels. "How come you went this way when you could have taken Little Fairfield and saved me some money?"

"It's not much more going this way; I drive in Arcata normally so sometimes I'm not familiar with the shortest routes."

"Well, how much more is it going this way? I have never had a cab driver go this way before. You're trying to take advantage of me, because I'm Hispanic."

Well folks, that's where she was wrong, but she wasn't listening to me, because she kept on bitchin.' So I told her the bad news.

"It's going to cost you about 40 cents more this way, but it's my mistake so I will deduct 40 cents from what you owe me."

She wasn't giving up.

"I'm going to call your boss the next time I get you and you pull this stunt on me."

"Lady, I told you I will deduct 40 cents."

"I'm still upset with you, because if I hadn't said say anything you wouldn't have offered to pay me the 40 cents."

I wasn't going to win this fight. I couldn't wait to get her home. After we left Eureka Market she didn't say anything else until we pulled up to her house.

"I live on the second floor, could you take my groceries up there for me?"

"I can do that."

I wanted to tell her how much I enjoyed her company, but I kept my mouth shut. Then she asked, "How much do I owe you?"

I pointed at the meter, because I didn't want her to think I made up how much her bill was and I told her to deduct 40¢. She paid me the full amount.

I handed her the 40¢ and she said, "Go ahead and keep it because I need you to carry my groceries up to my apartment."

I was thinking wow how generous of her, I just can't wait until I see her again someday. After I carried her stuff up to her apartment, she said, "Thank you," and handed me $15.

"What's this for?

"I always tip the cab drivers $15 for helping me with my groceries." I told her thank you, but I couldn't believe it; I just shook my head and laughed all the way to my cab. Just when I think I've figured people out, something like this happens.

CHAPTER 20

New Years Eve Log

CAB 10'S LOG; STAR DATE DECEMBER 31ST

The biggest day driving a taxi is New Year's Eve. It's always super busy and can be a very crazy night. Here's how last New Year's Eve was for me and my luxurious yellow cruiser.

12:30 p.m. Pick up Mrs. McCarty and take her to Safeway to shop.

12:45 p.m. Pick up Marion Patterson at Ray's and take her home.

12:59 p.m. Pick up Gene Wellington in McKinleyville and take him to Healthsport.

1:20 p.m. Go to Mad River Hospital Adult Day and pick up Dorothy Riley, Francis Anderson, Annie Suhovy and Margaret Robinson and take them to their homes.

1:59 p.m. Go back to Healthsport and take Mr. Wellington back to his home. Mr. Wellington has a radio show on KHSU Radio and also has a class on Blind Awareness at Azalea Hall in McKinleyville.

2:31 p.m. Go back to Mad River Adult Day and take seven more ladies home.

2:46 p.m. Go to Safeway and take Mrs. McCarty and her groceries back to Sunny Brae.

3:05 p.m. Put 20 gallons of gas in my luxurious yellow cruiser.

3:28 p.m. Go to St. Vincent's in Old Town and pick up a man who just purchased a used stereo system and take him home so he can get it ready for his new year's party he's having.

4:01 p.m. I'm driving down "E" Street, Eureka to 14th and there are about six police cars there. I asked what was going on, and they told me someone just drove by and shot about a dozen or so rounds with an automatic weapon. After hearing that, it's time for me to get the hell out of here.

4:05 p.m. Go to Ray's at the Bayshore Mall and pick up a

couple and their groceries. They need a ride home, but wanted to go to the Shell station to buy some cigarettes. I asked why they didn't buy them at the store. They said they were a dollar cheaper at Shell. They bought two packs and saved $2.00, but it cost $3.70 extra in cab fare because their house is in the opposite direction. They were happy. So was I.

4:25 p.m. Just passed the 100 mile mark for the day.

4:31 p.m. Go to the airport and pick up a man and a woman that need to go to Crescent City. During our ride, they are telling me about all the bad luck they have had getting home.

The man told me he was going to San Francisco Airport yesterday to catch his flight, when the cab he was riding in ran out of gas. The cab driver couldn't get anyone to bring him gas for about two hours (What a dummy). I told the guy he should've of gotten out of the cab and flagged down another one. Then when he got to Arcata Airport his luggage wasn't there.

The lady told me she was supposed to be here the night before. She was on a flight yesterday and they were in the air only about 10 minutes when she noticed out of her window that the metal shield around one of the jet engines was flapping up and down. Then it came apart and the wind was mingling it all up. She said it looked bad. She told the stewardess who told the pilot. In a couple of minutes the pilot came on the intercom and said they would be returning to San Francisco because of a mechanical difficulty. She was glad to be back on the ground.

6:30 p.m. Arrive at Crescent City Airport and head back to McKinleyville.

7:09 p.m. 200 miles and counting.

7:25 p.m. Passing through Orick. For all you people that wanted to know what you missed in Orick, the town is really quiet. Wait a minute, everyone is that the Lumberjack Bar partying? It looks like the whole town is here. Too bad—you missed it.

7:45 p.m. Stop at Cher-ae Heights Casino to wish my mom, dad and my wife Dannette a Happy New Year and, of course, to see if they had won any money playing bingo. Lots of people there. I grabbed a soda and some snacks and got back to work.

7:58 p.m. I'm now passing Clam Beach. Lots of fireworks going off. A lot of people there having a good time.

8:00 p.m. Picked up a lady in McKinleyville going to the Sidelines bar to party.

8:22p.m. I took a case of beer to a Humboldt State University dorm.

8:31p.m. My next call is up Fickle Hill and there are seven people going to a party on L.K. Boulevard. They were loud, but they were having a good time.

9:01p.m. Picked up a guy that just got off work in Arcata and took him to Sweetriver Saloon at the Bayshore Mall to party with his girlfriend. Nice guy, and a good tipper, too.

9:29p.m. Picked up two ladies and two babies at the Bayshore Movies and took them to Winco.

9:40 p.m. Next call is to Spear Avenue. I pick up Eric Younger, Ken (The Barrel) Bradbury, Scott Rocha and three others. They all our having a good time. They're yelling and screaming all the way to Sunny Brae.

9:53 p.m. Take a bottle of whiskey to a house on Ross Street.

10:05 p.m. Go to McKinleyville to pick up an old roommate of mine, Phil and Chelsea Sutter and Scott and Sherry Perry and take them to the Moose Lodge.

10:20 p.m. Now passing Central Station Cocktail Lounge; there's only about seven or eight cars in front but as usual everyone is hiding their cars out back.

10:24 p.m. 300 miles I have traveled so far.

10:49 p.m. Going to Northcoast Inn, some guy just passed me going about 85 mph. What a jerk!

10:52 p.m. Pick up my sister, Toni Collenberg, and her boy friend and take them home. Toni told me to wait a minute. Then Toni handed me a plate of salami, cheese, crackers and a soda. That's my kind of tip.

11:08 p.m. Pick up a bunch of beer drinkers in Sunny Brae and take them to the Sidelines.

11:31 p.m. Go to L.K. Wood and take a lady to the Pin Room. I was opening her door so she could get out when this guy I know walked up to me. He's drunk and wanted me to go into the bar and talk to this guy who wanted to fight him. I told him I had better things to do.

11:44 p.m. My next call is in 15 minutes, so I'm going to cruise the Plaza. I see Kevin Hoover, the editor of the Arcata Eye newspaper. He jumps in and we go around the plaza and talk about everything that is happening on the Plaza. He then jumps out, and goes looking for another story.

12:00 a.m. Happy New Year!

12:01 a.m. Everyone on the Plaza is going nuts. There are firecrackers everywhere. A smoke bomb goes off in front of Marino's Club. People are screaming and yelling, a pink Cadillac with three girls that are topless hanging out the windows is going by me slowly, and all right, you want to know more about the pink Cadillac. If I find out, you will be the first to know.

12:09 a.m. Go to Toni's Drive-in, where they have the best linquica omelets, and take a couple home.

12:16 a.m. Back to the Plaza. The pink Cadillac is parked by the Arcata Hotel. Circled the Plaza and I noticed everyone coming out of the bars. So I stopped in front of the Alibi and I saw two girls in leather coats that barely covered their butts. They were facing the large crowd, exposing themselves.

They would open their coats every so often and the crowd would cheer them on for more. Then I noticed a man dressed all in black; now I know what's going on. He's the owner of the Tip Top Club, a topless bar on Humboldt Hill; he was inArcata with some of his dancers doing a little advertising and handing out some discount admission tickets.

12:31 a.m. Picked up a man at Wildberries and took him to Elk River. Go to Ernie's bar in Eureka and take an old army buddy and his wife home.

1:01 a.m. Go to Harbor Lanes and pick up a couple that are going to Reco's bar. The guy is drunk and told me how a good mechanic he was and he can fix anything. He asked if we needed a mechanic. I told him I didn't know, but I told him when the bar closes, that would be a good time to stop by and get an application. He said okay. What a ding-a-ling!

1:11 a.m. Took a man from Old Town to Ridgewood. He went to see the movie *Titanic*.

1:20 a.m. 350 miles and still going.

1:28 a.m. Going to Arcata again. Only one car on 5th street. Everyone's playing it safe.

1:41 a.m. Pick up three guys and take them to Old Arcata Road.

1:59 a.m. Go to the Moose Lodge in McKinleyville and take Phil's party back home.

2:10 a.m. Go to Northcoast Inn and take three couples to the Eureka Inn.

2:40 a.m. 400 miles traveled.

2:51 a.m. Picked up at Summer Street and took a lady to a party in McKinleyville that's still going.

3:16 a.m. Next call to 14th and "H" and picked up three couples that wanted to go to Myrtle Avenue. One girl passed out. Then one of the guys is telling his wife that he didn't want to stay at their friend's house because he always sees demons there. She's trying to tell him he's nuts, but he keeps going on and on about all the demons that there are in the house. She told me he was a little crazy. He was crazy. He was serious. We finally got to the house that is possessed and they got out carrying the girl that passed out and almost dragging the demon hater.

3:41 a.m. Picked up at Club West on 5th street and took them to Spring Street.

3:48 a.m. Go back to Northcoast Inn again and take a lady to Pine Hill.

4:20 a.m. 462 total miles. My eyes are sore—what a night. If you stayed home now you have an idea what everyone else was doing. I hope you enjoyed your ride, I'm going home now, I'm tired.

Happy Tales and Trails everyone!

MIKE CRAGHEAD
QUALITY WEB DESIGN
WWW.NORTHCOAST.COM/CRAGHEAD/WEB
EMAIL:CRAGHEAD@NORTHCOAST.COM

HATE TO SEW?
CALL GINA LOYA AT (707) 825-7042.
SHE WILL TAKE CARE OF YOUR CLOTHES THAT NEED MENDING.
SEW PATCHES ON FOR YOU AND REPAIR THAT SPECIAL
STUFFED ANIMAL YOU CHERISH AT REASONABLE RATES.
CROCHET AND NEEDLEWORK LESSONS
FOR KIDS AND GROWNUPS.

WHEN DRIVING THE SCENIC ROUTE ON OLD ARCATA ROAD
BETWEEN ARCATA AND EUREKA, CALIFORNIA,
STOP AT BAYSIDE MARKET
ACROSS FROM JACOBY CREEK SCHOOL.
COLD BEER, SODAS, SNACKS,
ICE OLD FASHIONED HOT DOGS, JERKY,
SOFT SERVE ICE CREAM, CONES, CANDY,
FRESH BREWED COFFEE, AND A DELI.

ORDER ADDITIONAL COPIES OF
CAB10-THE WEST COAST CABBIE

Ship to: (please print)

Name_____

Address_____

City_____ State_____ Zip_____

Phone(_____)_____

Please send _____ copies @ $12 each _____
Postage and handling @ $3.00 per book in US _____
CA residents add 7.25% tax - $.87 per book _____
Total amount enclosed _____

Please make checks payable to Randy Collenberg.

Send to: Randy Collenberg
P.O. Box 290
Arcata, CA 95518

- -

Ship to: (please print)

Name_____

Address_____

City_____ State_____ Zip_____

Phone(_____)_____

Please send _____ copies @ $12 each _____
Postage and handling @ $3.00 per book in US _____
CA residents add 7.25% tax - $.87 per book _____
Total amount enclosed _____

Please make checks payable to Randy Collenberg.

Send to: Randy Collenberg
P.O. Box 290
Arcata, CA 95518

ORDER THE WEST COAST CABBIE NEWSLETTER

To read more exciting adventures of the West Coast Cabbie, sign up for the monthly newsletter.

Order your subscription today. Only $1.50 per month. We will mail your newsletter to you the first week of each month. Each newsletter will contain the real life stories of Cab10. It will contain all the wild adventures from the West Coast Cabbie weekly newspaper columns, jokes and other exciting facts. Join subscribers all over the US and several foreign countries that read the West Coast Cabbie monthly newsletter.

Name_____

Address _____

City _____ State _____ Zip _____

Phone(_____) _____

Subscription Options

3 months/ $5.00   ———
6 months/ $10.00   ———
12 months/ $18.00   ———
Total   ———

Mail your subscription order form with a money order or check to:
Cab10
P.O. Box 290
Arcata, CA 95518

Thank you for your order!

RIPLION

Dancing through the spiral

by

Barbara Gates Burwell

and

Betty Jean Wall

ISBN 978-1-4303-1882-8

Type Sb/Sc peculiar spiral galaxy NGC5364, in the
constellation Virgo, was imaged by the KPNO 4-meter
Mayall telescope in 1975, with permission from
NOAO/AURA/NSF/WIYN

"---at the still point, there the dance is,"

from "Burnt Norton," Eliot, T.S., 1943, *Four Quartets*, p.5, Harcourt, Brace and Co., N. Y.

CONTENTS

FOREWORD

RIPLION book came into being the fall of 1979.
Since that time we have continued to gain a wider
perspective of our lives. As we have evolved, so have
the writings in this book, for *RIPLION* book is an
opening to the universe through the earth, through us.

As physical beings, we talk about being grounded.
When we understand our connection with the earth and
know that the earth always supports us, then all that we
express can be from the center of us, supported through
the center of the earth. The earth, in turn, is a pathway to
the Universal Center to which we belong. *RIPLION*
book expresses the joy in this cosmic connection. This
book is to lift us up when we feel weighed down in
moments of separateness and to remind us of what we
already know we are: Cosmic Divine Beings.

RIPLION book is in three parts: The first part tells of
divine communication and the creation of the Riplion
Board. The Riplion Board is a gift from the Realms of
Light given to us in sacred trust as an instrument of
LOVE. When we have evolved to where we no longer
need such a spiritual lever "to open hearts to love" the
Riplion Board will have served its purpose.

The second part is devoted to "Declarations of Life."
The title for each declaration was received through the
Riplion Board. The writings themselves were spoken
out of our own awareness as co-creators with Godly
Mind. Along with these declarations we were inspired

to include quotes from the writings of other earth souls to enhance the divine expression we share with one another.

The third part is a collection of "Mullings" which Barbara was motivated to write after mulling over different ideas.

All human beings are ever unfolding.

WHY READ THIS BOOK?

The choices we make in the exercise of free will provide us with life "experience." How free is that will? How wise are the choices? On what ground do we stand? Where are we coming from? This book can help answer these questions.

RIPLION book is tuned into a dimension of Life beyond our three-dimensional physical life where Mind is free to create harmony, joy, and well-being. It is the dimension of consciousness called "inner knowing," an interior realm of spirit from where we receive inspiration. It is the dwelling place of intelligence. From there we take charge of our lives and know what choices are in our best interest.

This book, in spirit, is a "how-to" workbook. It offers guidelines on how to connect with this more aware state of Being. It clues in the reader to centers of "higher learning." Simply, in the reading of this book, spaces will open in your mind, allowing spiritual energy to flow in your direction ready to be claimed by your own creative aspirations. This book, acting as a stimulant to your desires, can help you activate "your own Inner Light."

Thus propelled by your intuitive imaginings, ardent listening, inspired ideas, glimpses of eternal truths, etc, your decision-making power becomes increasingly enlightened. Simultaneously, your sphere of influence enlarges, for light does not stand still.

Empowered by success, measured by the outcome of your choices, you begin to acknowledge your own validity. As you become aware of your virtues, you understand how to make wiser choices which makes you more aware of your true worth which, in turn, generates greater power to divine wiser choices. You are traveling an ever-rising spiral of Self-Discovery.

Life is the gaining of wisdom through the exercise of intelligent choices. Through experiences illuminated by wisdom you realize your way to become a fulfilled Human Being.

This book can help the process. The process works, and is work. Be patient with your self and proceed, mindful that forces of the universe are also working on your behalf. Above all, keep a lively sense of humor. Enjoy "The Work." As you build confidence in your ability to choose "The Righteous Path," you free your self from worldly distress and find your SELF dancing with delight on the heavenly Ground of Being.

THE DIVINE CONTENT

Whether we realize our divine connection and awaken to our true nature and purpose while we live on Planet Earth is up to us. In our search to see more clearly, many of us find useful ways to help our quest: meditation, prayer, yoga, visualizations, breathing and relaxation techniques, are some of the ways. Our desire is to learn more about the universe, who we are and why we are here, so that we can help to heal ourselves and the planet.

With this intent in mind, two sisters, Barbara and Dorothy, on November 6, 1973, used the Ouija Board for the first time. Here is the opening communication they received, given to them letter by letter:

"The inner ear

Visualizes

The Go with God

Giving with truth

Effect great thoughts

Every day

You came for GODLY MIND

CHRIST PSI ZEN"

Barbara and Dorothy were told that saying this prayer out loud at the opening of every session will always keep a person within the Divine Space of the Universe.

The prayer automatically attunes the participants with the beauty and love of the spiritual vibrations.

The following is their experience of communication with Godly Mind, as recorded by them:

During the first session they gave the name "Friendly Light" to the Light Being making contact. After several sessions they were given the understanding that Friendly Light manifests in the physical dimension of the earth plane as the North Star. In other words, the North Star is Friendly Light's physical manifestation. In fact, all physical reality, from stars and constellations to the stones under our feet, is manifestation of the consciousness of Divine Beings. From a universal view they called all these Light Beings "Infinite Intelligence."

This work has stretched their minds and hearts to the limits of their belief. Each session opened them to relationships beyond their wildest dreams and gave them information beyond their greatest imaginings. In awe, they thought of the opening of Psalm 19:

> "The heavens declare the glory of God and the firmament sheweth his handiwork. Day unto day uttereth speech and night unto night sheweth knowledge."

The messages received are directed to all of us on Earth, and invite personal contemplation. After some of the messages, we have made brief comments corresponding to our understanding of the communications.

As Christmas was coming in 1973, Friendly Light announced the good news with the message:

"Imagine

Christmas your mind

Meditate

Christ consciousness shall appear

Find your light with

Meditation

Creates mystical reunion"

In the quest for knowledge, the human mind has been constantly concerned with the question, "What is evil?" On November 11, 1973, the sisters asked Infinite Intelligence the same question. The reply:

"Your subconscious individualizes
cosmic power to please God
and in the process distorts good into evil."

We are to realize that evil is simply a distortion of good and has no essence of its own. It is we who give evil identity with our own individualized imagination as we exercise the Godly gift of free will.

The following day they received:

"Envision self realization

within motion of

Christ consciousness"

This message encourages us to continue unfolding
within the Divine Mind.

During a session on November 26, 1973, they asked
"Where do we come from?" They were told all human
beings come from conscious realms that manifest in our
universe as planets. It all seemed bewildering to them,
so during the same session Friendly Light said:

"Lighten your awareness
You are your load"

On December 3, 1973, Friendly Light spelled out the
word KISMIC, a new word for Barbara and Dorothy.
KISMIC means 'the relative' in relation to 'the absolute'
or COSMIC. They were told that the Little Dipper in
the heavens is the physical manifestation of KISMIC
consciousness (relative mind) while the Big Dipper is
the physical manifestation of COSMIC consciousness
(absolute mind). Thus, the Little Dipper and Big Dipper
are the KISMIC-COSMIC forms in the third
dimensional universe.

This information prepared them for the session the
next day, December 4, 1973, in which they received a

message from the Big Dipper consciousness itself! The message:

"Friendly Light is the day star of your being"

No wonder we steer our course by the North Star!

As we become aware of the love of Infinite Intelligence for each one of us, we will "OPEN HEARTS TO LOVE."

EVOLution of life is LOVE reflected. It is through consciousness that we empower the love force here on planet earth. As we raise our consciousness, the quality of consciousness shifts to a greater radiance and becomes more attuned to the Source of all power. Love is the immeasurable force that centers our vibrations to effect change. Love sets in motion the spheres, be they atoms, planets, solar systems, constellations, galaxies, or universes.

As doubt is a close companion of astonishment, Barbara and Dorothy began to question: "What is happening? Is this for real? Are we fantasizing? What's going on?" They stopped their next session the afternoon of December 6th, and said to whoever was listening that they needed a sign, a visible sign in order for to proceed. Within the hour as they went about their day, they noticed that clouds began to form out of a clear sky from one horizon to the other into seven rays arching overhead. Each of the seven rays was tinged with gold and silver light and permeated with the orange-pink of the setting sun. As the colors faded and the clouds disappeared, they rushed back to the Ouija Board and asked Friendly Light: "Was that your sign?" The answer was "YES." They proceeded. The next day the local newspapers had photos of this spectacular phenomenon (see Figure 1), without giving any satisfactory explanation.

Figure 1: Clouds formed into seven rays over Falmouth-Woods Hole on afternoon of Dec. 6, 1973, photo by Gordon E. Caldwell, published in Cape Cod Standard Times, Hyannis, MA 02601, Friday, December 7, 1973, photo permission granted from Cape Cod Times.

On December 16, 1973, Infinite Intelligence inspired this concept with the message:

"See your answer under the stars
Quark your mind"

Infinite Intelligence explained that "quark" is the love expression of the pure Godly Mind. The search for the "quark" is within the hearts of Human Beings.

In one session during the winter of 1974 when certain patterns of reply kept looping off the Ouija Board, in a jovial frame of mind they asked if Friendly Light wanted a larger board. The answer was an enthusiastic "YES!" Friendly Light commenced to give them detailed instructions: The kind of wood to use, size of board, design, etc., and insisted that they call the board RIPLION, a name meaningless to them at that time. And so the RIPLION BOARD was created. The shape and name of the planchette was also given: Arc Mutator (see Fig. 2).

Figure 2: Riplion Board with Arc Mutator in center

There are at present twenty-four Riplion Boards in existence. Whenever we ask if it is beneficial to humankind for us to go into greater production of the Riplion Board, the reply has been "No." Everything has its "good time."

On the reverse side of the Riplion Board are three prayers given to them by Friendly Light: "The Opening Prayer for Communication" (see page 11), "The Lord's Prayer for the Cosmic Mind," and "The Lord's Prayer for the Kismic Mind."

THE LORD'S PRAYER FOR THE COSMIC MIND

Our ETERNAL BEING
Thy Kingdom is becoming
Thy will be done together
Give us this day our daily WISDOM
Create in us the will to do Thy will
For therein is the KINGDOM and the POWER
and the GLORY forever and ever

THE LORD'S PRAYER FOR THE KISMIC MIND

Our ETERNAL BEING
Thy Kingdom is becoming
Thy will be done together here as it infinitely is
Give us this day our daily bread
So dwell in us that we may welcome each other
For as we open it will be opened unto us
Lead us out of ignorance into the
LIGHT OF KNOWING
For therein is the KINGDOM and the POWER
and the GLORY, forever and ever

On February 23, 1974, the following message came from a star consciousness in the Pleiades:

"Be! Our becoming being
Stars your hour"

The beauty of Being is that we are so bound together in evolution that my becoming affects your becoming and all together we are uplifted into greater realms of becoming. A new awareness trembles the whole earth, and the blade of grass smiles.

"For ye shall go out with joy and be led forth with peace, the mountains and the hills shall break forth before you into singing and all the trees of the field shall clap their hands." Isaiah 55: 11-12.

Each session on the Riplion Board is a meditation. It is a way to center on the inner Source allowing thought energy to spiral into an expression of awareness.

May 23, 1974:

"Center within

Let peace create"

June 7, 1974

"Strength is yours

Be aware

Quietude"

"Live as lightly as a songbird"

"ALL IS WELL"

Hopefully, we are consciously evolving so that some day the Riplion Board will no longer be a necessary tool for us in our learning. Until then we are using the Riplion Board to get to know ourselves and to reaffirm what we already envision through our "inner ear," i.e., "the Kingdom within." Many human beings can now tune into their inner knowing without the use of a tool such as the Riplion Board.

When the "Opening Prayer for Communication" was given to them in 1973, Barbara and Dorothy had little perception into its meaning. (It seems strange to visualize with an ear.) Now we know that when we are willing to listen to our "inner ear," then each of us will have the insight to visualize the "Go with God" and "effect great thoughts every day" – "The inner ear" is actually our sense of knowing. We "just know" by seeing with our "inner ear." The "inner ear" understands our true nature and purpose and knows what is appropriate and beneficial for all. The inner ear attunes us to universal truth shining through the Light of Knowing. Within that Light of Knowing our consciousness can effect great thoughts, which, in turn, is in tune with Godly Mind. We consciously can learn to act according to what we actually are:

COSMIC DIVINE BEINGS

Our divinity, however, is revealed through our daily living: "effect great thoughts every day." As we live each day, CHRIST, PSI, ZEN light the way in our DIVINE BECOMING.

Through the Riplion Board sessions, we have become aware of the multitude of Beings working in all dimensions to bring about peace and harmony on Planet Earth. We are beginning to perceive the magnificence of the universe to which we all belong. As participant in this universe, the more we live in harmony and love with all beings, the nearer we are to bringing about world peace and a healthy planet.

DECLARATIONS OF LIFE

The declarations of life are to help us realize that what we declare becomes reality for us. We can live each moment conscious of our wholeness, of our connection with all in the universe, or we can forget that we are divinely inspired as we focus on our daily activities.

We are often pulled down by the events we create, unaware that all is for our learning and growth, and, that from a wider perspective, "all is well." We live in a loving universe but can close ourselves off from that knowing. As we unfold into a collective consciousness that encompasses all of our creation we can use reminders of who we really are. The declarations act like tuning forks for well-being, for in the reading of them, an attunement to the joy, wisdom, and love of the universe takes place. From the horizon of our daily lives, these declarations can lift us up into the light of a higher view.

Infinite Intelligence spelled out the titles for these declarations through the Riplion Board. We were then asked to write whatever came to mind inspired by the declared titles. The quotes, interspersed, are other writings pertaining to the same themes which we were guided to include.

As you read, feel free to be where you desire to be and to enjoy who you really are.

BE CREATIVE POWER, BEAUTY AND LOVE

RIPLION - the soul-sound of the universe
Sound is empowered throughout the universe by THE WORD.
Declare the beauty of creation through sound, and life will be transformed into new life.
Connect all consciousness through sounding forth.

The Love of God

Trumpet the sound,
Hum it in your heart,
Know it in your mind,
Express it in your speech,
Shimmer the sound in sunlight,
Laser the sound to the darkest corner,
Be the sound.

Humankind is gifted with words.

Give word-gifts, for as we give we will receive.

Let all words fall with good intent on rich ground.

Send the sound of joyous words to the Universal Center to seed the joy waiting for expression.

Lift thought to the pinnacle of its highest potential.

Peaked with joy, our thoughts vibrate to form a circle of energy to be expressed in words.

Expression is the sound between thought and word.

Be kind in expression and the world will be a halo of light.

All sound is centered in the ONE VIBRANT NOW.

The pleasure is ours to sing sound in song.

GO TO HEALTH IN YOUR MIND

Be as you desire to be for being is the totality of your existence.

Do you desire to

See light?

Swirl in light?

Be light?

Know the balance of NOW?

Attune thought to spin your atoms according to the divine motion -

a constant spiral.

Be that divine spiral as you move through your existence.

Only you can be the expert of your experience.

You are unique. Your thumbprint is the outer expression of your personal self; your thought prints are the signature of your inner world. As your outer earth self attunes to your inner eternal SELF, a balanced vortex of healing energy radiates throughout the universe.

YOU are HEALING LIGHT.

Act with deepness, good intent, love, kindness, and you are bound to heal.

The healing light tunes all to oneness and so bonded together we dance the cosmic spiral in orbit with spirit.

Let your light shine on the face of the earth, for

"Something there is more immortal even than the stars." Whitman, Walt, 1861, "On the beach at night," *Leaves of Grass,* David McKay, Philadelphia, 1900.

GO TO LOVE

Love is the world - the world we live in.

Love is the heart of the matter.

Matter is the expression of love as we witness.

Divine your being, radiate love, and the darkness vanishes into its love-light.

Evil lives again within good intent and loses identity.

Goodness is Godness.

We manufacture our own gods, but we ourselves are created by the Oversoul God that vibrates love throughout infinity.

Recognize love vibrating within your soul.

Breathe the spark of love into a roaring flame.

"The sum of all love is the Great Principle, God. --- It is the Law that in Principle we live, move, and have our being." Spalding, Baird T., 1927, *Life and Teachings of the Masters of the Far East*, Vol. II, p.42-43, DeVorss & Co., Marina Del Rey, CA.

OPEN WILL TO LOVE

The willingness of the universe is waiting.

Open the door.

All will be as all beings are, true to the will of God.

Will you listen to that willingness within that delights?

Fill your will with laughter, love, and kindness.

Express that will within and the power of the universe is yours.

Work, move through love.

God is willing.

Heaven becomes and earth unfolds into heavenly becoming.

> "The year's at the spring
> And day's at the morn;
> Morning's at seven;
> The hillside's dew-pearled;
> The lark's on the wing;
> The snail's on the thorn;
> God's in his Heaven -
> All's right with the world!"
> Browning, Robert, 1841, "Song" from *Pippa Passes.*

LIVE YOUR LIFE TO LOVE – ENJOY

Joy is nearer than you think.

So do not think.

Imagine joy in color.

That is joy.

Imagine joy in the ocean wave.

That is joy.

Extend your joy to the tip of a star, and then swirl it around the tip of your little finger.

Play with joy.

See joy in the heart of all relationships.

Practice joy as you move.

Express joy with an airy smile.

Radiate joy with the look of the eye.

Praise joy and the tumult will echo with joyful sound.

It is fun to joy-ride the universe spiraling through space and then the true meaning of joy breaks into your consciousness.

You are the image of God.

Sing praise!

LIVE FAITH

Faith comes full blown.

Faith does not strive, is gentle, delicate.

Faith is the gift of our being, untouched by knowledge.

Without this gift humankind is lost to unfolding.

Faith is not ignorance, nor is ignorance faith.

Ignorance is a turning away from the light.

Faith is a moving toward the light.

Ignorance knows nothing beyond ignorance.

Faith acknowledges the beyondness of the infinite.

Faith is a process which yields to the Light of Knowing: the greater the knowing, the greater the faith.

Faith frees us from the bondage of the unrealized.

Faith spreads before us the excitement of the universe.

Follow your faith for it leads to greater gifts.

> "Faith is, above all, open-ness - an act of trust in the unknown." Watts, Alan, 1972, *The Book on the Taboo against knowing who you are*, p. 10, Vintage Books, NY, Random House.

WILL HONESTY TO WORK YOUR LIFE

Honesty is clean. Keep it polished. And in that shine let it reflect the openness in your heart. For honesty without love is brash and bristling. Only kindness can smooth honesty into rightful harmony.

Move your mind to love and your action will bring the divine to the discipline required. Action will be righteous and truth will expand into the deepest corners of darkness to create a brilliant masterpiece of light for all to witness

Nourish growth with honesty, gently.

The unknowing will discover knowing.

The lost will be found, the strayed will be pathed.

Bring back the wanderers with honesty.

Become disciples of truth.

The universe is impeccable.

WILL YOUR LIFE TO LIVE EASILY

Ease your life.

Round the corners and join the cosmic spiral dance.

Let it be simple.

There is no toil if you dwell in the center and allow.

All is open in that center where life dwells with all life.

It is easy to be.

We are born to be.

Accord yourself that right.

It just happens.

To strive makes life thick and opaque.

The quality of life is clarity.

You are a sparkling crystal.

Unpolished it appears lifeless.

All you need do is blow the stars of love, then shine your crystal with the smooth cloth of being.

Welcome ease.

> "To melt and be like a running brook that sings its melody to the night." Gibran, Kahlil, 1923, *The Prophet*, Alfred A. Knopf, NY.

GO TO LIVING WITH GOOD INTENT

Attend to your intentions.

They are intense with power.

What you intend lives.

The expression in events is the picture in your mind.

Watch carefully.

Intentions are self-fulfilling.

Though your outer consciousness may not be aware of their realization, all intentions find lodging.

Good intent is wholeness.

Without that goodness the dwellings are dark.

Light your intentions.

The good intent of the universe will respond in kind.

The Universal Vibration knows not darkness.

Unenlightened intentions are the works of stumbling humanity.

Remove the stones beneath your feet.

Strew the path with fragrant blossoms of good intent.

Smile through the universe.

The universe will smile back through you.

Live in wonder.

"in a way impossible to explain, the good intent of this atmospheric presence is such that any ill intent would dissolve within it, not to be annihilated, but transformed, automatically changed into its best expression; and at the same time I realize that destructiveness is simply the inadequate, or poorly realized expression of a good intent." Roberts, Jane, 1978, *The Afterdeath Journal of an American Philosopher, The world view of William James*, p. 168, Prentice Hall, NJ.

DO UNTO OTHERS AS GOD WOULD DO

God works in mysterious ways.

The mystery of relationships is hidden within the atom. The mystery of God is hidden within relationships.

Bring the mystery forth into the light and make it personal.

It is in the personal that we understand.

The God Force becomes personal through relationship. As the atom is "quarked" by love, so is the person.

"Quark," and God is doing. It is that simple.

The only reality we experience is through relationships. We are all related.

Be kind to your kindred.

Be kind to your self and you will be kind to others.

Start with the love of self and that love will spread throughout your own oneness to all oneness, and will shower into the life cells, bringing all cells of all selves together.

As God does, so do you.

> "and let us go on and on endlessly increasing our perception of the hidden powers that slumber, and the infinitesimally tiny ones that swarm about us, and the immensities that escape us because they appear to us simply as a point." De Chardin, Teilhard, 1961, *Hymn of the Universe*, p.79, Harper & Row, NY.

BE AWARE   GO TO WISDOM

How aware are we? Who knows? SELF knows, and we shout with joy at this knowledge. Without SELF our personality selves here on Planet Earth would scratch around blind and purposeless. To become aware of SELF is a challenge. Meet that challenge in whatever way. Start now and persist. For you are greater than you think.

Beginning the search for SELF, you will be relieved to find SELF right within you. Actually, you are the outermost expression of SELF. You are like a dew drop, a pendant at the end of a golden chain. You are fastened to that chain and always have been. That chain is a circle of SELF from which you have dropped into life experiences from generation to generation.

SELF is your best friend. For SELF opens you to the wisdom of the cosmos. Until you recognize this friendship, you will feel the isolation.

Move into awareness of SELF and you will realize your safety within the Godly order. Awareness lifts the darkness from your eyes and shows you the glory of your being. All is open to you. All you need do is simply recognize your own greatness. Why act small when you are great?

> "If I take the wings of the morning and dwell in the uttermost parts of the sea, even there thy hand shall lead me, and thy right hand shall hold me."
> Psalms 139: 9-10.

WISDOM IS LIVING

Wisdom creates.

The power of creation is within wisdom.

Without wisdom the void remains the void.

Dominate your thoughts with wisdom.

How do you know the wise choice?

Practice through experience.

Work with free choice.

Reflect on your actions.

Wisdom is earned.

There is no instant wisdom.

    The years roll by from life to life and your experience within that rolling creates a thin wisp of wisdom which is spun with gold and is your greatest treasure. Enrich that strand, plait it with your experience. Treat it with reverence and contemplation. Patterns of your daily choices design knowledge into wisdom - The divine wisdom of knowing.

Intelligence of Spirit permeates wisdom.

Wisdom is patient.

It grows straight, cannot be bent to self.

Self aligns with wisdom in order to follow the spiritual path.

Wisdom is generous and open to the grandeur of adventure, firm in principle, serious but not solemn.

Look carefully for the twinkle.

Without the twinkle, life would be heavy laden.

Be loyal to wisdom, in that loyalty you will win your reward.

> "Do you need proof of God? Does one light a torch to see the sun?"
>
> Oriental Wisdom

JOY PEACE LOVE

Joy, peace, love enfold your being,

Otherwise you cannot be.

Your existence would disintegrate without these forces.

They hymn your harmony and sing praise.

The perfectibility of your soul rides the waves of the sounds: joy, peace, love.

Let the sound waves surf onto the beach of your existence.

Let them inundate you with new sounds beyond, which refocus the particular, de-crystallize the hard, and float on the sea of spirit.

All knowledge will come forth as you swim that sea.

Joy, peace, love, this trio musicale concerts your life.

> "Ocean: ---by the light
>
> Of wave reflected flowers, and floating odours,
>
> And music soft, and mild, free, gentle voices.
>
> And sweetest music, such as spirits love.
>
> Apollo: ---I hear
>
> The small, clear, silver lute of the young spirit
>
> that sits i' the morning star."
>
> Shelley, Percy Bysshe, 1901, *Prometheus Unbound*, Act III, Scene 2, *The Complete Poetical Works,* Houghton Mifflin, NY.

LIGHT OF KNOWING

Divine Intelligence is Perfectly Present throughout all creation. On this plane of creation Humanity is central to the unfolding of that Perfect Presence. How do we unfold the Perfect Presence here on Planet Earth? Through conscious choice, the divine gift of free will. In other words, "the lifting of the veil," revealing the wondrous Oneness, relies upon our own activity of creative Mind as we experience life.

Time flows through us, moment by moment. As we look to each day, each one of us yearns deeply for Happiness. We are restless for fulfillment now. Some call it "finding a meaning in life," others call it "seeking God." When we come to the realization that ALL IS GOD manifesting the Divine Presence in ALL, the indwelling spirit of "the light of knowing" vitalizes our Being, and our lives become a joyful voyage of discovery.

Very few of us receive instant enlightenment. Most of us need "to labor in the vineyard" (Matthew 20). But as we open our hearts to share ourselves with others, together we become a radiant circle of living light, and we know that we are ever being fulfilled within the vibrant NOW of daily life.

"Let there be light, and there was light"

Genesis 1:3

"ALL IS WELL"

BARBARA'S MULLINGS

GOD: IMPERSONAL AND PERSONAL

ONENESS IN RELATIONSHIP early February 1981

Attunement: Initiated by us to understand ourselves and our oneness - brings at-one-ment. No longer out of balance, we join the great balancing act of the universe. When we are in dis-harmony (self-ish), the wholeness is disturbed. We are "missing the mark" (Greek definition of sin). The separated self is disconnected from the Godly Force and is the obstacle to the divine current; we short circuit the light into "darkness."

The "trick" is to so attune that the Godly Light can shine forth on planet earth through us as conductors.

The Great Rejoice, described in the Parables of the Prodigal Son and the finding of the lost lamb (Luke 15), is that that return has brought the universe back into balance. . Creative Energy can flow again in all its Glory.   (Those who cry of doomsday cut off the potential for return - if doomed, there is no salvation).

This yearning for wholeness is the propelling force of evolution: survival yes, but for what, in order to consciously return to perfection. Falling out of our God-given perfection (the Garden of Eden, Genesis 3) through our free choice "to have it our way," we can now consciously find "our way" HOME. The technique is the art of attunement.

And attunement implies relationship. Someone does the attuning and there is someone or something to attune to. Attunement also implies will and desire. – We do the desiring through conscious will.

Happiness is in the journey, not at the end of the road, the journey to become ONE (or PERFECT).

Any journey is relationship: going from place to place, going from lesser awareness to greater awareness toward the GREAT HARMONY. Take the first step, play the first note and you are on your way, to travel the universe composing your own symphony in harmony with the MUSIC OF THE SPHERES.

How do we start that first step or strike that first note, by doing a loving act. Love dissolves the obstacles blocking the way. Love is attunement, and attunement is love. As we attune to our "inner" relationship with our Self, we will attune to our "outer" relationships with our neighbors. GOD, LIGHT, LOVE is very much alive in our life.

As we "GO WITH GOD" we become increasingly conscious of our Godly State of Being. When in harmony, a chord is struck of greater richness and power than is achieved through a single note; a chord is a quantum jump behind the relationship of notes. It is its own Being.

The Japanese-Zen approach to wholeness is "Let go and let God," i.e. get oneself out of the way (self-less) so that the oneness can manifest. It is their approach to the Impersonal God, the void (the ineffable, the unspeakable).

When one is in harmony with ONENESS or when one is ONENESS, there is no separation and the LIGHT OF HEAVEN CAN SHINE THROUGH.

On the other hand (God has many "hands"), many of us are more "at home" with a personal God to whom we can relate. We personify "the void." The Ten Commandments (Exodus 20:2-17) would be useless if we were stranded alone on a desert island. They speak to relationship, the personification of the impersonal.

God is personal and impersonal. We personify God through attunement and at the same time, through attunement we are God through oneness.

"My Father and I are one."

CONSCIOUSNESS, SUPER CONSCIOUSNESS, SUB-CONSCIOUSNESS AND UNCONSCIOUSNESS
February 19, 1981

What is their common denominator? Awareness, the degree of awareness defines the various levels of consciousness (Analogous to brain-wave cycles which have been arbitrarily divided into Beta, Alpha, Theta & Delta). CONSCIOUSNESS: What we experience in the Now of the present moment as it relates to the past and to the future here on the three-dimensional level, includes feedback from our 5 senses. We cannot separate consciousness "out from life's experience," very simply, consciousness is what we are. The nature of each of us is subjective and relative - no two people measure exactly the same in regard to consciousness.

We are each unique therefore our experience is equally unique. And this consciousness forms our own reality - so each one of us lives in our own reality - through which we can recognize and relate to the realities of others. Although we use a common language to express our realities, "my joy is not the same as your joy" though we react in a similar manner to that feeling and the nature of our joy is of the same substance.

Consciousness is manifested intelligence.

SUB-CONSCIOUSNESS can be described as the level of suppression. What we filter out to forget stays at the sub-consciousness level. We are no longer conscious of that experience. The psychiatrist focuses on bringing back into memory these suppressed experiences and suppressed thoughts so they can be dealt with consciously. This level is full of emotions which have not been resolved and integrated into one's total life awareness.

The UNCONSCIOUS is the level of non-experience, we are not aware of what is happening there - if we were conscious of it, it would join our conscious experience. Many describe the unconscious level as the spiritual level - where the realities of facts exist - the unknown level. Belief in the unknown is the foundation of faith. Faith is a conscious understanding that there are areas of reality which we cannot measure nor experience - yet. Once we do experience the spiritual, then it is part of our conscious reality.

The SUPERCONSCIOUS is consciousness which includes the spiritual realm. One is consciously aware of the reality beyond the five senses. The yearning of the human species is to bring the super-conscious into consciousness so we can live in the LIGHT OF KNOWING.

This is an on-going process until we become ONE with "GOD" - and as God is Infinite, the process goes on infinitely. This is our purpose on planet Earth, to unfold our consciousness. As our soul evolves through millennia of experience, our consciousness unfolds to greater and greater awareness of the Godly nature of our BEING. There are those who equate consciousness with GOD.

Super-consciousness is Universal Mind - All-Knowing (Omniscient) = is the God Mind - we can experience Godly mind as we unfold our consciousness until we are God.

The salvation of the human spirit is that we each have a spark of the Godly mind within us. It is up to us to fan the flame into LIGHT. U.S. Anderson wrote a book called *Three Magic Words* (1972) - I AM GOD - We can get in touch with our "I AM" (some call it Higher Self). The Joy in recognition of our basic perfection (Godliness) is the urge which keeps us moving toward that PERFECTION. The Fall was a falling out of that Perfection (Garden of Eden) to which we are consciously returning - that is why we live in a dual world of love-hate, joy-pain, good-evil. Unless we can compare our present existence, feelings, etc. with something else, it has no meaning for us. We are now moving consciously from that dual world which we needed to jolt us into understanding. We needed a reality of contrasts to move our consciousness along "The Way," to relationship - everything is relative to everything else: AGE OF RELATIVITY. Physicists are now talking about reality as relationship. There are no things anymore - only interrelationship of energies which, when we form a relationship, appears as "things." From the Age of Relativity, we are coming into the Age of Oneness where reality is different aspects of the same ONENESS.

Oneness is expressed by Gibran: "What is evil? Evil is good tortured by its own hunger and thirst." There is no evil; it is good out of balance. There is no darkness; it is the absence of light.

The Old Testament experience is one of the wraths of God - the New Testament experience is of the love of God. The new age is built on the love of God of which wrath is love out of harmony.

In the past we have understood God as "He," image of the Father, existing at the astral level of consciousness which is non-tangible, above this earthly plane, yet is equally full of good and evil, positive and negative forces - creatures of our imagination.

We are now moving toward another level of consciousness -we will witness God no longer as a person, not even as Father-Mother God, but as revealed as a universal level of consciousness.

We will recognize "The Heavens," the stars in the sky as manifestations in our direction of the Godly MIND. "The Heavens declare the Glory of God and the

firmament showeth His handiwork. Day unto day ---"
(Psalm 19:1)

Calling God "Creative Energy, Supreme Intelligence, The Ground of all Being," does not meet the emotional needs of our present day consciousness. Even God as love, life, light is too abstract - our three dimensional world is one of relationships (Father, Son, and Holy Ghost) - and that is all well and good as we make the next quantum jump of consciousness into "Father-Mother, Son-Daughter, and Holy Spirit" - which will unfold into even greater awareness of God: our Eternal BEING.

BECOMING   February 20, 1981

We are made in the imagination of God. God is made in the imagination of man. As we become more aware, as we raise our consciousness (i.e. bring more of the unconscious into our consciousness), our image of God changes, and change implies time and motion from our point of view on planet Earth (a 3-dimensional reality). Thus we see everything as BECOMING, including God. All is evolving, including God. Actually what is evolving is our soul-selves, as our consciousness unfolds and our relationship to God becomes greater, God expands. The Perfection expands. It is the relationship that "becomes."

Deep within us we know that God is PERFECT, COMPLETE, WHOLE, ABSOLUTE, as we are when lifted into that Ultimate Dimension of Reality.

Evolution is involved in revealing the perfection. "Be ye perfect, as your Father in Heaven is perfect" (Matthew 5:48).

Our consciousness through the ages has encountered God at the astral plane, full of personified forms, both good and evil, human and inhuman, running the gamut of emotional expression: love, anger, compassion, jealousy, etc.

Our astral "bodies" are the blueprint for our material bodies. As above, so below. The "above" refers to the astral level for most of us.

There are those who have evolved beyond the astral to a higher dimension of consciousness where God has now become more universal. This has been expressed by those who have become world citizens, identified as ONE with God, no separation and in paradise.

The astronomers are looking for intelligent life on planets in other solar systems, in other galaxies and even perhaps, in other universes. Someday we may identify ourselves as citizens of the universe.

THE INSEPARABLE PART   February 25, 1981

Yes, that is you, each one known to each other as separate personalities with given names. Each of us is partial to our self and from the perspective of that self we reach out to relate to other individuals, i.e. in division we connect and weave a web of relationships.

And that is good. In our world of reality, we focus on "real things," to state our condition of perception we see objects of materiality and recognize the existence of the physical universe including our own bodies. Thus, the name of the game is how to relate all the objects into a meaningful mosaic. Each person creates his/her own mosaic, guided by culture patterns and inspired by intuitive thought. That is the outer image. However, we all know that we are not our bodies. We are not merely objects of materialization, but expressions of "something more" to state it vaguely. And if we are "more," then everyone else is more too. What is this "more-ness?" An attempt to answer that question has been the root of all religions.

We intuit that we are part of a greater part, which is part of a still greater part. From self to Self to SELF to the infinite "I AM" or God, Consciousness itself. But notice we still keep the "I." "I AM THAT I AM" (Exodus 3:14). Could we say we go from ego to Ego to infinite EGO? Beyond that there must be "the AM that AM," where God is no longer personified even as an impersonal SELF.

We are caught in a web of BEING, and BEING implies existence of something, and we are back to where we started.

Let us start from another perspective. Start with the Void, the non-being. The problem is we have to express through words, already limiting the ineffable.

"In the beginning was the Word---" (John 1:1). What does that mean? We have been told that God is eternal. If there is eternity, then there is no beginning. Even the word eternity implies time. Eternity is timeless, that seems to be the only way we can describe it. Round and round we go, be it Christopher Robin's mulberry bush or other bushes (Milne, A.A., 1926, *Winnie the Pooh,* Illustrations by Ernest H. Shephard, E. P. Dutton & Co., NY). In our awareness, the bushes get in the way!

If we start with where we "Are" in our awareness, the goal of our evolution is to become closer and closer to the Godly MIND, to become more God, to understand better the nature of God and to act according to that nature.

One way is through meditation: to get one's little personality mind out of the way and allow consciousness itself to be, remove the obstructions of personality, "to let go and let God" is the popular expression for this approach. Usually we can only clear the channel to the astral realm and what comes through are images from the astral plane, be they Godly images or any other kind of images. *The Tibetan Book of the Dead* (1957, Oxford University Press) is dealing with consciousness at the astral plane. So is Job in his imagery of God. We see God "astrally," and the so-called enlightenment is astral plane enlightenment where we become "One" with our inseparable part at that level. Light shines on the astral as we are illuminated at that level of awareness. This is where God is personified, Father imagery, visions of the Virgin and Christ are visions of the Godly essence personified.

Our awareness determines the Way and we can become ONE with God at whatever level of awareness we know to be the truth for us.

We must always keep in mind though that it is a relative truth. The Absolute Truth can only be seen from one relative plane to the next, and each plane has its own nature of illumination.

And to reason we can become ONE at any plane of reality is because we are an inseparable part of the infinite wholeness. We go from completeness at one level of understanding to completeness at another level of understanding, from a oneness at one level to a oneness at another level. Is there a final ONENESS? That is unanswerable because at the level of awareness of most of us, the answer can only come from the astral plane.

Like in quantum physics, we can view awareness as a spiral staircase, with steps, not as a gradual incline or gradual revelation. Revelation comes in leaps, steps up, not slides up.

We go to perfect awareness from level to level, go from perfection to perfection. We perfect our understanding of God, by becoming One with God at each level until we come to GREAT PERFECTION, whatever that is. Then perhaps we have finished with the cosmic universe and go into a whole different universe of awareness.

BE UNASSAILABLE!   March 5, 1981

Do not let things get to you in such a way as to assail your being. Of course, if you do not know your BEING, then you are vulnerable to all sorts of "---slings and arrows of outrageous fortune---" (Shakespeare, Hamlet, Act III).

A clue to understanding who you are is to take a look at your fears. Fears are the expression of doubt about your Self. They worm their way into the nooks and crannies of your person opening up greater cracks in your condition. What is your condition right now? What is your greatest fear? What is a "little fear" you have to face today? Is anyone threatening you? A person without fear does not even recognize a threat, for no threat exists.

It is a great honor to be in the presence of a fearless person, they are very rare. Those who come to mind are Socrates, Jesus, St. Francis, Lincoln, name your own. I have decided fearlessness has to do with absolute integrity. You do not have to know much or even have a strong faith. Sometimes I have noticed that those who profess to have a strong faith are very fearful. Their faith is built on fear, not love. Ask them to give up their faith, and they would panic.

And you can not have integrity unless you do know and understand yourself. You have made a firm commitment of honesty to your Inner BEING; a relationship exists that is built on a mutual conscience which is inviolate. You are One and the same.

The result is that your actions on planet Earth find their source in your Soul-Self - your personal EGO is so attuned to Soul-Self (Ego does not step aside, it disappears in its attunement - impossible to separate out, cannot distinguish it, but does not mean it is extinguished). And your "Higher" Self has nothing to fear because it is vibrating at an entirely different level of frequency - does not tune into the "lower" vibrations of earth plane. (Just like a radio - tune in to a certain frequency, and it is undisturbed by the other frequencies.) Be a clear frequency - as Don Juan said: "Be impeccable,"(Castaneda, Carlos, 1968, *The Teachings of Don Juan: A Yaqui Way of Knowledge*, Pocket Books, Simon & Schuster, Inc., NY) then you are the truth and the truth will set you free.

THE TWO-LANE HIGHWAY (no stop sign) March 6, 1981

PRAYER	and	MEDITATION
Asking		Allowing
Relative (Kismic)		Oneness, Universal (Cosmic)
Focusing		Expanding
Outreach		In reach
"Little Self"		"Big Self"
Personal		Impersonal
Third plane consciousness		Cosmic Consciousness
Aspiration		Inspiration
Conception		Perception
Change		Accepting
Lack		Abundance
Tuning in		Tuning up
Words		Symbols
Attachment		Detachment
Time & Space		Timeless-Space-less
Desire		Inquire
Out-going action		In-coming
Project-ing		Introspect-ing
The Conscious		The Super-conscious
Hope (Future)		Being (Now)

AWARENESS: What is really happening is that as our awareness unfolds, we experience God in different aspects or as manifesting at different levels. And right now we are beginning to go beyond the astral awareness.

"Good intent" is the force that increases our awareness.   Jose Silva's Mind Control "password:" "if it is beneficial to mankind," whatever you project in your thought has to be beneficial to mankind in order for it to manifest (Silva, Jose, 1977, *The Silva Mind Control Method*, Pocket Books, Simon & Schuster, Inc., NY). Your "good intent" overrules or bypasses the reactivity of the astral as does LOVE now.

The battle of LOVE & HATE at the astral is over. The Angels of LIGHT have won. Lucifer has been freed, and man's awareness is now on the "upswing" toward Heaven. Hell has no power and dies as more people become aware. At present many of us still see God only in the astral aspect of God.

Jesus' God also dwelt at the astral, but he portrayed the positive aspects which also "live" at the astral plane, LOVE as personified by angels, positive as symbolized by the "Father," masculine, full of strength.

We realize that all is GOOD! Gibran realized this aspect of God, so did William James (at least after his death. See: Roberts, Jane, 1978, *The Afterdeath Journal of and American Philosopher, the world view of William James*). We live in a universe of Good Intent., a caring, friendly universe.

"WHAT IS EVIL, BUT GOOD TORTURED BY ITS OWN HUNGER AND THIRST" (Gibran). March 8, 1981

God manifests as good in our three-dimensional world, and "evil" is tortured life, i.e. disturbed and out of harmony or life going "backward;" turning around back to the good, EVIL becomes LIVE.

And who does the turning? We do, the persons caught in our own fears, emotions and unhappiness. Our souls are reflections of the Light. Our "souls" are happy and full of "fiery enthusiasm" (Strong, Mary, ed., 1948, *Letters of the Scattered Brotherhood*, p.75, Harper & Row, NY). We as personalities, are inherently particles of that Light, but through our own free will take the torturous path full of boulders and scraps causing us to stumble and stagger. The shadows fall on our Light and we think we are in darkness; the cracked branch over our heads turns into a venomous snake in that darkness; and for us in that state the experience is reality. Not until daylight comes or unless we know the branch personally and see its own beauty, regardless of the circumstances, do we rest our fears.

There is no darkness; only for us seeing is there less Light. Our eyes can only focus on a small spectrum of Light, outside that framework, it appears dark to us.

But what about the animals and birds who can see in the night? It is only our own reference points that give the aspect of darkness.

Yes, evil takes on a force of its own, and we feed that force with our fears and imagination. The force becomes stronger and evil appears more and more a reality, we force feed it. Take away from it foods of fear and it will starve to nothingness.

The fear in our culture and myths create the evil, and yes, then evil becomes real for our third-plane consciousness, at the fear level of vibration. But were we to dwell exclusively in fearless higher vibration, all its food would disappear and evil would be eliminated.

GOOD FRIDAY   March 9, 1981

Why good? The Christian church sees that day as supreme suffering (Matthew 27) - we bring all our burdens to Christ on that day - we feel so guilty and so in need of repentance - can we even atone for our sins? Lord, Lord, have mercy on us! We, "the Great Betrayer" - oh, yes. It is a relief to put the blame on Judas (Matthew 26); he carries all our guilt for us. Thank goodness for Judas. He is really our hero.

Christ, on Good Friday, is trying to draw our suffering out from us - cleanse us of that concept of sin. He is saying: "Don't you SEE? Why do you forsake me in the moment of Glory? You lay all the suffering on me, when laying down my body is nothing. I'm suffering because you want me to suffer. My suffering has nothing to do with the suffering you are talking about. I suffer and weep because of your lack of insight." He wept at the tomb of Lazarus (John 11) for the same reason - not because he felt compassion for Martha and Mary in their mourning, but because they had so little faith - he wept because they, after all his teachings, did not see the LIGHT.

And so Christ "suffered" on Good Friday because "his people were so limited in their vision." All the moaning and groaning were not for him. They could only see a narrow band of Earth's truth - death of the body. He knew that his BEING, expressed as SOUL on earth, was inviolate, only the expression of soul experiences in the third-dimension of awareness was ending. The load of earth plane life was being lifted. "Come to me, ye who are heavy laden, and I will give you rest." The people's limited awareness was the load weight holding them in darkness. As the Riplion Board message says: "Lighten your awareness, you are your load."

The more limited your view, the greater your suffering. Suffering has to do with limitation. There is NO SUFFERING, only your viewpoint binds you to that role. Spring free from your prison. Live according to the wider view of your SELF where your natural condition is one of joy and exultation.

BEING   March 9, 1981

Being means existing now. Notice the "ings," that means action. It is in the expressing that we live. It is in the singing that a song comes alive; it is in the doing that thought becomes real. We cannot sit on the thought of a chair. It is in the making of the chair that we appreciate the chair. God is our Maker; it is the making of each of us that we are on planet Earth.

So to be a BEING, we need to act. The personification of BEING is expressed in action. A beautiful BEING brings beauty to life. A happy BEING brings happiness.

EVOLVING FROM 3rd PLANE CONSCIOUSNESS TO UNIVERSAL CONSCIOUSNESS:

3rd Plane Consciousness	Universal Consciousness
god	GOD
self	SELF
personal	impersonal
self-limiting	unlimited
in time	timeless
a-part (particle)	whole
incomplete	complete
finite	infinite
imperfect	perfect
unconscious	conscious
focused	everywhere
crystallized	unbounded
material	spiritual
manifest	manifold
scarcity (lack)	abundance
measurable	immeasurable
described	indescribable
human	divine
now	IS
evolution	involution
form	formless
earth	heaven

terrestrial	celestial
division	vision
presence	essence
diversity (the many)	unity (the one)
identity	entity
disease	ease
doing	being
becoming	coming of Christ

DIVINE SOUND   March 13, 1981

"The Inner ear visualizes The Go with God." i.e. the inner ear "sees" (is aware of, is tuned in, resonates with) the TRUTH. The inner ear is part of the inner being or soul-SELF and thus, in touch with the Divine within. As the inner ear "hears" the Divine sounds, it visualizes (makes visual) those Divine sounds through the mind's inner eye or imagination. These Divine sounds translate into symbols which we see in meditation. Meditation is a way for bringing the Divine into our experience.

The transformation of the Divine sound seen by the inner ear produces imaginative pictures according to individual energy patterns. One's own unique energy field (aura) will determine the imagery or symbols one receives. My imagery will be different from your imagery. Both will be the expression of the same Divine sound. The imagery we create is the result of the interaction of a divine vibration with our personal vibration. What we "hear" with our inner ear is what we "see" with our inner eye which is the experience we have through our Mind's eye. One might say that Mind is a mental expression of our inner Being.

And the quality of our mind will determine the quality of our outer body, we are expressions of Mind.

So, Divine sound, an aspect of Divine Mind, comes through according to our individual Mind patterns.

We have thoughts, and our thoughts are determined by how aware we are - what level of Divine consciousness we have unfolded in our being.

Life is Divine energy, how we live our lives is the

expression of Divine energy manifesting at the level of Divine consciousness that we are aware of, our on-going process of revelation.

THE NOBLE CONCEPT   March 15, 1981

One may artfully say: Powered/ "quarked" by LOVE, energy becomes a wave through the process of TIME to form a particle in SPACE empowering/ "charming" MIND.

These four forces LOVE, TIME, SPACE, and MIND, are manifested physically as FIRE, WATER, EARTH, and AIR in the world of Nature. And Nature's laws - our physical universe, are the interplay of these four forces, and their effect on ENERGY.

What is energy? Energy is intelligent Spirit in motion and manifests in a myriad of ways, or one might say "waves" because how it manifests depends on its frequency or vibration at any given moment. At one wavelength it will manifest one way, at another wavelength it will manifest another way. This is mathematically expressed by $E = MC^2$ (Einstein). At a particular frequency, or rather band of frequencies, spirit manifests as matter (fire, earth, water, air), or what we call our three-dimensional physical universe. At the etheric dimensional universe it manifests as "LOVE, TIME, SPACE, and MIND."

Using the language of Spirit, one can identify LOVE with the CHRIST, TIME with DIVINE RELATIONSHIP, SPACE with the COSMIC, and MIND with ONENESS (as expressed in the Trinity).

Energy is always moving - and, for our understanding, motion implies TIME and SPACE. To move means crossing a certain space in a certain length of time, i.e. frequency. However, whatever moves changes its quality in that motion. MOTION is a process. Nothing in motion remains the same - we live in a dynamic universe continually in change - a world of action. In the physical realm, fire acts to heat, water acts to cool, earth acts to "form," and air acts to "evolve."

The actions at the etheric level are comparable. Love acts to heat, time acts to cool, space acts to form, and mind acts to evolve. Or to say it another way, it is the energy of these four forces which causes the heating (expanding), cooling (contracting), forming, evolving.

"Spaced" energy is formed (or manifested physical) energy. "Timed" energy is processed energy.

So far the scientists have seen energy both as a wave (timed energy) and as a particle (spaced formed energy). It is more difficult to see energy as "LOVED" or as "MINDED." Though it is recognized that the experimenter is a participator in the experiment, he/she is part of the experiment and influences the experiment. Physicists may come across the manifestation of "LOVING" as they have already identified the manifestation of "TIMING" (i.e. wave) and manifestation of "SPACING" (i.e. particle). The manifestation of "MINDING" may one day be measured. Thought is "minded" energy and one day may be measured. And LOVE is certainly an energy force.

It is very exciting to read that physicists no longer talk about "things" as reality, but as the relationship as the reality, it is the relationship that matters (or manifests).

LOVE "quarks" - fire

TIME processes - water

SPACE forms – earth

MIND "charms" - air

The motion of energy determined by these 4 forces creates a pattern or energy field.

THE CONSCIOUSNESS REVOLUTION   May 8, 1981

Awareness opens the gate to Being. As perfect Beings we are totally aware. We cannot isolate Beingness from awareness. Knowing this, we can walk through the gate to the welcome of who we really are - the name of the game is SELF-realization and the ground rules could not be simpler - use awareness to become REALIZED – "that's for real."

The problem is we give so many reasons why we do not know how to play the game. Why do we feel so fragmented? - So cut-off from our completeness? The answer is lack of awareness. The first step is to be aware that we are perfect. How many of us believe that?

We see ourselves as separate, individual, "an island unto myself." By so doing we do not see ourselves as part of a greater whole. Our awareness rests with our separateness. That attitude is the barrier that interferes with our wholeness, and we see that our individual selves are far from perfect.

We strive to make our "little personality selves" greater, what a struggle! If one can visualize oneself as that greater Being of which one is a part, then the scene shifts and conceptually one can breathe a sigh of relief and say "of myself I am nothing," I'm really not here. What is here is an expression of one aspect, a part related to a greater whole and that wholeness is wholly conscious and therefore, in charge.

Our problem is that we are so focused on "me-ingness" that we cannot see the "Thou-ingness" of ourselves.

We are afraid that if we lose that focus and turn our minds elsewhere we will lose our identity, what are we afraid of? Loss of ego. It is an act of faith to be willing to experience the loss of ego. But the beauty of letting go is that "the nothing" we fear turns out to be everything we desire! Christ said "those who are willing to lose their life will find it" (Mark 8:35).

Of course we want to lose ourselves, if we come to that point, but "our" way. We want to be in charge of "the losing." Don't we bring up our children to be independent? "I'll do it myself" is what we instill in our children.

How much wiser it would be to allow someone wiser than ourselves to guide us. All we need do is give permission to allow it to happen. We have clothed ourselves in our own ego-belief. We need to take off "our clothes" as Peter, the disciple did, and jump overboard (Matthew 14:28-31). Do we dare see if we can "walk on water?" We are so concerned about blowing our own horn we cannot hear the angel's trumpet.

Yes, we get discouraged in our lives - at least most of us do. We do not seem to be getting anywhere. How does one become courageous? The greater the belief in SELF, the greater the courage. Actually, courage is in the "eye of the beholder." If one holds a strong belief about anything, it does not take courage to act on it. It looks courageous to the person who does not hold that same belief. What is courageous to one person is not to another.

The glory of humankind is its awareness. We know that we know. We recognize ourselves as conscious: self-recognition. We all manifest in our dimension of reality as material three-dimensional form. That is the milieu of our Earth-bound awareness. As we have evolved we reached a stage in physical body-brain development to a point of enlightenment where we became SELF-conscious and know that there is an overall guiding SELF in charge of our physical bodies, a

SELF greater than the sum of its parts. This process of SELF-realization moves in quantum jumps, from atom consciousness, cell, molecule, organ, body, species, planetary, star, solar systems, constellations, galaxies, universes. At the planetary level, there is an overall consciousness, "Mother Earth" of which the earth is the body.

All planets are the manifestations in our reality of conscious beings. The same can be said for solar systems, constellations, galaxies, universes. All these conscious beings recognize each other.

We are each consciousness itself and are each a conscious being, influencing one another.

MULLING TO SELF   May 24, 1981

"Strike your own true tone!" That's what Seth says (Roberts, Jane, 1977, *Unknown Realities,* Vol. 1, Prentice Hall, NJ). If the realities are "unknown," what's the point? Unless you can tune in to your "unknown realities," and make them known, how can you "strike your own true tone?" I find it discouraging.

One thing for sure, I know I'm "bogged down" in my physical reality, my wrist has been hurting for six months, I've got a pile of weeding, etc. to do in the garden, I'm out -of- sorts with my husband, I resent being interrupted to cook meals, I'm already fed up with planning for my Mother's 90th birthday and it's still a month away. If I knew my "unknown realities" would I have as many complaints? "Live as lightly as a songbird" says "Friendly Light." La-di-da!

CLEAN UP THE UNIVERSE   May 27, 1981

I am beginning to wonder if "little ole me" has a good deal more power than I ever even dreamed of. I have "heard" that if I raise my arm, the whole universe changes. I can "buy" that: all is in constant motion and a blink of the eye obviously has some impact, because the blink is part of the motion. Physical motion makes sense to me, but what about psychic motion? Does my tiniest wispiest thought also change the universe? Is my mind charged with a universal energy that I am in charge of? If so, I must be very thoughtful about what 1 think! We tend to laugh when we hear the admonition "be careful what you wish, because it may come true somewhere!" After reading Jane Robert's *Unknown Reality* (Vol. 1, 1977, Vol. 2, 1979, Prentice-Hall, NJ), I am beginning to think carefully (I like that word "carefully," we need to fully care about "all that is"). Does whatever I think, whether I act on it or not "have a life" of its own? Do all my thoughts affect me and others? I find the idea mind-blowing!

And what about this concept: the quality of my thoughts manifest "concretely" in the universe, for example, affecting "stars," the more positive and "light-bearing" my thought is, the brighter the star shines. Maybe a negative or "dark" thought is diminishing to me or someone or something.

The stars in our heavens are physical manifestations of Conscious Beings. It is the way conscious-entities create an expression of themselves according to third-plane-three dimensional world. That really is not such a far-out idea. Before we create physical things, such as chairs, automobiles, doorknobs, etc., we have the idea first, they are created by our thoughts, so why not the creation of stars by star-conscious Beings? Actually a better analogy would be the creation of our physical bodies by our Mind-Being. We are bodily what we think. The stars are bodily what star-conscious Beings think.

So let us think LOVE and LIGHT and all worlds will shine, shine, shine!

"THE SPACIOUS NOW"   May 20, 1981

Seth in *Unknown Reality* speaks of the spacious present which has durability, I like that.

One can get so hung-up on the meaning of "The Now," it can be an infinitely small "piece of time." Theoretically, one can keep dividing it in one's mind ad infinitum. Space is compatible to the same theory of infinite division, as is physical matter. But what is the point of all that? Where does it get one? What does it solve? One cannot practically live in the infinite instant. But ah! "the spacious moment," that has meaning and momentum for me! It can be all inclusive of past, present, and future if one is elevated enough to comprehend. The common analogy is of standing on the top of a mountain and looking down a roadbed seeing a car pass from its past into its present and able to see into the future as one's eyes follow it. Actually within that heightened vision one can see where the car has been, where it is any instant, and where it is going all at once.

One can take the present NOW and give it "durability" and "space" by viewing one's current awareness of experience in a wider context, a context that includes one's past, present, and future.

Christ said "take no heed of the morrow, --- sufficient unto the day---" (Matthew 6:34). "The earth is the Lord's, and the fullness thereof---" (Psalm 24:1). That used to make my practical self feel very impatient. If I do not plan for the morrow, when it becomes today it would be a mess. I resented that admonition, for in order for "my life" to be productive and "run smoothly" I spent a lot of energy planning for the morrow.

What I believe Christ was saying was to see "life" within the context of "the spacious moment," rise above and see the fullness of the moment, be totally present in the situation no matter what it looks like, allow oneself to relax, to just BE.

Linear time is piecemeal and short of sight. Vertical time is complete, has depth, and is full of insight. Focus up like a fountain, not down.

And then move a step "higher" and see one's present life charged with one's past lives and future lives - all is part of the Eternal Now, infinite space of all BEING.

LOVE, LOVE, LOVE! June 5, 1981

Be a messenger of love! Open hearts to love! We love you!

Love Is the "Ground of All Being," the ineffable substance, the context of Life according to the "view from the Riplion Board." It seems to be "all there is."

What is this "thing" called love? I have an uneasy time with the word. Why? Is it because our culture focuses so on physical love, which can bring us much sadness, tragedy, and violence, as it can bring joy, happiness and peace here on planet Earth?

It is difficult for us to disengage ourselves from the sexual aspect of love, nor do we want to. Do animals comprehend love beyond the needs of physical mating? Are swans monogamous because of an understanding different from polygamous birds? Is love merely an appetite, like the need for a hamburger? We "hunger and thirst," but is it "after righteousness?"

I take it for granted that most of us realize there is a difference between the love that Christ is talking about and the love that is "researched" in human behavior, both speak of joy as the counterpart to love however.

So what do I think? If Christ talks about "loving your enemy," then I know he is not talking about the love between one person and another person. Personal love can be a fragmentary expression of Christ's love, but it certainly is not "the real thing."

So let's leave personal love within its own framework and mull over Christ's Love. First of all, I understand that it has no conditions, unconditional love has no prejudice, no discriminating criticism, is all encompassing: murderers, enemies, dictators, etc.

So, Christ must be talking about a Love that speaks

to the Soul of Humankind, to one's "higher self," one's Perfect Being. We are all perfect at the level of Christ consciousness.

Also, at that level we have reached "oneness with God," we are all one. So of course you love "your enemy," because the enemy is you? The individual self is like a cell of a greater body, "the temple of the Lord," and as "God" is in charge of that greater temple, we are part of the temple. We may be an individualized part; we are not apart. We are ordained with "free will" to say "No" to that greater temple, but implied within the "No" is a resounding "Yes." We cannot escape our godliness. Every "No" is merely an obstacle, a boulder, blocking our godliness. Roll away the stones from your tomb (where you lie dead) and all is life, love, and light! It does not become life, love and light, it already is!

The Love Christ is talking about is our birthright, that is where we are and who we are. If the "little self" can attune to the "greater SELF," then all is in harmony, balance; integration brings oneness. We are righteous, impeccable, true to God-form. The path has been cleared (by our consciousness-will) of all its stones on which we stumble and falter. And we have instantly reached the summit. The view is glorious from the top of the mountain.

But, what is the purpose then of being born again and again on planet earth, stumbling along through evolution, becoming. I have a poster that says "Happiness is found along the way, not at the end of the road" (Updeglaff). That is the point of choosing life on planet Earth, to see if we can "make it to the top of the mountain," in spite of the obstacles. Otherwise, there is no point in choosing life here in the three-dimensional earth plane.

So the "name of the game" here on Earth planet is to overcome the obstacle course: make end runs, kick the boulder out of the way, pick them up tenderly and throw them away, climb over them any way that is best for you in order to reach the top, your awareness will tell you how. And there are as many ways as there are people living on planet Earth.

To help yourself, use your vision, stand at the top (where your SELF is) and watch your Self climbing - view your Self as you make your way - encourage your Self, stretch out your hand, send light to your little Self, and above all, LOVE your Self.

"ACCEPT THE SITUATION AS PERFECT FOR WHAT YOU NEED TO LEARN." June 11, 1981

How many of us really believe that? Most of us would reply "few and far between." We say: what a "Pollyanna" statement in the face of the tragedies, "grim realities," and nonsensical happenings of life. And yet, if we can believe that statement, how much more joyous would be our lives, because then we would see life as an opportunity rather than as an oppressive necessity.

Musing over that statement from "Infinite Intelligence" I can see that believing it would make me infinitely intelligent! Life would have meaning, and could lead me, ever alert, into greater understanding of people and places. I must say it takes a great leap for me to believe that the famine in Somalia is "perfect" for the people who live there. And we all need to learn not to ravish the land and each other.

I have decided that we do create our own reality and thus are responsible for whatever situation we are in, to an extent. Am I equivocating? Am I making exceptions? When a drunken driver crashes into me and I end up in the hospital, is it my fault? Am I responsible? Well, I did decide to go driving on the highway that day at that time. Actually, what makes more sense to me is that I am responsible for the response I have to the accident. I can say "Now I can read Tolstoy's *War and Peace* (1865-69) which I have always wanted to read and never taken the time to do, or I can bemoan my fate and rail at the drunk. I can wonder why the driver of the other car was drunk and ran into me, or I can wish the driver a long jail sentence "to teach a lesson."

Each event is perfect for what we need to learn. The secret is to find the perfect response. And what is that?

Each of us must find that alone. No one else can tell us. And when we do find it, we will know.

BE A SERVANT OF THE "THE LORD," WHAT DOES THAT MEAN? June 12, 1981

Servants are not supposed to think for themselves. They are just "door mats" hiding their own light under a bushel. That is not what "the Lord" had in mind! To be a "true" servant one must be a self-realized Being, because unless one is fully-aware one cannot be the perfect servant. One needs to be perfect (fulfilled) if one is to be the ultimate servant.

"The Lord" has been interpreted as "the law" in the minds of some. Most of us think or imagine "the Lord" as a personified Being. The Lord is the Loved one, the ONE who loves us. Can "the Lord" be impersonalized: the Law? Sure, because the LAW of the universe is LOVE! LOVE is the strongest force in the world! LOVE, and you are all powerful.

We live in a physical world of emotional attachments, so the idea of the Lord being "supreme Intelligence" or "first cause" or the "cosmic current" or "profound substance" or whatever, leaves me cold. To warm us up we need the strength of personal relationship.

That is why we like to think of ourselves as servants to the Master. It is an effective way of saying "we are nothing, the Lord is everything." It puts us in our place. But, our place is "at the Right Hand of God" (Luke 22:69). That is where we belong! It is our rightful righteous birth right! Glory hallelujah! What a spot to be in! Why grovel on the ground when one's seat of honor is beside the Lord God?

Mankind has freely chosen to separate self from SELF, leaving the throne of SELF-BEING empty. Now mankind, through self-realization, is free to choose to occupy that throne! Only will one BE "the true servant of the Lord" when one becomes enthroned. So, fill the empty seat with LOVE, for through LOVE we claim our royal heritage.

COINCIDENCE   June 26, 1981

We tend to be so dense about coincidence. There are a myriad of "coincidences" which happen in our daily lives which we ignore. It is only the large coincidences which capture our attention. We are truly living in the cosmic flow but we interrupt that flow with our stores of emotion, prejudice, ignorance, and down-right ornery-ness (when flow of self is like a bottle-stopper - nothing can flow out or in).

So, the first step is to be alert to "the coincidences" that happen all the time, and like a rolling snowball, more and more "coincidences" will accumulate in your everyday life. By just being aware, the blockage melts away, and there you are, standing in the flow!

You see, coincidences are merely points of meeting which pierce into our reality - all meet in oneness within the godly mind - and coincidences are merely intermittent points of oneness exposed to earth plane consciousness. We are all grounded in Being, it is our individual egos which supposedly disconnect us one from another - when "coincidences" happen, they are expressions of that oneness which cannot separate us or our experience one from another. Why we so delight in coincidences is that what we think to be separate phenomena suddenly coincide and we recognize for a moment the unity and belonging, our true nature. It is the togetherness which gives us joy.

All is so intricately interwoven within the cosmic flow of which we are a part that we cannot extricate ourselves (though we may think we can). So to stay in the flow, count the number of "coincidences" that happen to you everyday, and you will be amazed at how often they happen - until finally you will realize that Life itself is a "coincidence" - that all coincides with all.

WHO IS WRITING THE SCRIPT?   June 30, 1981

Driving to a wedding last week I was following a car with the sticker: "Just for the record, God is writing the script."

It really got my attention. Thank God, my car sticker as I drive through life with all the traffic, noise and pollution, is not that. But what is it? "Just for the record, God loves you?" or "Just for the record, laugh?" or any one of the "sayings" that have come through the Riplion Board, such as "Lighten your awareness, you are your load." Actually the "Just for the record, God is writing the script" is perfectly true. It is my interpretation of it that is the "burden" - because I imagine the people in that car as structured with moral attitudes - they see God "in my mind" as a great white father sitting in Judgment and writing out sentences for each soul. But maybe, just maybe, that is not the way the car occupants look at God at all! If God is LOVE, then one can say "Love is writing the script" - and I am all for that, or as we are each a spark of Godly substance, one can say "I AM writing the script." I am for that too. I AM THAT I AM.

So I guess I will back away from my original judgment on the car people - in fact, maybe I will put the same sticker on my car and see what kind of reaction I get from my fellow travelers.

I AM PERFECT July 6, 1981

Check One: #1 ▢ I AM PERFECT
#2 ▢ I AM IMPERFECT

I bet you checked #2! But the directions are to check One! So you did not follow directions and checked two! So you must be imperfect (or followed your own negative interpretation of the directions. So round we go in a dizziness of confusion as to our state of being.

Our "fall" from the Garden of Eden has been so ingrained into our conditioned self that we flow on all the dents (sin so-called) in our Being. We need to take a big sledge hammer and un-dent ourselves! Or maybe we can do it through LOVE, or maybe we can just change our focus! The dents have been made in the perfect body. It is not that the perfect body has been made out of the dents.

One has to start somewhere, and I am going to start with the Perfection. "Be ye perfect as your Father in Heaven is perfect." Just BE perfect! Believe in the abundance (those who have, more will be given unto them). Believe in Health, Be Health - and concentrate on the harmony and balance of life accorded us through Divine Righteousness.

One can beat one's chest and feel a "miserable sinner" pleading for atone-ment and redemption - or one can thank God for the Divine Spark which automatically makes an at-one-ment with God, our Divine Heritage.

Concentrate on your Divinity –"Seek ye first the kingdom within and all else will come unto you" (Matthew 6:33).

O.K. - If I am Divine, then I must be in Perfect Health! But I have had a painful wrist for eight months! It is so much easier to visualize my dis-eased wrist than to kid myself into thinking "all is well." My wrist is "Not" hurting - but it is! But why does one consider pain as an expression of imperfection? Isn't it fantastic that there is such a process in the human body that when something does go wrong we are alerted by pain or fever or some discomfort? Perfect feed-back. With no feedback we would suddenly, for no apparent reason, keel over and die.

Pain tells one, O.K., this area is no longer in perfect running order. So pay attention and do something about it. What a blessing to be given this guidance! Mind your health. Start with the concept of ease which at times is constricted and we feel dis-eased. As darkness is the absence of light and has no strength or power in itself, so disease is the absence of health and has no strength or power in itself. It is our attitude and thoughts which energize the disease. Step aside and allow yourself, your "higher" perfect SELF to shine through. As we create shadows by stepping "in front of the sun," we create disease by obstructing our soul-SELF - with our "little" personality self as we struggle to be in charge. What we need to do is dis-charge our personality self, or, to state it another way, charge it with our Divine Being or Soul-SELF.

And if your Soul-SELF is in charge, then all Is perfect. Whatever situation you are in, see it as the perfect way for you to claim your perfection. Every situation is perfect for your growth: "See joy in everything," quote from Riplion Board), - to jolt you into righting wrongs, to challenge you to stay on "the right path." Life is a great balancing act on the high wire! The wire is charged with Divine Love and it is up to each of us to focus on that wire. Walk it gracefully in balance and harmony - and even if we stray and fall off, there is a net to save us from destruction – "God's hands" will be there to catch us and boost us back onto the heavenly wire.

Christ said "I AM THE WAY (Luke 14:6). Follow me - only through me can you reach the kingdom" - meaning if you follow me on the high wire through life I will lead you safely to "the other side," "Lead, kindly light---" (John H. Newman, 1833).

Those experiencing a painful and terminal disease may well be fiercely angry with this mulling. All I can say is that I believe all is for the good. There is a "wider plan" - if mind, spiritual body and soul are wholly in balance. Thus the physical body can be sloughed off when no longer needed. We see this all the time in nature. A butterfly leaves behind its cocoon. The snake sheds its skin, the lobster its shell - all in the process of greater growth. And I am told billions of our cells are dying everyday and being replaced by new ones.

CURRENT   July 7, 1981

I have been mulling for some time over the relationship between intelligence and energy. If thought has energy, i.e. the thought actively sets up a vibration - a movement - what is it a movement of? Particles? Does thought rearrange particles which then bombard our brain which, in turn, responds by sending signals out? A signal is a flash of light, a feeling of pain, our emotional reaction (emotional = emotes motion - the verb to emit means "to send forth") - something that we sense with one of our five physical senses. But maybe movement is primarily a difference in relationship between two "things." Webster's Dictionary (1942) defines current (electrical) as "what results from difference of potential between two points just as a current of water results from a difference of level or head." Without this difference there would be no motion or vibration - all would be static and "dead?" - Or maybe instead of "dead," the word ONE is more appropriate.

If one sees our universe as "one big thought" or as "one big vibration" with infinite varieties of that vibration within it, then the vibration itself was "caused" by the "difference of potential between the God point and the universe point" or to bring it to our point of awareness, between the God point and the human point. One might then call that current "Spirit in motion" between the level of God consciousness and human consciousness-- that moving spirit (Holy Spirit) PREVAILS - is current. i.e. belonging to the present time or season (Webster, 1942) - it circulates - it flows, moves (part of French verb courir: to run). Webster's (1942) first definition of current as adjective is "hastening to aid an ally" - that definition makes me feel so good. The currency we know most about is "money" - it circulates from hand to hand, hopefully "hastening to aid an ally."

I seem to have mulled a far distance removed from the idea of intelligence and energy. But have I? Maybe Supreme Intelligence is "hastening to aid an ally" - and that is exactly how I see all the beautiful Beings making up "our universe" - from cherubims and seraphims - to Heavenly Host Being - with Humankind somewhere in between. The universe is energized by the differences in our thoughts - and as we are all unique, each creature creates a unique thought pattern which inter-reacts with all the other thought patterns in the universe which together create reality. How we think makes a difference in how the Holy Spirit flows! We are part of the great universal stream of consciousness!

The God current is the swiftest part of the stream - we can be "eddy back-water" off the main current, forcing our own ego-consciousness to buck the ongoing cosmic flow - but where does it get us? We just go round and round in small whirlpools. So let us join "THE MAIN" - for ONE, it is more fun. For TWO, it is more exciting - it will bring us to new lands of beauty and understanding, and for THREE, we will feel free! As part of the MAIN CURRENT we become all powerful - the KINGDOM-QUEENDOM is now our DOMINION.

THE SOUND OF BEING   July 17, 1981

I have been mulling a lot about sound. I feel stuck - no break-through into the creativity of sound. Some insight is missing. I have adequate out-sight: a sound is a vibration which we hear. But that is a very limited definition and totally unsatisfactory. I suspect we also see, touch (feel), smell and taste sound. And, as all "things" have their source in "THE INNER," I can "see" inner sound as being picked-up by my mind's eye and transmitted through a prism which, in turn is picked-up by my five senses. So I visualize sound striking the prism of third plane reality to radiate outward according to my awareness and creating a "rainbow of sound" divided into the five categories humankind has designated as seeing, touching, smelling, tasting, and of course, hearing.

I just looked up the word "sound" in Webster's dictionary. Among other definitions it defines sound as (1) vibrational energy (as in sound the trumpet! (2) forming a channel between mainland (God Self) and an island (us Self) (physical example is Vineyard Sound - between Cape Cod and the island Martha's Vineyard), (3) founded in truth and right (a sound principle), (4) to measure the depth (making a sounding), (5) healthy, firm (sound body). Sound, say it out loud. It seems to encompass ALL - I see the sound as reaching out to embrace the universe with its touch. It sounds complete, in perfect equilibrium, carrying within it the harmony and power of an ordered universe.

Gee, that sounds Godly to me!

BLOW-OUT? July 21, 1981

"I have yet many things to say to you but you cannot hear them now," John II 16:12.

I am curious about those "many things." Christ was talking to his disciples at the time - not to us "ordinary" people, but to those he had chosen to spread his Spirit, and even they were not ready to hear those "many things." What was it he had in mind that was too much of a burden?

What they could not hear was some kind of truth. Perhaps it was the truth of their inability to really understand who He was. Had the "many things" to do with the future of Humankind? I am not sure I want a clairvoyant look into the future myself.

Are any of us ready yet to know about those "many things?" Am I (for one) ready to risk the burden? I doubt it, though I am tempted. But Christ knows what I can bear and what I cannot, and as he knew with his disciples. He knows what to say to me NOW and what to wait until my awareness has reached a greater understanding. He will not tell me something that I cannot bear - He knows how much "suffering" I can bear - it is not that I won't suffer at all. This idea of suffering has me confused, though. I contend that if I understand a situation from a wider viewpoint, if I see purpose in that suffering, then it is no longer "suffering," but merely a means to a greater end. It is only our limited awareness that causes us to suffer.

Yet Christ is portrayed as the Supreme sufferer. How can that be if He was totally AWARE? Christ's suffering must have been of a different order of magnitude or quality. We see suffering as we see love - identified with our emotions, physical being and human relationships. Unconditional love or the Christ love is beyond these human experiences - and so must unconditional suffering be beyond our human experience. What would unconditional suffering be? It would be beyond physical pain (crucifixion), despair in being misunderstood ("forgive them because they know not what they do") and utter loneliness (no friend).

Could his unconditional suffering be in his relationship with God rather than man? (As unconditional love is a relationship with God, which then manifests in our relationship with man). Did Christ feel He had failed God? And, as He knew "I and the Father are One," had God failed to reach mankind? Can there be any greater suffering than that? And surely the disciples were not ready to hear that kind of unconditional suffering.

Maybe the "many things" had more to do with Christ as the bearer of unconditional LOVE - that God is HERE and has not failed to reach humankind. The LOVE force is very powerful and unless one is in harmony and health one can be physically short-circuited by the LOVE charge (see Spangler, David, 1976, *Revelations,* The Rainbow Bridge, San Francisco, CA). Perhaps that is one of the problems with the mentally ill - the Love charge was too strong for their brains to handle. It is an observation that many of them have delusions of being the Christ and have to save the world. Maybe they were trying to take on the Christ vibrations and "blew a fuse" - and yet still experience, in a distorted way, that love force.

"Many things" are the manifestations of mental energy forces and so, for the moment, at least, I understand John 16: 13 to mean that the disciples' energy patterns of consciousness were not "geared-up" enough to harmonize with and accept the powerful ideas that Christ had in mind. Are we more ready now?

MIND SYMBOLS   July 28, 1981

After reading *Psychic Politics* (Roberts, Jane, 1976, Prentice Hall, NJ), I decided to experiment with mind symbols as she does in her quest to understand consciousness. She would blank her mind and then see what came to mind. Then, in the course of the day, or several days, she would see if the symbols related in any way to any conscious experience.

So, I thought I would try my "luck" too and see if I could "conjure" up symbols which could be identified as premonitions to something that would happen in the near future. Immediately before I even began the exercise (and just after I decided to limit myself to five symbols) a lemon popped into my mind, and trailing it, the word "Sunkist." I thought to myself "that does not count because I was not ready," I let it go and the next visualization was of a jagged line - like lightning, full of power, renting or slashing through something - I felt it was an ominous sign - strong and cutting. I quickly identified it as a "razor's edge" and thought of Somerset Maugham's book *The Razor's Edge* (1944, Doubleday & Co., Inc) - that made me think of a delicate balancing act on a tightrope - I wanted to get away from the visualization of a cruel angry slashing out. My third symbol was a strong right arm - bare and powerful. Then the word "crank" came on my "mental screen" followed by a billowy cloud, gaily sailing through space - white, puffy, and "blowing into the wind." Those were my five symbols, counting the lemon, which I decided to include because the cloud symbol seemed a good symbol to stop with.

Thinking over these five symbols, I intellectualized that perhaps they were a warning about a car accident. I saw myself driving a lemon of a car, then getting a flat (to the right-rear tire for some reason) which caused the accident (slash of tire? - jagged line representing accident?) I needed my strong right arm to crank up the car to change the tire, then went on my "merry" way. All was O.K. I had escaped serious Injury.

The next day I went on the Riplion Board with a friend. The Arc Mutator refused to move. I thought this is "strange" because she has strong energy and it had always moved well for us. Then very slowly, heavily, laboriously, it moved. I felt we were dragging something up out of the deepest darkest pit imaginable. The object was dense, black, strong and powerfully masculine, slowly and with great effort "we" cranked it up into the LIGHT, the Arc Mutator twisting counter-clockwise.

We asked for interpretation and this is what we understood. The "thing" cranked up was represented in our universe by the back or dark side (razor - slash) of anything (symbol: jagged). In this case, it was the dark side of the sun, which was transformed into light (by the sun's kiss? Sunkist lemon?). By balancing our energies with those of the universe - a mighty balance act supported by (the strong arm?) spirit, we (cranked? transformed) the dark energy into LIGHT OF LOVE (cloud?).

How about that? Did my five mind symbols of the day before clue me in to this experience through the Board, an experience outside of my wildest Imagination before it happened? Or so I thought.

FEAR   July 29, 1981

Fear: that is a loaded word! I even hesitate to mull over fear because just the thought tends to open me up to fear - but I will be brave and see what happens.

What is fear, why do we fear? We do not fear wishy-washy like, there is always an object of our fear. We fear something. The wrath of God immediately comes to mind. Wrath! That is a nasty word. It is much more than the word "anger" because it implies vengeance, punishment, retaliation. I cannot even say the word "wrath" without screwing up my face in an unattractive contortion. Try it. On the other hand the word "anger" I can say with cool control.

Well, now. Is God an emotional being like us? Does "He" (masculine, of course, since it is a case of discipline and punishment) oscillate from one extreme (wrath) to the other (love) depending on whether or not his head aches, his stomach hurts or his bowels are moving? If He is like little emotional me, I should think He would find it very difficult to be wrathful if He felt good; I will have none of it. Job (see Book of Job) can envision that kind of God if he wants, but not me.

How about Joshua's God? "---Be strong and of good courage, be not afraid, neither be thee dismayed, for the Lord, thy God is with thee whithersoever thou goest" (Joshua 1:9). Well, since I cannot ever rid myself of God, and I am not to be afraid, no matter what, then that God must be more loving, merciful, supportive, etc, than I can possibly imagine, and must be able to take care of my fears, before I have any fears. That is the kind of God I like to have around! I cannot ever lose God if I tried!

Fear of loss is one of our greatest fears, especially of one we love either though death or disaffection. Life on this three-dimensional plane matters - it is experienced physically through our five senses. We relate to the physical beings and objects surrounding us. Thank God that God is not physical, otherwise we would lose God overnight.

Fear has to do with separation - and that has to do

with our belief about "sin" - being separated from God because we feel very guilty about that famous apple in the "Garden of Eden." Do we choose to believe in sin? Just because we are not attuned to God does not mean God is not attuned to us! The "Great Art" is being in tune with all - whatever is happening, whoever is doing the happening, etc. God is "in tune" with the separation through Love. It is up to us to heal that separation also with LOVE.

LOVE DEEDS   August 15, 1983

"DELIGHT IN UNCONDITIONAL LOVE DEEDS" and when we are in touch with cosmic consciousness all is DELIGHT. The phrase "unconditional love" has never set right with me ever since it has been banded about by all of us striving for the "new age." Love is love and is neither conditional nor unconditional. Any relationship that even implies conditions (or the opposite un-conditions) is not love, but a pact, a treaty, an agreement. The Hebrew Covenant is not love – the Old Testament God is an emotional God full of wrath if the Covenant is broken. The Ten Commandments (Exodus 20:2-17, Deuteronomy 5:6-21) are demands on human behavior, not love. The first Commandment "Love thy God with all thy heart, etc." is a command, not love. Love cannot be commanded.

The difficulty is that we are "quantity thinkers," "Oh ye men of little faith," why the "little?" We either have faith or we don't have faith. When we condition love we break it up into bits and pieces and love becomes unrecognizable. Does one recognize a person by focusing on one attitude or one appendage, or that person's deeds? When one of our attitudes or one of our appendages does a deed, we can extrapolate a good deal about that person. Take a "hand," it can caress or collect something, it can slap or sooth, it can stir a pudding or lay idle in the sun to tan. Its action at least gives us a clue as to its purpose at the moment, whereas merely describing the hand or even describing how the hand works does not enlighten us. It is in the action that a hand delights, and so it is in the action (the deeds) that love delights. It is in action that all delights! Movement, change, flux and flow are inherent in our universe. Nothing stops. Isn't that beautiful? We can never become stuck, regardless. The great urge of the universe urges us on.

Love is love and cannot be conditioned, because conditions are static, they try to stop a relationship. Conditions freeze a monetary relationship, conditions are like footprints in cement: they become obsolete as soon as they have been cemented. We even say "let us do this or that (condition) to cement this relationship, and immediately that relationship becomes fossilized.

The pulse of the universe is at our fingertips. Let us use our hands to feel that pulse, to feel the ongoing unfolding, to allow the energetic essence of BEING its full expression, ever changing, here on planet earth.

Let us delight in LOVE DEEDS.

COLOR   April, 1984

From the Light, all expressions radiate out as vibrations/spirals – be they physical form, thought, colors, numbers, sounds.

Everything spirals, and everything spirals everything else. God is the supreme Spiral, the Master Vibrator, starts everything to vibrate/spiral with the spark. All begins with a spark. We all begin our sojourn on Earth with the spark of Life.

"Breathe on me, Breath of God, Fill me with life anew, That I may…" (from the Hymn "Breathe on Me, Breath of God" by Edwin Hatch, 1835-1889 and Robert Jackson, 1842-1914, John 20:22) breathe out love, or as my sister Dorothy experienced, "God breathes me." God doesn't breathe on me, or through me, God breathes me into LIFE beginning with the spark. That spark contains within it the potential for the whole being, and is the Light.

I see color as active, a verb, not just a descriptive word; the color moves; it is vibration. I wonder what color breathing is. Each color must have its energy pattern, its own moving identity. Colors may be expressed in complementary numbers and sounds. Each color may express a distinctive quality. Is each color perceived differently by each person, influenced by individual life experience? Does love have a color? Is the color of love "radiance" or "rose?"   What are the colors of joy, praise, laughter, gratitude, balance, peace, silence?

Alice Bailey (Theosophist, 1880-1949) has seen the

colors of thought forms; and many people can see the colors of auras, the energy patterns surrounding the body. How we are at a particular time may show up as a different color of the aura.

Each of us has the free will to choose, to become more aware, to see the world differently, and to see with a wider perspective, to have a spiritual sight beyond this 3-dimensional world. Our task is to see what is needed in the world, and to bring these visions into reality.

We can imagine everyone filled with love and light.

FLAME   April 11, 1984

What a powerful color: flame! We imagine flame as fire, the spark, the force that ignites life, the fiery dance of the soul as it agitates to become incarnate.

Fire burns away the dross, purifies, and disconnects the whole into its separate parts: each part maintaining all the qualities of the whole, we are soul-sparks for the "Oversoul," later to be consumed and reconnected with the Eternal Flame.

The Sun (Son) flames forth its Glory – radiates its love. Fire is a symbol of Love – totally envelops, more than that, it transforms, so we can develop into our perfect selves - or more accurately for my understanding, burns away the dross, so our perfect selves can shine forth in Glory.

Our perfect selves are flames. Flame does not burn away flame, flame acting as flame adds to the glory, intensifies the glory!

Let us stand up together in glory!

MIND GLINTS   July 2, 1984

Objects are often invisible, particularly those at a distance, until the sun shines on them at a certain angle, then they burst into Light – "they catch the light" – that is what we human beings must do: "catch the light" so we can shine. Otherwise we remain invisible.

What is that magic angle? We can only find out by experimenting and trying – at least that is the western cultural approach – action. The Easterner would say – don't try. Just reflect – i.e. meditate and willy-nilly without effort, suddenly you will "catch the light." It is the invisible light that we are trying to catch, how to make it visible.

I had a sudden glint the other day – I wonder if we are just as invisible to the angels as they are to us! Our vibrations are so "heavy" or "low" that "the angels are bending low to earth to touch our hearts with gold" – they are trying to find us as much as we are trying to find them! When the angels make contact they sing "Joy!"

Imagination may be the contact angle!

I AM A STAR   January 16, 1985

It is through imagination that we can leap "outside of ourselves" or leap "inside of ourselves." To help myself in my own imaginations, I like to not think of "without" and "within," but "through" – we live through the universe. The universe lives through us. The barriers are down and we are all part of the whole. We live

through God and God lives through us. All is ONE. A drop of water lives because it is water, not because it is a drop. We live because we are made in the image of God, or shall we say we live because we are God.

I prefer image – the idea of being God is beyond my imagination. I can't be consciously aware of being God until I act like God, also love as God loves, and I'm far from that. Yes, I, in theory have the potential of being God.

The purpose of our being in this dimension is to bring to this planet both individually and collectively the consciousness that dwells in "greater" dimensions of mind, to bring "heaven" to "earth," not escape earth to go to heaven. We don't have to go anywhere, just open our hearts to love.

Each of us is a STAR.

SPACE-TIME   January 2, 1985

We know that all substance is in motion and thus intrinsically there can be no substance (materialization) without time, nor does time exist without substance – space-time is inseparable; take away space and there is no time, take away time and there is no space.

And because we live in the milieu of space-time we filter all earth experience; i.e. all our hearing, seeing, smelling, tasting, and touching is through the space-time grid.

There are those who are able to experience other realms through what is called the sixth sense. When we visualize in meditation or hear other voices, or have an "out-of-body" experience, we use our five senses to describe the experience within the space-time mode. Our imagination may be tuned to other realms, but the other realms are experienced according to the manifestations we recognize here on third-plane awareness – we can only visualize the colors we know; we can only hear voices speaking the words we know; we can only see "angels" in the forms we know; we fly through space-time in "out-of body" experiences. "Out" implies movement (takes time); "body" implies substance (fills space). Though we can experience life only as it is perceived here on the three-dimensional world, we can contact Beings in other realms who can express in our language how "they" see. They can relate our seeing to the perceptions of a space-less-timeless life.

Life-love-light is expressed in an infinite variety of ways – the ways of and the how of expression are God's gifts to conscious Beings. We are conscious Beings of Life-love-light in the earth mode in order to grow and to learn: to self-consciously realize that we are individualizations of the ONE journeying creatively within space-time which, in turn, is within the timeless-space-less ONE

I AM   May 20, 1985

I feel a veil or separation between us here on planet Earth and the Light beings in other greater dimensions. What flashed through my mind is that we are the connection to those Light beings. There is no way we really can be separated - because we are the Light beings who intentionally made a choice to come to planet Earth in this physical form. Without us (the human being) there would be no connection, that is, no conscious connection. We have unfolded our awareness century following century to this realization – and we have come to this realization through Self as expressed here in the third dimension. We ARE the perfection, the personification, the particularization (call it what you will) of those Beings we have had glimpses of, or heard voices singing from, or felt a touch of love from. Logically we can carry the idea a step further, because "they" are perfection, personification, particularizations of "higher Beings, until we all meet in the Godhead," or until we realize we are the God-mind in all its wholeness or holiness. We are IT. I AM THIS I AM!

Now maybe the birds, the bees, the rocks and the trees have known this all along, but the wonder is that we have learned this knowledge, have earned this knowledge through the experience of free choice.

We are living beings with the full capacity to learn through experience. Many other living beings live through instinct, and because of that, the instinct overwhelms, in most instances, their experience. Our experience can overwhelm our instincts, and by so doing, we become more and more aware of who we truly are: cosmic divine beings, imaged by "God" or as some state it, "the all in all." God "on High" is unnamable, unspeakable, unimaginable, but we can know "ourselves!" That is the way to the unnamable, the unspeakable, and the unimaginable. We might ever call ourselves, "God" on "low." We're God in low gear, and our destiny is to love ourselves, up to be God in high gear! The New Age is a changing of the Gear!

LIFE   November 15, 1985

Life! What is life? Who is life? Down through the ages Mind has wondered and watched humankind gazing into the sky for answers. Are the stars heavenly Beings? Who ignited life, the fiery flame, the spark of energy that catapulted into life on planet earth? My heart is filled with love, my mind with knowing and my pen with the light of expression. We are all kindred spirits to enliven each other with the luminous, intelligent spiritual all powerful light of love.

My desire is to serve here, to listen carefully to hear the words so that we can live life according to Mother Earth's vibrations, a scintillating, extravagant, effervescent LIGHT. Speak through me; open me to Oneness. I know we are ONE. Express through me that ONENESS for all to hear and know the Joy we are.

I am open. May we be free to move throughout the cosmos.

Life is everywhere, in all manifestations of word and deed. All is in mutual accord, no longer the duality of discord: no good, no evil, no sin, no sinless, all is unfolding before our eyes of awareness, all encompassing, no beginning, no end, no out, no in, no higher, no lower.

All is the same center from which we enter our being in third-dimension, from the oneness of the white light we journey through the rainbow colors within earth's sphere. We are made of the same stuff, energized by the same fire; we dance our dance with the angels' dance of life.

Nothing is new; nothing is old; no-thing is. Time is a creature of habit addicted to space. Let us give up our focus on space-time and free ourselves from the shadowed caves of our thoughts, from our fears, from thinking we are winged bats of darkness in battle, to knowing we are winged Beings of Light in common. Dissolve the scales blinding us so that the all-seeing EYE can inspire us to perceive the answers to the questions of life.

JOY   November 19, 1985

Joy! Does that ring bells? The ringing of bells – that is the sound of joy! We live in a loving universe bursting with joy (like a spring bud bursting into bloom). When creating heaven and earth, God said: "It is good" and that is all there is! Goodness or Godness – there is nothing else. We create the other stuff through fear, judgment, insecurity, ego, etc. Have faith in the goodness, regardless. Build your own city of Joy, that is the beauty of Being, we are free to choose and create whatever we so desire – God gave us that gift - before we left paradise.

The time has come for us to claim our own Divinity! No longer are we just "enlightened animals." Hidden within the outer physical manifestations has been our divinity, lying dormant from the very beginning; the mind of human consciousness is essentially Divine.

Back to faith and joy, etc., it takes awareness that we have a choice to allow divine knowing to become part of our experience. We are saved through faith in believing there is something beyond our animal nature; we can know who we really are – Divine Cosmic Beings!

GOLD   November 21, 1985

GOLD! Oh, the magic in that word! How humankind has longed for gold from earliest times – not so much the ore as the aura! The ore has become the symbol of wealth, abundance, richness, enlightenment – "Lay not up for yourselves treasures (gold) on earth---, But lay up for yourselves treasures (golden energy – supreme consciousness, etc.) in heaven---" (Matthew 6:19-20). The ore is left behind from lifetime to lifetime. However, the riches of consciousness we take with us through lifetime after lifetime.

The alchemist strived to transmute base metals into gold with actual earth-bound elements. The true alchemist knew that the richness of mind and heart which opened up the person to cosmic consciousness was the real goal of humanity – how to make that connection between "heaven and earth."

The gold at the end of the rainbow is stepping out into a higher world of God's love of Divine life – the rainbow is the bridge – it arches over the river of experience from the banks of earth to the banks of heaven. The rainbow is a myriad of colors – each color its own true and unique vibration of energy – the total rainbow symbolizes what we draw-up from the waters of experience on earth that we treasure – the essence of experience which is, no matter what the experience, embedded in our Being. We, in fact, are that rainbow: unique, beautiful, multifaceted, sparkling soul. The energies of soul are love, joy, laughter, beauty, harmony, kindness – the ingredients or expressions of the rainbow of our Being. These energies move us into light; without the rainbow we remain lightless, caught in the shadow of death. As the rainbow, we can welcome death to shine in the light, and death itself becomes part of our own walk into the light over the golden rainbow bridge. Seeking gold – it is the urge for enlightenment, the craving to return to "our Father's house."

If we have merely secured that gold for selfish earth-focused needs and used that physical gold to become grand in our own eyes, we have really secured nothing. A lifetime on earth is a mere blink of the eye in eternity. Our greatest challenge is to be awake. We may shine forth in all our splendor when we open the heart to love and divine knowing. We will be what we really are, the gold at the end of the rainbow! Glory hallelujah!

WHO AM I?   February 8, 1986

Who do I believe I am? – Do I truly know? I live in the milieu of my own beliefs. Whoever I am, my beliefs hold sway. I am on a merry-go-round with my beliefs which are jostled by my experiences which, in turn, are drawn to my beliefs – a continuum of cause and effect – a relationship like space-time where one cannot exist without the other. I witness the merry-go-round of belief-experience as a spiraling wheel of change – a wheel within a wheel within a wheel… (Ezekiel 1) and my response to belief-experience is the crux of the matter. In my attitude is my reality. My response to my belief-experience centers me or flings me out to chaos. Joel Goldsmith (*The Infinite Way,* 1948) calls it "attitude of mind." And how does one reach "attitude:" through will power. Will directs the response. Will is the master, the belief-experience the servant.

Whoever I am, I am not alone. I am "a part of all that I have met," also a part of all that I have not met. A visualization of a tapestry comes to mind. I see myself as a golden thread aware through an inner seeing that something is happening that includes me – something greater than the experience I am having as a thread-self. Am I part of a great weave and is there a weaver? Is there a weaver with designs on me to create something of which I am a part? Do I play a vital and essential role in the creation? Something beyond my understanding is going on, and I am going on within it?

Who is the weaver? The best definition I have received so far for my understanding is that the weaver is a "luminous, intelligent, spiritual, all powerful Light of love." Others call the weaver God, Allah, High Self, Creator, Supreme Being, Universal Mind, etc. – the All in All. I can merely say "I sense God" and leave it at that …

Who am I? Maybe I am an idea in the mind of some Being who is focusing thought energy to create a Being like Itself. Suppose I am an idea in the Mind of God? If God is "all that is," there is no-thing but God, then God knows only Itself and can only create an idea in Its own image! That sounds familiar. I am made according to the totality of all that is (microcosm – macrocosm) – I am the image of God's idea of total Being in all its perfection. "I live and move and have my being" within the totality of God-Mind. There is no way I can escape from that idea because I am that idea.

How about free-will? I am free to stand in the full light of the noon-day sun, i.e. be the idea in all of its fullness, or I can turn my back on the idea and live in my own shadow – the shadow of the idea – creating the illusion of separation.

And that is what much of humankind has chosen – to turn its back on the Light and live within its own collective shadow where it is too dark for us to see one another in the outer gloom.

But I am still "the idea," not the shadow! Through an act of will power I must pierce the outer darkness with a laser beam of Inner Light to dispel the sense of separation. I could easily just turn to face the light again, but the darkness of the collective shadow would still exist. I am part of all that I have met and until all humankind faces the Light, I am still in the shadow.

To gain our freedom we must break the chain of "old" beliefs holding us within our own shadow of disobedience, and form "new" beliefs which will, with "fiery enthusiasm," lead us to "march gaily on up the road obedient with every breath" (*Letters of the Scattered Brotherhood*, p.70). Then living within "The Light of Knowing" I will know who I am.

God is Being me through Love

God is en-Joy-ing me through Light

God is growing me through Life

And if these "new" beliefs don't work for me?

I will rest on the wings of the angels

And be borne to a far-distant star,

I will fly to the arms of my loved one

To circle the earth from afar.

But I do believe that:

Love spirals the Light of the Cosmos

To planet the stars out in space

And the life that is born to that Love-Light

Embodies the whole Human Race.

So:

Let us dance on the Ground of our Being

To center soul now in this sphere

And the joy that we feel, is the knowing

We star in the cosmic plan here.

"Few people know their exact destination, and the ones who think they do, often find another place than the one they imagined. If you knew your exact arrival point, there would be little spontaneity or choice in your journey. In the same way, if you knew before hand just how you were going to write a book, it would no longer be an act of creation. But even if one does not know one's arrival point one can and should, I believe, have a direction."

Lindbergh, Anne Morrow, April 12, 1978 lecture, "The Journey Not the Arrival," from Smith Alumnae Quarterly.

Since the above "Mullings" were written about 20 years ago, many people have become more aware. For example, the molecular structure of water has been studied by Masaru Emoto, and he has found that thoughts and music of love and harmony will cause the molecular structure of water to be shaped into beautiful crystals while thoughts and music of disharmony will cause the molecular structure to look disorganized.

When we check on the internet for the subjects: color healing, healing sounds, visualization in healing, thoughts and healing, there were millions of different listings for each subject. So much is available for different aspects of healing, that each could be a lifetime study. Books have been written, workshops and lectures given about healing sounds by Alfred Tomatis, Ron Minson, Jonathan Goldman, Mantak Chia, Mitchell Gaynor, to name a few; Andrew Weil has a CD called "Sound Body, Sound Mind." Thomas Ashley Farrand has books and CDs giving mantras that one can repeat aloud to bring about healing, each mantra for a particular condition. There is now being distributed a CD of the Dalai Lama chanting for healing. The sense of smell is also used to heal with aromatherapy, using essential oils that bring about healing of specific ailments. Bruce Lipton has written a book: The Biology of Belief, in which he says that what we believe determines our physiology, thus our health. The field of healing has increased so much that one can find health practitioners to assist physical, mental, emotional, and spiritual healing wherever one lives.

GO TO FORCE IN YOUR LIFE

A   Creative force

B   Holy force

C   Cosmic force

D   Becoming force

E   God force

F   Imaginative force

G   Manifestation force

H   Accepting force

I   Oneness force

J   Force of good intent

K   Motivation force

L   Self-realization force

M   Authority force

N   Universal spiral force

O   Divine relationship force

P   Peace force

Q   Questioning force

R   Love force

S   Spiritual force

T   Service force

U   Consciousness force

V   Free choice force

W   Transcendent force

X   Christ vibration force

Y   Happy force

Z   Connecting force

SOUNDS OF KINDNESS

G H   All is well

V O Q   Harmony in relationships

R O Q   To open hearts to love

M L   To live in love

XXX   To awaken Christ consciousness

Y Z   To love all in universe

By repeating these sounds of kindness, we can bring ourselves into each state of harmony and awareness.

    May *Riplion* book inspire every one of us toward a renewed dedication, to know who we are, to be here as sons and daughters of the universe. May we remember that all of us are to live together in peaceful cooperation with each other. We all depend on each other for our breath and our life: air, earth, earthworm, plant, sun, rain, insect, fish, bird, rock, and flower. May we all awaken and bring about peace with each breath.

About the authors:

Barbara Gates Burwell was born in New York City, and moved to Cambridge, Massachusetts at an early age, with summers in Woods Hole. She graduated from college, married a medical student, Lang Burwell, and spent the following years raising four children. With a global outlook on life, she welcomed into the family many foreign students and started various United Nations projects in her community in Woods Hole on Cape Cod, particularly the UNICEF Halloween Program. She has always participated in community affairs. Among other projects, she helped to initiate the Shining Sea Bicycle Path. She has been interested for years in spiritual questions. That search has led her to much reading, contemplation, meditation, visualization, and living her life as a guiding light for all who come to her.

Betty Jean Wall is a Chinese-American who was born and grew up in a small town in the south. Betty has been a student of biology, religion, and all aspects of life as long she can remember. Her parents emigrated from China, and opened a grocery store where Betty and her three brothers worked while they were growing up. Although they went to school and all received advanced degrees, the family store turned out to be a significant classroom about life.

Betty enjoyed working in the laboratory and published extensively in the field of biology. After about 20 years of doing biological research, she changed her career. For over 25 years she has been studying various types of healing work, and practices in Boulder, Colorado and Woods Hole, Massachusetts. Please visit:

www.bettyjeanwall.com

Printed in the United States
210066BV00001B/190-198/A